T0355141

Campus Misinformation

Campus Misinformation

The Real Threat to Free Speech in American Higher Education

Bradford Vivian

OXFORD
UNIVERSITY PRESS

OXFORD
UNIVERSITY PRESS

Oxford University Press is a department of the University of Oxford. It furthers
the University's objective of excellence in research, scholarship, and education
by publishing worldwide. Oxford is a registered trade mark of Oxford University
Press in the UK and certain other countries.

Published in the United States of America by Oxford University Press
198 Madison Avenue, New York, NY 10016, United States of America.

Library of Congress Control Number: 2022941524

ISBN 978–0–19–753127–3

DOI: 10.1093/oso/9780197531273.001.0001

1 3 5 7 9 8 6 4 2

Printed by Sheridan Books, Inc., United States of America

For all my students—past, present, and future.

SOCRATES: Then let me raise another question; there is such a thing as "having learned"?

GORGIAS: Yes.

SOCRATES: And there is also "having believed"?

GORGIAS: Yes.

SOCRATES: And is the "having learned" the same as "having believed," and are learning and belief the same things?

GORGIAS: In my judgment, Socrates, they are not the same.

—Plato, *Gorgias* (c. 380 BC)

The great truth was proclaimed by an ancient, *that there is no royal road to learning.* . . . The teacher who professes to possess a steam-rate conveyance for instruction, not only deceives himself, but will assuredly find his own errors produce a corresponding ill effect upon the improvement of his pupils.

—J. Tourrier, *A Treatise on Jacotot's Method of Universal Instruction* (1852)

Contents

Acknowledgments

The Department of Communication Arts and Sciences at Pennsylvania State University supported this book in a variety of ways. I benefited from the diligent work of my graduate student research assistants: Breanna Mapston, Caroline Koons, and Dominic Manthey. I am grateful for their assistance. Any errors in what follows, however, are mine alone.

I am also indebted to several of my departmental colleagues. Jim Dillard, LJ Shen, and Michael Steudeman shared their combined expertise with me about various aspects of social science and higher education. Mary Stuckey provided sage advice in early stages about conceptualizing this book and finding the right audience for it. Rachel Smith generously reviewed early drafts of Chapter 4 and offered extensive consultation about the kind of scientific research that it examines. I am fortunate to have such supportive colleagues.

The subject matter of this book concerns several intersections between the state of higher education and that of democracy. My ideas and arguments about this subject matter were aided, indirectly but no less meaningfully, by the supportive institutional environment in which I worked throughout my research and writing. Two simultaneous service roles (as director of undergraduate studies in my home department and as director of the Center for Democratic Deliberation in the McCourtney Institute for Democracy at Penn State) enriched my understanding of the reciprocal relationships between healthy education and healthy democracy. Defending one is a way of defending the other.

Meredith Keffer at Oxford University Press generously supported my development of this book, with wise editorial guidance, into what I hope readers will find to be a constructive contribution to vital public as well as academic matters. I am grateful for her insights, and for the work of those at OUP who helped prepare it for publication.

I am also thankful, as ever, for my wife Anne's extensive support—including her enthusiasm for the very idea of this book before I had put a single word on paper, and for her encouragement at every stage until I completed it.

I dedicate this book to all my students, regardless of their individual beliefs, opinions, or personal backgrounds. The opportunity to help them on their way in learning and in life has been, and will continue to be, a privilege.

Introduction

Casual references to *what's happening on college campuses* are now common in public debates about a wide variety of perceived social and political ills. I started to encounter this phrase, here and there, in the mid-2010s. I overheard it in casual conversation and noticed it in news stories. The question of what's happening on college campuses became prominent during and soon after the presidential election of 2016. Students and colleagues at the university where I work talked about meeting people who presumed that awful things were transpiring on college campuses across the nation. This colloquialism crept into discussions about the state of politics and the fabric of society. The phrase was always uttered with a sense of foreboding, even dread. It suggested the revelation of a dark and troubling secret. "Can you believe what's happening on college campuses?" Seemingly anyone who used the phrase did so in hushed tones, as if relating a shadowy conspiracy.

I am a professor in one of the United States' largest university systems. I have taught as a university instructor, at one professional rank or another, for more than a quarter of a century. I have taught hundreds and hundreds of students at four different institutions. Two of those institutions were private schools; the other two were public land-grant universities. I have taught students at institutions in southern, northern, and mid-Atlantic states. I have also interacted with undergraduate students at these institutions outside of the classroom, on committees and in service roles dealing with student affairs. And I had no idea what people were talking about when they started, not long ago, to angrily condemn "what's happening on college campuses." Ominous stories about universities kept appearing that bore little resemblance to the places where I worked, the students whom I taught, or the colleagues with whom I worked.

What was allegedly happening on those campuses? Why did so many people who neither work nor study at universities become so troubled and enraged about so-called campus culture? For most of the past decade, a spectrum of pundits, politicians, and even some university faculty have popularized specious and exaggerated claims about college campuses. Promoting misleading claims about higher education has become a cynical but fashionable way to project intellectual superiority and attract public followings.

Many readers of this book will probably accept the following distortions, for example, as obvious truisms: Undergraduate students today are badly coddled. The smallest obstacles and disagreements trigger them. Students desire safe spaces and constant reassurance. The overly emotional whims of undergraduate students now run the show at colleges and universities. Most students, not just a few of them, think and act in such frenzied and domineering ways. The culture of most college campuses now represses free speech, diverse viewpoints, and constructive disagreement. That culture threatens not only higher education but democracy writ large.

Critics of higher education insist that a willingness to reconsider personal views based on reasonable arguments is essential to quality education and democratic disagreement. If so, then my basic appeal in this book is for all readers to consider the following argument with an open mind: the increasingly accepted claims about campus culture listed in the preceding paragraph are misinformation—exaggerations, distortions, and mistruths—about higher education that did not accurately describe college campuses when those claims first emerged in the mid-2010s and do not accurately describe them now.

In this book, I examine the evolution of that misinformation from its origins to its present state. I do so to underscore how it endangers both academic and democratic freedoms. Ominous stories about what's happening on college campuses evolved into a reactionary and antidemocratic political vernacular during the 2020 presidential election. Diatribes about *coddling, trigger warnings, safe spaces, mobs, cancel culture, illiberal liberalism, Marxism, ideological orthodoxy*, and *critical race theory* originally applied to college campuses. Throughout the 2020 election cycle, however, self-described conservative politicians as well as the national Republican Party adopted and amplified those diatribes in their core political appeals.[1] Falsehoods about mobs overtaking entire college campuses in the late 2010s evolved into false but politically potent claims about liberal or Marxist mobs threatening to dismantle traditional US culture. Conservative campaign messaging in the presidential and state elections of 2020 was thick with promises to ban the teaching of critical race theory in schools, end the rise of an allegedly authoritarian liberal orthodoxy, and defend traditional culture against so-called cancel culture. The sum of these promises constituted a politically reactionary pledge to defend the greater United States against the supposed evils of universities. Such caustic and largely fabricated political appeals appear poised to continue shaping—or corroding—national public discourse for the foreseeable future.

I oppose erroneous diatribes about college campuses, not because many self-described conservative figures adopt them, but because they promote dangerous, quasi-authoritarian ideas about both higher education and First Amendment freedoms. Numerous forms of misinformation currently threaten civil society and democratic decision-making. Proliferating but increasingly popular falsehoods about democratic elections, climate science, vaccines, and alleged anti-American plots deep within federal agencies are all prime indicators of democratic erosion in the United States.[2] Journalist Brooks Jackson and professor of communication Kathleen Hall-Jamieson stress the importance of citizens finding ways to understand the huge amounts of "outright dishonesty, misrepresentation, and a lack of respect for fact" seen "far too commonly today in politics and business alike."[3] The need to add rising popular hostility against higher education to this list is acute: anti-university campaigns are an early warning sign of rising authoritarian sentiment. What I categorize in this book as *campus misinformation* is a threat not only to academic freedom; it also endangers civil liberties in US society writ large.

Campus misinformation deserves greater public scrutiny, even from people who do not work or study in universities, because higher education is one of society's most important bulwarks against all misinformation. Authoritarian populists commonly target centers of higher learning along with other forums of free speech and open debate like the free press and voluntary political assembly. The propagandistic premise that university life weakens young adults and inspires them to adopt radical, unpatriotic ideas is common in periods of rising authoritarian sentiment.

Anti-university campaigns in such countries as Russia, Hungary, Poland, and Brazil from the 2010s forward were key elements of larger authoritarian populist movements to restrict civil liberties. Political figures in those nations sought to normalize the idea that specific aspects of independent universities represent existential threats to society. Leaders like Vladimir Putin (Russia), Viktor Orbán (Hungary), and Jair Bolsonaro (Brazil) frequently targeted academic discussions of diversity and equality based on race, sex, or gender as well as favorable intellectual views of multiculturalism and democracy.[4]

Authoritarian figures in this mold often claim that universities censor free speech. Such claims reflect a deceptive code, not sincere commitment to civil liberties. Teachers and researchers at universities expose scientific and historical falsehoods in authoritarian propaganda. Authoritarian figures falsely allege that universities restrict free speech precisely because those academic communities pose an obstacle to the spread of political misinformation. The specious and exaggerated claims about US college campuses that I have described resemble such aspects of ongoing anti-university campaigns in Russia, Hungary, Poland, and Brazil.

Campus misinformation in the United States promotes distortions about universities to generate pretexts for political attacks on free speech rights and academic freedom beyond higher education. Numerous proposed or ratified measures in Republican-controlled state legislatures from 2020 forward were designed to politically regulate or censor academic activities on some college campuses, but even more so in public schools. The most infamous of such measures were bans on the teaching of critical race theory in K–12 education. Local governments also attempted to censor materials from libraries, mostly by Black authors, amid this wave of legislation.[5] Targeting pro-diversity messages and critical race theory reflects a core premise of campus misinformation: namely, that college campuses are corrupting youth and fomenting radical or unpatriotic ideas. Once again, I do not oppose partisan measures of this sort because Republican-controlled legislatures embrace them. I oppose such one-party actions because they normalize government censorship and interference with academic freedom.

The scope of campus misinformation extends far beyond hyperpartisan pretexts for political interference in schools and libraries. Throughout this book, I show that such misinformation has also helped popularize misleading ideas about free speech, academic freedom, and voluntary political organizing. Common tropes and argumentative conceits reappear throughout different strains of campus misinformation. Its characteristic language promotes the paradoxical notions that pro-diversity messages on college campuses are discriminatory, that criticism of spurious and bigoted views is censorship, and that the political speech of some social groups is illegitimate because members of those groups are inherently irrational. These notions are inconsistent with a nuanced understanding of the First Amendment and a broad commitment to civil liberties, yet degrees of popular acceptance for such claims illustrate how misinformation typically operates. Misinformation does not persuade people intellectually; it acculturates people in ways of describing reality that satisfy preexisting prejudices and provide seemingly simple explanations for complex affairs.

I therefore focus, throughout this book, on the characteristic language and standard argumentative premises that constitute campus misinformation. Many current debates about higher education reflect borrowed terms and hypotheses from social scientific fields like social psychology and political science as well as broad legalistic arguments about free speech. I question many of those dominant terms of debate. I do not simply attempt to make a case against the typical language and standard argumentative premises of campus misinformation. I simultaneously advocate for a more empirically accurate, multidimensional public discourse about higher education and the state of free speech within it.

Each of the chapters in this book examines a key element of misinformation in popular discourse about universities by focusing on a prominent term or closely connected set of terms. Examples include *diversity, trigger warnings, safe spaces, mobs, free speech*, and *orthodoxy*. Yet portions of those chapters also indicate accessible and practical ways to elevate the quality of popular discourse about higher education—or, by extension, any important public debate. Such techniques include replacing exaggerations with empirically responsible claims about people or institutions, interrupting cycles of outrage with dialogue from multiple perspectives, and resisting stereotypes in favor of democratic engagements across sociopolitical differences.

The Language of Campus Misinformation

I do not attempt a rose-colored argument about higher education. Contemporary universities face many challenges, even looming crises. Manufactured outrage about so-called free speech crises and pseudopsychological speculations into the mental health of thousands of college students do not meaningfully inform the public about the most serious challenges to higher education today. Free speech and academic freedom on college campuses *are* endangered—but not in the ways that agents of campus misinformation insist.

The most critical threats to free speech, academic freedom, and the free-flowing exchange of ideas in universities today are external rather than internal. The current wave of one-party political efforts to regulate or censor academic content in colleges and public schools did not appear out of nowhere. Gene Nichol, professor of law and former president of the College of William and Mary, warned in 2019 about increasing "governmental suppression of academic freedom—in particular, legislative and political interference with academic inquiry."[6] Such attempted governmental suppression emerged in several notable forms over the course of the 2010s. Republican-controlled legislatures used the threat of severe budget cuts to compel changes in academic and administrative policies from state universities. Such legislatures frequently sought to punish faculty and student groups for freely protesting Israeli policies toward Palestinians.[7] Political appointees to governing boards of state universities increasingly included hyperpartisan actors hostile to publicly funded education and to pro-diversity messages on college campuses. The Goldwater Institute—a partisan think tank not accountable to the public—drafted model "campus speech" legislation and promoted it among Republican-controlled legislatures. The misleadingly named and highly punitive Campus Free Speech Act was designed to intimidate students and faculty from engaging in free political speech or assembly under threat of accusation and punishment from other members of those campuses.[8] Legislatures in Arizona, Georgia, North Carolina, and Wisconsin advanced measures modeled on this template in the late 2010s. "These efforts, funded in part by big-money Republican donors," the *New York Times* reports, "are part of a growing and well-organized campaign that has put academia squarely in the cross hairs of the American right."[9] Formidable threats to free speech on college campuses are quite real—but not because of coddled students or censorious diversity policies.

These individual threats, moreover, are unfolding against the backdrop of global trends in eroding academic freedom. Scholars at Risk, an international network devoted to documenting threats to scholars around the world and providing sanctuary for them, characterizes the sum of international attacks on academic freedom as "a crisis moment." The accelerating attacks on academic freedom that it documents range from "wrongful imprisonment and prosecutions of scholars" to "lawmakers' efforts even in more open societies, including the United States (U.S.)," that "seek to restrict what can be taught in lecture halls."[10] The increasing popularity of campus misinformation coincides with such increasing governmental curtailments of academic freedom.

I classify campus misinformation as a mode of popular discourse that helped rationalize attempts to inhibit free speech and open inquiry in US higher education from the mid-2010s forward. One of the most common claims of such misinformation—that college campuses now predominantly censor free speech and restrict diverse viewpoints—mirrors the semantic ploy of the Goldwater Institute Campus Free Speech Act. That erroneous assessment of campus culture rests on a specious premise: namely, that universities must demonstrate commitments to artificial parity or balance among liberal and conservative viewpoints to truly safeguard free speech and academic freedom. Such highly circumscribed and punitive definitions of free expression artificially promote the speech and ideas of some at the expense of others—even endangering some marginalized groups through attempts to criminalize on-campus activities.

The language of campus misinformation has helped to normalize the idea that something deeply wrong is happening on college campuses or that large majorities of deluded faculty and students have adopted radical ideas. Describing university administrators as ideological overseers, portraying politically active college students as pathologically triggered, and mocking institutions of higher education as safe spaces became fashionable ways to assert one's intellectual bona fides. In this context, self-described conservative and libertarian figures have sought to capitalize politically on those largely false assumptions, but cynical tropes about campus culture grew in popularity across many different social and political groups.

In the chapters to come, I therefore examine campus misinformation as a kind of language unto itself. Such language offers a way of talking about college campuses that confirms existing prejudices and provides seemingly simple explanations, if not scapegoats, for complex shared problems. The following excerpts provide a brief introduction to the common script that reappears in different sources of campus misinformation. Attorney Greg Lukianoff and social psychologist Jonathan Haidt published an influential 2015 article in *The Atlantic* about alleged dangers of "trigger warnings" on college campuses that read, in part,

> The ultimate aim, it seems, is to turn campuses into "safe spaces" where young adults are shielded from words and ideas that make some uncomfortable. . . . This movement seeks to punish anyone who interferes with that aim, even accidentally. . . . It is creating a culture in which everyone must think twice before speaking up, lest they face charges of insensitivity, aggression, or worse.[11]

President Barack Obama made the same argument, during a political town hall in Des Moines, Iowa, the very month that Lukianoff and Haidt's article appeared:

> I've heard of some college campuses where they don't want to have a guest speaker who is too conservative, or they don't want to read a book if it had language that is offensive to African Americans or somehow sends a demeaning signal towards women. . . . I don't agree with that either—that when you become students at colleges, you have to be coddled and protected from different points of view.[12]

Breitbart News, a hyperpartisan website frequently accused of promoting nativist and ethnocentric ideas, was one of many such outlets that retold the same story during the late 2010s:

> Universities were once a beacon of free speech, but today, measures are being put in place to stifle speech under the guise of protecting students. . . . Today, speech is subdued by creating and implementing concepts such as "free speech zones,"

"safe spaces," and "trigger warnings," among many others. These all act to censor speech and shield students from hearing opinions that differ from their own.[13]

In March 2019, President Donald Trump cited this common script to justify a constitutionally questionable executive order that targeted higher education:

> Under the guise of speech codes and safe spaces and trigger warnings, universities have tried to restrict free thought, impose total conformity, and shut down the voices of great young Americans.[14]

The adherence of so many different sociopolitical figures to the same tropes and argumentative conceits suggests degrees of commitment to normalizing a contrived worldview rather than fully informing people about the complexities of higher education. My approach to misinformation, based on this illustration, does not amount to an attempted debate with any one kind of public figure or organization. I assume, rather, that misinformation develops through the recycling of key tropes and argumentative turns among several different groups. Eventually, a comprehensive vocabulary emerges that helps members of those groups make preferred, albeit questionable, sense of the world. The benefits of making sense of the world in those preferred ways may override habits of critical thinking even for distinguished and learned public figures.

In this context, two features of the common script about college campuses that I have illustrated deserve particular mention. First, unconventional key terms or tropes reappear across the previously quoted statements from remarkably different social and political figures: *trigger warnings*, *safe spaces*, *speech zones* or *speech codes*, *oversensitivity* among college students or a desire to be shielded and protected from ideas that make them uncomfortable. Second, these nearly identical key terms or tropes, sustained over a period of years in many different public forums, reflect a relatively common underlying worldview, which coalesces in the following core assumptions: *College campuses dangerously cater to undergraduate students. Those students irrationally crave confirmation of their existing naïve and radical ideas. Such irrational entitlement leads students to frequently shut down campus events and even assume power over entire universities. College campuses are therefore proving grounds for radical takeovers of civic institutions.* This kind of language turns fixations with occasional conflicts on specific campuses into sweeping condemnations of higher education in general. That language also turns speculative theories and stereotypes about large groups of students and faculty into allegedly accurate depictions of their supposedly dangerous psychology or motivations. Extensive portions of this book explain how such tropes and argumentative conceits reflect, at best, exaggerated claims about incidents on a small number of campuses and, at worst, demonstrable falsehoods about higher education in general.

I do not rely on the language of political stereotypes to examine the tropes and conceits that typify campus misinformation. I have already indicated that a notable variety of public figures and organizations sponsor the language of campus misinformation, from lawyers and social scientists to presidents and hyperpartisan media. That list will expand in subsequent chapters to include partisan pundits, op-ed writers, and some university faculty themselves. One of the most misleading parts of such misinformation is the tendency to measure questions of free speech and intellectual diversity on college campuses according to political stereotypes. The notion that so-called liberal students and faculty cannot stand to encounter dissenting conservative ideas suggests a myopic understanding of the many forms of First Amendment expression and intellectual exploration that universities support. I do not take a position *against* conservative viewpoints *in favor* of liberal ones. I encourage, rather, a different framework of debate that better informs the public about issues of academic freedom from multiple constructive viewpoints. Understanding how stereotypically liberal and conservative viewpoints operate within social groups is important. Using those political stereotypes as a dominant lens to assess the complexities of higher education can be reductive and misleading.

That dominant lens of partisan identity has already contributed to the erosion of public confidence in crucial civic institutions. In Chapter 1, I argue that claims about insufficient viewpoint diversity among liberal and conservative views on college campuses do not reflect a novel philosophy of higher education. Those claims echo longstanding political pressure on journalists to prioritize artificial ideological balance among so-called liberal and conservative perspectives over quality of public information—a template now applied to university teaching and research. I hope, over the course of this book, to demonstrate the benefits of engaging in public dialogue about important civic institutions without relying on stereotypes about conservative and liberal identity as a primary, all-purpose analytic lens. Moving beyond this partisan lens can empower even people who do not belong to universities to better understand the most serious threats to free speech and academic freedom on college campuses—and, by extension, threats to civil liberties writ large.

Free Speech and Intellectual Diversity

I frame the chapters to come by emphasizing two broad claims. First, many institutions of higher education protect First Amendment freedoms more effectively than most other parts of society (not *perfectly*, but *more effectively*). Second, many college campuses are now more intellectually diverse than at any prior point in history (not *ideally* diverse and democratic, but *far more so* than in any prior era).

The fact that many universities protect First Amendment freedoms better than other parts of society, especially relative to the private sector, does not rest on any single study or data set alone. Several indices support that claim. For example, layers of federal and state legislation, which do not apply to the private sector, require universities that receive public funds to demonstrate protections for personal expression, open inquiry, and equal access. "The Bill of Rights," *Business Insider* explains, "doesn't protect workers in the private sector from being fired over speech in or outside the workplace—it only prevents the government from infringing upon citizens' speech."[15] Protections for personal expression and equitable treatment that do not exist in the private sector do exist in higher education.[16] Lee Bollinger, a First Amendment scholar and president of Columbia University, thus argues that "universities are, today, more hospitable venues for open debate than the nation as a whole."[17] One of the major sources of animus in campus misinformation—diversity policies or pro-diversity messages on college campuses—are additional evidence of First Amendment protections in higher education. The purpose of those policies is to convey a commitment, often in compliance with relevant statutes, to maintaining diverse faculty bodies, student communities, and campus organizations so as to encourage new and diverse perspectives—that is, free speech.

Cycles of manufactured outrage about student protests on college campuses reflect an exceedingly selective focus when it comes to free speech and academic freedom. Sigal Ben-Porath, a professor of education, political science, and philosophy, observes that most of the controversies over campus speech "that animate public debate occur outside of class"; yet "the most meaningful and productive opportunities for discussion, the development of knowledge, and the free exchange of ideas" occur "inside the four walls of the classroom."[18] Michael Roth, president of Wesleyan University, adds that controversy over "high-profile speakers" on miscellaneous campuses has "little to do with the ongoing education project of colleges and universities."[19] Even a relatively small liberal arts institution of only a few thousand students holds hundreds of individual classes every week of an academic term. Each one of those individual classes is, in principle, a protected First Amendment forum. Now multiply the example of a relatively small liberal arts institution to encompass the approximately five thousand institutions of higher learning across the United States.[20] Those approximately five thousand institutions include Ivy League institutions, private Christian colleges, large state universities, historically Black colleges and universities, tribal colleges and universities, vocational schools, and more. Many individual state university campuses alone support tens of thousands of students and faculty—the size of small municipalities. An average university hosts on-campus events throughout an ordinary week of a given academic term. These, too, are protected forums across thousands of institutions. During the same week, numerous committees of faculty members, students, and administrators will convene on myriad college campuses. Protections for free speech and freely chosen academic activities apply to such meetings as well.

The reality that many campuses protect free speech better than other parts of society goes hand in hand with the intellectual diversity of numerous universities today. The era of legal segregation in higher education is still within living memory for many Americans. During the 1950s and 1960s, large mobs of white southerners violently sought to prevent the enrollment of even one qualified Black student at institutions like the University of Alabama and the University of Mississippi. Other universities throughout the nation, including northeastern Ivy League campuses, used a variety of discriminatory measures, from standardized testing to quota systems, to prevent qualified women and people of color from joining them.[21] Throughout most of the twentieth century, moreover, the high cost of higher education meant that colleges were the domain of mostly privileged social classes. Although such measures did not directly regulate speech, the purposeful exclusion of large segments of the population from access to higher education dramatically limited the kinds of speech and ideas that could circulate in academia.

Making higher education more accessible to qualified students and faculty introduced greater intellectual diversity into many universities. People who experience differing degrees of freedom, privilege, and social mobility frequently express contrasting intellectual perspectives. Demographic diversity commonly promotes intellectual diversity and positive educational outcomes.[22] The relative diversity of many student communities and faculty bodies today exemplifies notable changes in higher education compared to a historically recent time when belonging to a university signified membership in a socially and intellectually exclusive group.

Trends toward more equal access to higher education and enhanced sociocultural diversity within are excellent evidence of improved conditions for free speech and intellectual diversity on college campuses. Relatively new fields like African American studies, women's studies, and sex and gender studies, as well as nontraditional interdisciplinary programs, have opened up areas of study and invited perspectives long excluded from academia. Increasing numbers of international students and faculty also bring new perspectives. A predominant trend in higher education since the late twentieth century has been significant movement *away* from institutions governed by a lack of diverse viewpoints, or inflexible intellectual orthodoxy, in pursuit of greater academic freedom and intellectual diversity.

The modern university is not a utopia. Many college students and faculty perceive power disparities and gatekeeping methods in higher education as impediments to personal expression or academic inquiry. Self-described conservative members of universities and those who advocate for social justice within them might experience similar frustrations, albeit for different reasons. I do not claim that *all* college campuses protect First Amendment freedoms diligently or demonstrate meaningful organizational diversity. As a class of institutions, however, universities protect First Amendment freedoms and intellectual diversity more effectively than many other parts of society based on the structural characteristics and historical patterns that I have summarized.

Indeed, the institutional variety and decentralization among colleges and universities that I have described means that sweeping narratives about free speech emergencies and a dearth of intellectual diversity throughout higher education are substantially false. There is no one system of US higher education per se. That so-called system is, in truth, a decentralized network of several thousand dissimilar and inconsistently affiliated schools. Such features prevent anyone from arguing, in an empirically responsible way, that a restrictive political or intellectual culture has overtaken college campuses writ large.

A reasonably informed dialogue about free speech and open debate in higher education would explore specific institutional problems as well as successes on a case-by-case basis. Many universities resemble one another in terms of academic curriculums and administrative hierarchies, but student and faculty perceptions of individual campus climates can vary in important ways. Evolving trends in more inclusive and diverse campus communities, as well as notable exceptions in lingering forms of inequity, should motivate us not to preserve the status quo, but to continue reinventing higher learning for multicultural democracy. Reducing deliberations about higher education to discussions of stereotypically liberal and conservative viewpoints does not promote that laudable goal. Neither do polemics that try to absorb colleges into manufactured culture wars or promise to impose corporate standards of efficiency and productivity on them. If we can agree that universities should exemplify ideals of free speech and pluralistic exchange, then our public discourse should help those institutions build their capacities for modeling such civic goods—not popularize distorted and politically reactionary narratives about them.

Throughout the chapters to come, I not only analyze key elements of campus misinformation, but also attempt to provide empowering information that can lead to more constructive, multifaceted discourse about the state of higher education. Chapters 1 through 5 tell the story of how campus misinformation came to be in its present form. The seemingly intellectual doctrine of *viewpoint diversity* is central to this story. This new iteration of a longstanding reactionary conceit—that university diversity policies designed to welcome all views restrict conservative views—has provided a faux intellectual basis for hyperpartisan invective against college students and faculty. Orienting readers, in Chapter 1, to the circumscribed definitions of academic diversity that polemics about viewpoint diversity entail is necessary background for the rest of the book.

Chapter 2 explains how polemics about viewpoint diversity influenced public discourse amid sensationalized reports of trigger warnings and safe spaces beginning in the mid-2010s. The chapter shows the value of a historically informed perspective on academic affairs that resists the impulse to treat isolated incidents as representations of higher education in general.

In Chapter 3, I explain how this alarmism about trigger warnings and safe spaces spiraled into hyperbole about a full-fledged free speech emergency in higher education. Such developments throughout the late 2010s established campus misinformation as a staple of opinion columns and intellectual commentary distinct from investigative reporting in higher education. I argue that this mode of commentary offers a metadiscourse rooted in reactionary nostalgia for past eras of higher education rather than informative analysis of higher education in the public interest.

Sources of campus misinformation, I show in Chapter 4, frequently sought to prove broad and largely inaccurate assessments of so-called campus speech emergencies with specious uses of scientific evidence or even blatant pseudoscience. My examination of these suspect appeals generates practical guidelines that readers can use to distinguish between abuses of scientific evidence and sound scientific claims in public argument.

Escalating cycles of campus misinformation eventually helped to popularize one of the most deceptive and corrosive premises about higher education today: that violent student mobs shut down or cancel most invited speakers on most college campuses. Chapter 5 shows how that premise rests on wildly exaggerated uses of anecdotal evidence. I hope to empower readers to recognize abuses of such evidence in any given form of misinformation.

In Chapters 6 and 7, I examine antidemocratic ideas about free speech and political protest that campus misinformation has helped to normalize. Campus misinformation promotes, on the one hand, selective interpretations of First Amendment freedoms. Such interpretations emphasize decorum and civility to characterize the counter-speech of disempowered groups as suspicious, radical, or mentally unhealthy—and therefore less legitimate. Campus misinformation promotes, on the other hand, dystopian narratives about ideological orthodoxy to delegitimize the freely chosen ideas and political activities of historically disenfranchised groups. This strain of discourse falsely reduces the disparate academic studies and freely articulated views of myriad college students and faculty to a nefarious leftist orthodoxy. Both major themes of Chapters 6 and 7—circumscribed definitions of free speech and fantastical tales of warring ideological forces—are consistent with rising authoritarian sentiment.

With this book, I intend not simply to underscore the dangers of campus misinformation. I also hope to motivate readers to advocate for truly constructive public dialogue about higher education. I therefore conclude by outlining essential principles of a more historically informed and nuanced framework of debate about what's happening on college campuses. I intend such campus *information* to explain that many universities warrant public support because they generate safeguards against rigid orthodoxies and offer important resources for encouraging the kinds of free speech and open debate that are essential to democratic society.

1

Diversity and Viewpoints

Debates over how to define diversity in universities have been central to the state of US higher education for decades. Contests over the meaning of diversity in this context typically concern a variety of issues, from the content of classroom instruction to the demographic or socioeconomic makeup of student and faculty bodies. Persistent disputes over what counts as beneficial diversity in higher education and how to measure it reflect the legacy of the desegregation era during the second half of the twentieth century. Federally mandated desegregation of US public education not only made higher education more racially diverse over time. Other legal and political initiatives in the same period made higher education more accessible to women and more affordable for applicants from all economic classes. Ongoing debates over diversity on college campuses thus reflect the still-unfolding legacy of a historically recent time when higher education was patently un-diverse: overwhelmingly segregated by race, sex, and gender as well as financially or intellectually elitist.

The doctrine of *viewpoint diversity* is one of the newest and most consequential additions to recurrent debates over diversity on college campuses. The term itself is not new. Social scientists study viewpoint diversity in public and private institutions to try to understand how organizations or communities function in light of the opinions or beliefs that their members hold.[1] Over the last several years, however, viewpoint diversity has assumed new rhetorical life in popular intellectual commentaries and punditry. In these more polemical versions, viewpoint diversity has become a goal that someone advocates, seeking to correct perceived imbalances among conservative and liberal views, rather than a phenomenon that researchers analyze. Advocates for viewpoint diversity in this mold claim to operate as centrists because they seek an ideal balance between stereotypically liberal and conservative views in higher learning.

Advocates of viewpoint diversity further claim that ideological imbalances between conservative and liberal views on college campuses are scientifically measurable. For this reason, the language of viewpoint diversity in polemical forums borrows heavily from fields like psychology, social psychology, and political science. Champions of viewpoint diversity claim that they oppose imbalances among ideological views in higher education not for partisan motivations, but to understand better the psychological, social, and political roots of human behavior. (I address the scientific claims of this movement at length in Chapter 4.)

New, centrist, scientific: the positive appeal of these connotations helped this movement grow in popularity and exert influence over higher education policy. These connotations, however, are strategically misleading. This chapter shows that the allegedly fresh doctrine of viewpoint diversity is a semantic repackaging of unscientific partisan polemics. Political operatives have used polemics of this sort, from the late twentieth century forward, to oppose the diversification and democratization of university campuses according to race, sex, and gender in particular. Self-described conservatives have alleged imbalances between liberal and conservative views in national media and higher education as part of a larger coordinated strategy for decades. That strategy never promoted a genuinely diverse spectrum of social, political, and economic views, but sought to limit the increasing democratization and multiculturalism of public institutions. The increasingly popular and influential language of viewpoint diversity performs a deft linguistic trick: it refashions an old partisan argument into a seemingly new and centrist one while promoting an un-diverse definition of diversity.

Insisting that intellectual diversity hinges on the obligatory inclusion of one or two partisan perspectives is a recipe for artificial *viewpoint parity*, not a truly diverse spectrum of social and political perspectives. Diversity defined as equal time among standard, oft-repeated liberal and conservative viewpoints is not diverse. Such a definition suggests, instead, a desire for carefully managed parity among a small number of sanctioned perspectives. This approach to diversity risks excluding more viewpoints than it includes— especially when translated into education policy. Framing educational exchanges according to such narrow ideas about intellectual diversity harms students and faculty of all kinds—from those who self-identify as either liberal or conservative to those who do not. When put into practice, this definition narrows what counts as a diversity of viewpoints instead of cultivating an open intellectual environment for truly diverse forms of knowledge, insight, and perspective.

Recent political events illustrate the dangerous effects of mandatory viewpoint parity instead of true diversity of thought and opinion. Conservative legislators in various states have invoked the cause of viewpoint diversity in proposed measures to monitor First Amendment rights on college campuses and thereby achieve so-called ideological balance. In June 2021, Republican Florida governor Ron DeSantis signed a bill that requires state universities to annually survey their campuses to assess "viewpoint diversity."[2] Such language positively characterizes state monitoring of personal views or beliefs on Florida campuses. A wave of state legislation designed to correct alleged imbalances among partisan perspectives on college campuses is the clearest outcome of viewpoint diversity polemics in higher education. (I examine these measures further in Chapter 6.)

Legislative measures of this sort threaten federally protected First Amendment rights and academic freedom. Creating novel forms of state monitoring and regulation in systems of higher education only makes the First Amendment rights of *all* students and faculty more subject to state interference. Recent one-party political initiatives in this vein prove that the increasingly popular and influential conceit of viewpoint diversity is a highly partisan argument in semantic disguise. Such developments indicate that the cause of so-called viewpoint diversity is already a tool for regulating speech in higher education for political purposes, not for protecting First Amendment rights in a nonpartisan manner.

The constructive lesson of this chapter is that obligatory parity among two dominant political ideologies is not meaningful intellectual diversity. Neither does such parity foster meaningful social diversity—diversity of knowledge, experience, values, histories, and more. This perspective is fundamental to examining, across later chapters, how elements of campus misinformation advocate highly qualified definitions of diversity and thereby misinform the public about numerous aspects of contemporary higher education.

A robust commitment to institutional diversity entails proactive measures to include and value a wealth of people and perspectives. This kind of diversity requires going far beyond privileged identity categories or partisan stereotypes. Welcoming many kinds of knowledge and experience in a common learning environment typically strengthens the value of academic pursuits within it.[3] A robust commitment to diversity cuts *across* categories like race and ethnicity, culture and nationality, gender and sexuality, religious and political affiliation, health and physical ability. Forums of genuine ideological diversity bring representatives of those categories together in an intellectual climate that allows them to reframe existing forms of knowledge, discover novel intellectual questions, and develop new terms of debate. Such a commitment to diversity does not evaluate conditions for intellectual pluralism according to competitions for ideological hegemony among a small number of already-prominent partisan perspectives. Substantive commitments to genuine intellectual diversity seek, instead, to acknowledge a diverse spectrum of opinions, experiences, forms of knowledge, and identities that established partisan labels or ideological stereotypes cannot accurately describe.

My claims in what follows are not defined by a partisan perspective. My claims reflect a concern for how a prime source of manufactured controversy over free speech on college campuses—the self-styled viewpoint diversity movement—promotes misinformation about diversity itself. The conceit of viewpoint diversity has been used to constrict, rather than encourage, the healthy flow of information and independent thought. We should avoid replicating those results in higher education at a precarious time for US democracy.

Defining Diversity and Discrimination

Advocates for affirmative action policies throughout the 1960s and 1970s argued that proactive measures to include people of color and women in higher education would enhance education by ensuring a greater diversity of experience, thought, and expression. Diversity policies of this sort pursued two primary and intertwined goals. First, affirmative action policies sought to ameliorate historical injustices (specifically, the systemic denial of equal access to US higher education for people of color and women). Second, proponents of affirmative action simultaneously sought to enhance the quality of teaching and research for all students and faculty by including people and perspectives from noncanonical or non-elite backgrounds in university life.

These kinds of arguments have traditionally cited empirical data concerning evidence of structural discrimination.[4] For generations, colleges and universities predominantly denied entry to qualified people of color and women. Institutions of higher education also typically failed or outright refused to recruit and hire professors of color and women faculty. University teaching and research in those same institutions reliably prioritized traditional Western or Eurocentric perspectives as universally representative academic models—a narrow range of potentially much more diverse sources of knowledge. Advocacy for affirmative action in higher education mirrored, in these respects, advocacy for equal treatment in multiple arenas of public life, including housing and employment. Proponents of affirmative action often used scientific data to emphasize anticipated benefits of diversity in experience, thought, and expression for all applicable social or economic communities.

Politically conservative leaders, however, soon realized the threat that such arguments posed to the social, political, and economic status quo. In August 1971, Associate Justice of the US Supreme Court Lewis F. Powell Jr. issued a confidential memorandum to the Education Committee of the US Chamber of Commerce.[5] Powell warned that "the American economic system is under attack," which he additionally defined as "the free enterprise system," "capitalism," or "the profit system." This "attack" on the nation's economic system was, for Powell, related to a more general attack that ultimately threatened "the strength and prosperity of America and the freedom of our people." He listed the alleged sources of this attack: "the college campus, the pulpit, the media, the intellectual and literary journals, the arts and sciences." Powell implied that "minorities" gained an outsized influence in these groups because "these often are the most articulate, the most vocal, the most prolific in their writing and speaking." Powell's memorandum depicted a more diverse economy and society not as a public good, but as a threat to existing American "freedoms."

This document is now called the "Powell Manifesto"—such was its eventual influence in modern conservative circles. Powell's depiction of college campuses in 1971 is tellingly similar to depictions of higher education in contemporary viewpoint diversity polemics. Both hyperbolic portrayals encourage the public to imagine agents of potentially violent leftist revolutionary tendencies routinely welcomed as campus speakers, classrooms dominated by the mindless repetition of leftist slogans instead of rational thought, and false assertions that members of university campuses mostly favor socialism over free enterprise. Then as now, the argument goes, policies intended to ensure more just and equitable inclusion of ethnic minorities and women in higher education allegedly replaced substantive education with ideological indoctrination.

The 1990s witnessed intensified conservative efforts to contest definitions of institutional diversity historically aligned with affirmative action and appropriate the language of diversity itself. Conservative figures abhorred increasing public acceptance of "multiculturalism" and "postmodernism"— or, respectively, favorable opinions of cultural diversity and pluralistic approaches to knowledge, truth, or values. Yet the same conservative figures recognized the broad popular appeal of multiculturalism and the political capital of depicting conservative groups as true champions of diversity. That narrative framing simultaneously portrayed conservative people as victims of diversity measures intended to counteract systemic discrimination against people of color, women, and LGBTQ people.[6]

One of the most prominent advocacy groups in current debates over campus speech, the Foundation for Individual Rights in Education (FIRE), was established in this period.[7] Its founding was inspired by the publication, in 1998, of historian Alan Charles Kors and attorney Harvey Silverglate's book *The Shadow University: The Betrayal of Liberty on America's Campuses*. The authors echoed contemporaneous partisan equations of affirmative action with threats to student and faculty liberties. Such partisan discourse equated university affirmative action programs with stifling of free thought and expression, symbolized in the phrase "sensitivity police."[8] No such police exist on college campuses—particularly on publicly funded ones controlled or influenced by state legislatures. The phrase itself is a tool of misinformation that falsely depicts diversity and inclusion efforts, which multiple stakeholders in universities collaboratively debate and ratify, as policies conceived to target conservative viewpoints.

Throughout the 1990s, conservative and libertarian groups promoted an alternative index of diversity. This competing measurement echoed the logic of the Powell Manifesto; it held that institutions like the ones that Powell named—particularly higher education and the national media—were not truly diverse unless those institutions featured relatively equal conservative membership and viewpoints. By the 1990s, self-styled pro-diversity conservative figures like David Horwitz or members of the American Enterprise Institute promoted the idea that diversity measures created to address race, sex, and gender injustices necessarily constituted *active discrimination* against conservative viewpoints in universities.[9]

This politically motivated redefinition of diversity during the 1990s led to vigorous debates over the legitimacy of affirmative action policies in college admissions as well as multiple lawsuits against those policies. Such debates were especially intense surrounding the Supreme Court decision in *Grutter v. Bollinger* (2003). The majority ruling in that case has been cited to uphold the principle that college admissions boards may consider race, without harming nonminority students, as part of their admissions criteria.[10] In September 2019, a federal judge upheld Harvard University's race-conscious admissions policy following a more recent major court challenge.[11] As these examples indicate, legal challenges to race-conscious admissions policies target both public and private institutions.

By the turn of the century, the principle of diverse political views, in contrast to race-based diversity, offered a competing measurement of diversity itself (sometimes subsuming racial diversity, sometimes contrasting with it). Nonpartisan educational policy experts and partisan political actors both invoked the category to question whether affirmative action policies were the most effective way to promote diversity at all.[12] The rhetoric of so-called pro-diversity conservatives understandably sowed strategic confusion over the meaning and value of diversity in colleges and universities during the early twenty-first century. Efforts to spread confusion by promoting partisan broadsides about culture wars as treatises on higher education continue today: in Chapter 7, for example, I explain how viewpoint diversity warnings about the "leftist orthodoxy" of campus diversity policies strongly resemble conservative Christian warnings about the threat of "secular orthodoxy" to US institutions.[13]

Affirmative action policies in higher education responded to measurable histories of systemic discrimination across multiple public institutions—against people of color and women based on who they were *as human beings*. Those factors included employment rates, admissions data, discriminatory policies, unequal institutional opportunities for educational or professional advancement, and so on. Social scientific research into structural inequality in employment, housing, and other areas has historically met a high bar for providing empirical proof of discrimination.[14]

Protesting an alleged lack of *viewpoint* diversity is a way of saying that institutions actively and knowingly *discriminate* against specific socio-political perspectives (most often conservative or libertarian). Advocates of this premise insist upon that interpretation—intentional and systemic discrimination—as a starting place for discussions about the perceived he-gemony of liberal versus conservative perspectives on college campuses. Yet such extensive and conscious discrimination has not been empirically proven in the same way that structural discrimination in higher education has been proven—as a lynchpin in larger patterns of discrimination also ev-ident in other social and economic institutions. Characterizing conservative viewpoints as targets of *discrimination* due to their alleged unpopularity on college campuses implies a rather bold equivalence between structural dis-crimination and ideological disagreement.

Furthermore, arguments that posit an equivalence between racial or gender discrimination and viewpoint discrimination occlude another cru-cial fact: each claim of discrimination relies on a fundamentally different def-inition of unequal treatment from the other. Systemically denying people of color and women equal access to public institutions, or treating them une-qually within, constitutes a form of discrimination for unjust and undemo-cratic reasons. Such discrimination does not target people of color and women because of their ideas, abilities, and credentials, but because of the false belief that they are genetically different or inferior as a class of humanity. A defining goal of democracy is to form consensuses, ideally through open and plural-istic debate as well as reasonable evidence, about which views should drive policymaking. Systematically excluding particular *people* from opportunities for collective participation and self-advancement, however, is anathema to democracy. Discrimination of this sort excludes people so that they and their views cannot even receive a hearing.

Viewpoints constitute a fundamental part of our individual and collective identities, but those viewpoints are not genetic characteristics. Viewpoints are not intrinsic features of one's person; they are subject to debate and frequently change. Choosing to reject someone's viewpoint is not equivalent to treating that person as a fundamentally different or inferior human being. A substantive and historically informed understanding of discrimination acknowledges that discriminatory policies and practices target people based on the false belief that they are genetically different and inferior as a class of humanity, often based on scientific falsehoods. The long history of systemic political disenfranchisement, so-called race science, the denial of economic opportunity, and legacies of institutional racism or sexism that still plague higher education all prove that discrimination targets the perceived inferiority of specific human beings across multiple public institutions, not their social or political views.

The history of standardized testing in US education powerfully illustrates structural discrimination—that is, discrimination built into the very functioning of various institutions. In the early twentieth century, Princeton University psychologist and president of the American Psychological Association (APA) Carl Brigham used the results of IQ tests administered to soldiers to "conjure up a genetic intellectual racial hierarchy." Stanford University eugenicist Lewis Terman developed the IQ test and relied on a model of "general intelligence" that supposedly demonstrated substantial differences in intelligence based on race.[15] Brigham also developed the Scholastic Aptitude Test (SAT) long used in college admissions. These tests were scientifically specious from the beginning; they "failed time and again to predict success in college and professional careers or even to truly measure intelligence."[16] The true purpose of those tests was to "rule non-Whites (and women and poor people) intellectually inferior, and to justify discriminating against them in the admissions contest."[17] This account is not in dispute: the APA itself recently acknowledged such long-standing discriminatory measures and apologized to people of color for them.[18]

The well-documented history of racism in standardized testing severely challenges the idea that institutions of higher education have resolved long-standing systemic discrimination based on ideas about human hierarchies. Thousands of colleges and universities still use SAT results from hundreds of thousands of undergraduate applicants in admissions decisions every year. The format and content of the SAT has changed significantly since Brigham first developed it, yet realities of inequality and discrimination continue to shape the outcomes of standardized testing. Data indicate that standardized test scores correlate with socioeconomic status, particularly family wealth.[19] The hypercompetitive academic culture of standardized testing, increasingly supported by expensive SAT prep courses, presents another disproportionate financial barrier to students from a variety of historically disenfranchised groups.[20] The single example of the SAT suggests that the most proactive affirmative action policies constitute relatively modest efforts to address generations' worth of systemic efforts to prevent equal access in higher education.

Discrimination in its most pernicious forms goes far beyond stubborn ideological or intellectual disagreement with the views of other people. Yet the idea of calling strong disagreement with conservative viewpoints a form of discrimination has benefited advocates for the enhanced inclusion of conservative voices in universities and the media. Greg Lukianoff and Jonathan Haidt revivify the argument that diversity policies predicated on race, sex, and gender equality lead to discrimination against conservative viewpoints in their bestselling *The Coddling of the American Mind.* "In recent decades," they write, "the professoriate and the student body have become more diverse by race, gender, and other characteristics but less diverse in terms of political perspectives. We suggest that universities add 'viewpoint diversity' to their diversity statements and strategies."[21] The authors frame this recommendation by positing an incompatibility between advocacy for social change, based on progress in racial and gender inclusivity, and the allegedly fundamental goal of higher education: truth based on viewpoint diversity. Lukianoff and Haidt "disagree" with "some students and faculty" who posit "a telos of change or social progress" as a primary academic goal because a search for truth involves viewpoint diversity as they define it and a commitment to social progress involves a fundamental lack thereof.[22] The authors buttress this argument by implying that some historically marginalized groups who continue to perceive injustices in higher education might suffer emotionally or psychologically from overprotective patterns of personal and social development, potentially requiring cognitive behavioral therapy.[23] Truth and social progress, in this influential formulation, are deeply incompatible.

A problematic paradox lies at the heart of such arguments for even greater diversity, open-mindedness, and constructive disagreement on college campuses. The claim to "expand" formal measurements of diversity to emphasize "viewpoints" means, in practical terms, assigning less priority to existing measurements of diversity like race, nationality, sex, and gender, if not eliminating them as formal measurements altogether. That proposed expansion, in other words, is a de facto argument for *contracting* measurements of institutional and intellectual diversity.

Viewpoint diversity polemics thus reflect a socially or politically *reactionary* response to formal measures that have created more socially and academically diverse institutions of higher learning. My claim in this regard hews to standard definitions of reactionary attitudes in political science literature: such attitudes evince desires to restore a prior status quo following significant expansions of social, political, or economic rights and equality.[24] Appeals to *viewpoint* as an allegedly superior index of diversity, intended to make diversity criteria themselves less diverse, have specific meaning in this context. The viewpoint diversity philosophy acknowledges that the categories of race, sex, and gender were used to exclude entire communities from higher education; but it also holds, paradoxically, that tools used to counteract those structural exclusions are themselves discriminatory. Separating "truth" from "social justice" therefore implies an effort to limit intellectual debate to comparisons of already normative sociopolitical views while giving less priority, or none, to questions of power, history, and systemic injustice. In effect, the doctrine of *viewpoint* diversity claims to champion openness to dissenting views while seeking to limit definitions of diversity to a narrow range of stereotypical ideas.

Viewpoint diversity polemics thus repurpose reactionary arguments traditionally used to undermine affirmative action policies in university admissions by redefining what counts as an optimal index of diversity in higher education. The majority Supreme Court decision in *Regents of the University of California v. Bakke* (1978) famously upheld affirmative action in university admissions but declared the use of "racial quotas" unconstitutional. Lewis Powell himself, in the court's plurality decision, expressed concern that affirmative action policies on campuses might entail discrimination against "the white majority" and thereby restrict the intellectual climate in higher education.[25] Conservative and libertarian thought leaders around the turn of the century muted such concerns about the fate of the "white majority,"[26] but retained the premise that proactively encouraging sociocultural diversity in university admissions fosters un-diverse teaching and research. For example, in *The Diversity Delusion: How Race and Gender Pandering Corrupt the University and Undermine Our Culture*, Manhattan Institute Fellow Heather MacDonald argues that affirmative action policies designed to promote racial and gender equity harm students by stifling independent, ideologically diverse thought in higher education (meaning, in large part, expressly conservative ideas).[27] Viewpoint diversity polemics about college campuses thus depend upon dated reactionary arguments. Such arguments posit that institutions of higher education have achieved enough racial and gender parity; existing diversity policies, according to this logic, now constitute discrimination against members of campus communities with conservative worldviews who favor a traditional status quo in university admissions and academic content.

Arguments that depict the pursuit of knowledge as separate from the pursuit of a diverse learning environment are more ideological than empirical in nature. Data suggest that integrated schools often yield higher average scores on standardized tests.[28] Anti–affirmative action arguments obscure the well-documented truth that affirmative action policies demonstrably benefit white students and students from privileged economic backgrounds in addition to their intended beneficiaries (that is, students of color from historically disenfranchised communities). In *The Shape of the River: Long-Term Consequences of Considering Race in College and University Admissions*, former Princeton University president William Bowen and former Harvard University president Derek Bok argue that "diversity has a number of positive effects" for both white and Black students, including "increased student acceptance of other cultures, participation in community service programs, and growth in other aspects of civic responsibility."[29] Additional research includes reports of "greater cognitive capacities" gained through practice in analyzing topics according to more diverse perspectives, histories, and forms of knowledge.[30] In *The Difference: How the Power of Diversity Creates Better Groups, Firms, Schools, and Societies*, political scientist Scott Page posits that integrated or more diverse classrooms can, under the right conditions, foster general academic success by boosting all students' ability to engage in critical thinking and problem solving, including economically advantaged white students.[31]

Quality education based on consideration of many different sociopolitical viewpoints and the goals of demographic diversity are frequently harmonious goods. Institutions do not need to choose between robust education and diversity so defined. Documented educational benefits for all kinds of students from proactive diversity and inclusion programs contradict the false dichotomy that colleges must prioritize one over the other. Treating quality education and diversity measures designed to create more just and equitable learning environments as distinct or conflicting goals suggests an artificial separation. Numerous governing boards and admissions deans at both public *and* private universities routinely create policies to recruit students or faculty from marginalized communities for the positive academic and social effects that such measures produce.[32] The fact that such policies are so normal and internally desirable in both public and private institutions of higher education invalidates claims that diversity and inclusion programs operate on a zero-sum competitive basis, in which policies designed to help historically marginalized student groups automatically harm historically privileged ones. Considerable amounts of research shows that the opposite is true.

"Viewpoint" means "point of view" or "opinion." To disagree with, or choose not to consider, a particular viewpoint is not the same thing as applying law or policy unequally to persons based on who they are as human beings—so long as people remain free to express that viewpoint in society at large. A lack of so-called viewpoint diversity in institutions does not prima facie indicate discrimination against particular classes of human beings in the same way that a lack of proportional racial, sexual, or gender diversity in institutions indicates discrimination against historically disenfranchised groups.

Deciding not to embrace a viewpoint, or preferring other viewpoints, is not discrimination—it's disagreement. Deciding not to agree with a freely spoken viewpoint, without taking steps to suppress that viewpoint in other forums, is neither censorship nor persecution—it's having a different point of view. Someone might argue that people *should* consider such viewpoints; but they do not *have* to do so. Members of a democratic society are free to take a different view, so to speak. Communities and institutions are free to choose—within reason, so long as First Amendment rights are protected—which *viewpoints* they wish to consider within open and accessible forums and to ignore or reject those that such communities and institutions deem less relevant to their pursuits.

I previously noted that Powell addressed his foreboding memo to the *Education* Committee of the Chamber of Commerce. Conservative thought leaders like Powell have long portrayed educational institutions as central ideological battlefields among larger social, political, and economic contests for power. Political pressures for greater ideological balance or viewpoint diversity in mainstream journalism—frequently on behalf of conservative interests, to counteract a presumed hegemony of liberal voices in the media—have therefore mirrored arguments about perceived leftist dogma on college campuses for decades. Any consideration of viewpoint diversity as an educational philosophy is incomplete without exploring this well-worn connection with news media.

Viewpoint Diversity and Political Media

Conservative figures in the postwar period alarmed by popular support for New Deal economic programs and liberal political power frequently cited a slogan from the world of broadcasting: "equal time." The phrase symbolized a case for ideological balance on college campuses and in the media.[33] Clarence Manion, for example, was not only an influential conservative radio and television host from the mid-1950s forward, but a former professor and dean of Notre Dame Law School. He helped to pioneer the argument, as part of a multifaceted partisan strategy, that universities and the national media both embraced so-called liberals while stifling conservative voices, frequently arguing that "the Conservative point of view should be given equal time."[34] *National Review*, which significantly shaped the modern conservative movement, was founded on the same premise. William F. Buckley Jr.'s mission statement in its first issue, published in 1955, claimed that "radical conservatives in this country" are "being suppressed or mutilated by the Liberals." The intellectual and commercial selling point of *National Review* was "to encourage responsible dissent from the Liberal orthodoxy."[35] The examples of Manion and *National Review* illustrate how claims of anticonservative suppression in the name of "equal time" were partisan marketing appeals, designed to grow an audience and generate profit, rather than sound historical or journalistic claims.

The fact that such influential claims about anticonservative discrimination in higher education were demonstrably untrue when figures like Manion or the founders of *National Review* made them is an index of their partisan nature. Widespread enthusiasm for Anglo-Saxon ideals of patriotism, cultural superiority, and masculinity became common in all forms of schooling (including northeastern Ivy League institutions) after segregation between white and Black people became legal around the turn of the twentieth century.[36] University teaching and research predicated on the alleged superiority of white people over Black people, of men over women, of European culture over other cultures, and of Judeo-Christian traditions over other belief systems was standard in the humanities and sciences. Such views were not wrong because self-identified conservative figures espoused them; they were wrong because those views are empirically inaccurate, as numerous academic disciplines have repeatedly demonstrated. The legal and social machinery of segregation still pervaded higher education at the time of Manion's early broadcasts; federal desegregation measures had only just begun in the mid-1950s. Thousands of predominantly white Americans engaged in self-described massive resistance to court-ordered desegregation for years to come; they sometimes used mob violence to prevent even a handful of Black students from officially enrolling in all-white institutions.[37] Higher education would remain either financially or practically inaccessible for women and people from lower-class backgrounds well into the late twentieth century.[38]

Granted, some self-described leftists—even self-described communists or Marxists—did join universities throughout the mid-twentieth century as those affiliations and systems of thought became more fashionable in labor organizing during the New Deal era. Faculty and students of this sort advocated for European-style socialist or communist programs in political circles. Yet the ranks of those openly leftist faculty and student groups were generally small within higher education, and educators with communist sympathies often reserved those sympathies for "civic life rather than the classroom."[39] The more accurate and comprehensive truth is that strident anticommunism was "central to American identity" in the postwar period.[40] In this context, college campuses remained predominantly elite, traditionally Christian, white, and male deep into the twentieth century.[41] The conceit of anticonservative or overwhelmingly leftist campuses echoed the contemporaneous Red Scare, or political hysteria about communists infiltrating the federal government and civic institutions, which led to some of the worst abuses of civil liberties in US history. Arguments about the necessity of giving equal time to conservative viewpoints from figures like Manion or periodicals like *National Review* make sense as analogous overreactions to the simple presence of so-called leftist ideas in some academic circles, not as accurate descriptions of higher education in general.

Manion, Buckley, and other self-described conservative figures told stories of discrimination against conservatives on college campuses to hold the line against post–World War II efforts to make college more accessible for all kinds of students. Ending discrimination against people of color and women in university admissions and making advanced education more economically affordable would substantially transform institutions typically reserved for socially privileged and financially elite classes. Strategic conservative messages about the need for equal time from the mid-1950s forward were flawed as empirical claims but highly profitable as political and commercial devices—staples of partisan identity and addictive narrative entertainment on talk radio and other media platforms for decades to come.

The corrosive effects of partisan pressures for equal time or ideological balance in political journalism illustrate the danger of applying those same standards to university teaching and research. After all, conservative thought leaders have long sought to exert partisan influence over both types of institutions with the same general doctrine. Nonpartisan researchers generally agree that redefining political journalism as a relatively free-for-all competition between stereotypically conservative and liberal viewpoints has been disastrous. The Telecommunications Act of 1996 included the internet in Federal Communications Commission policy for the first time. The act overhauled decades' worth of telecommunications law.[42] It was designed to eliminate barriers to competition in media markets by permitting greater ownership consolidation. The elimination of those barriers raised the question of whether consolidated private ownership of multiple media channels in a given market would restrict "viewpoint diversity."[43] For this reason, credible researchers have analyzed issues of viewpoint diversity in peer-reviewed scholarship on affirmative action policy and media ownership.

Overtly partisan organizations, however, appropriated the ideal of viewpoint diversity in those same contexts to claim alleged political or ideological biases in news media. "Viewpoint diversity" sounds politically neutral in theory; in practice, the cause has served narrowly partisan interests, in media ownership and programming, to the detriment of the public at large. Promoting greater diversity of political views in news media meant setting aside equal airtime for one type of viewpoint in particular—not for ensuring coverage of a genuinely diverse array of social and political views.

Such advocacy does not promote substantively diverse social and political perspectives. It promotes artificial viewpoint *parity*. A degree of elitism is coded into this preference for ensuring "ideological balance" by comparing "viewpoints": the viewpoints in question typically reflect the established sociopolitical platforms of already empowered officials and spokespersons.[44] Powerful groups thus pressure political journalists to provide equal airtime for partisan viewpoints and entertaining narratives that they wish to publicize. This scenario can lead journalists to function, in the words of political scientist Jonathan Mermin, as "transcribers of official utterances"[45]—even if those utterances contain falsehoods or distorted narratives.

Commitments to viewpoint diversity based on a perceived imbalance among partisan perspectives have undermined quality public information in a variety of ways. Debates in the news media intended to demonstrate ideological balance occupy significant amounts of airtime on cable news television or radio and often shape discussions of critical issues in traditional print media. Typically, however, those debates are not substantive exchanges of ideas or arguments but forms of political theater that diminish public understanding of issues. A dominant trend in political journalism over recent decades has been reporters conspicuously positioning themselves as seemingly impartial mediators of so-called conservative and liberal spokespersons rather than as advocates for evidence, truth, and overall quality of information.[46] Pressures to provide "balance" of this kind encourage news organizations to prioritize entertaining clashes among talking heads who offer simplistic talking points in place of substantive information.[47] Such talking heads engage in partisan messaging instead of modeling collaborative cross-party dialogue or problem-solving. Pressure for "balance" is one of the main reasons that cable news networks and some mainstream news outlets book professional political consultants or members of partisan think tanks to comment on critical issues like climate change, reproductive health, or gun violence rather than, say, climate scientists, doctors, and nonpartisan researchers.

In the event, these journalistic tendencies promote a kind of misinformation about conservatism and liberalism as well. Journalism designed to provide consistently substantive and nuanced comparisons of conservative and liberal policy proposals would benefit the public. Centering political reporting on talking heads paid to stage combative clashes for entertainment purposes does not achieve that goal.

Powerful partisan figures increasingly apply the same pressure for ideological balance to social media.[48] Conservative officials and their supporters claim that social media corporations like Facebook and Twitter censor their free speech—despite the fact that conservative groups have used such platforms with impressive fundraising and electoral success in recent years.[49] Accusing social media companies of a lack of viewpoint diversity or ideological imbalance exploits how those platforms market themselves to the public: as virtual unregulated marketplaces of diverse ideas and free speech. In fact, platforms like Facebook, Twitter, and others are heavily regulated—not by the government, but for corporate profit.[50] The algorithms of those platforms identify the tastes of different users and feed them addictive, revenue-generating content.

Those algorithms have made misinformation not only prevalent but also profitable. Facebook alone is now a quasi-monopolistic entity home to significant overlap between baseless conspiracy theories and self-described conservative group interests.[51] False conspiracy theories about immigration, voter fraud in the 2020 presidential election, COVID vaccinations, radical political indoctrination in public schools, and many more thrive on Facebook as well as other popular social media sites. In October 2021, a Facebook whistleblower provided a trove of internal documents to Congress that detail internal company research. According to those documents, Facebook officials long knew that their company was not an open marketplace of constructive ideas and free speech but an extremely profitable engine of addiction to political disinformation and cycles of outrage that it foments.[52] Pressuring social media companies to ensure that they achieve ideological balance is a disingenuous ploy that does not address the most serious problems with social media giants.

Such disturbing outcomes in political journalism and social media offer cautionary tales. Those outcomes demonstrate what can happen when institutions that claim to provide fact-based information in the public interest filter such information to ensure viewpoint parity or demonstrate artificial ideological balance. We should seek to prevent equivalent definitions of viewpoint parity as true diversity of independent thought and opinion from becoming the dominant terms of debate in disputes over free speech and academic freedom in higher education. Or, as I explain in the next section, we should prevent even further acceptance of artificial viewpoint parity in higher education than has already occurred.

Viewpoint Parity in Higher Education

Interest in discredited but cleverly repackaged forms of "race science" has risen over the past several years.[53] Disinformation networks have attempted to normalize the idea, particularly in academic circles, that some non-Western peoples are genetically different and therefore threatening.[54] Advocates of such "science" erroneously posit fundamental differences among human beings based on invented racial classifications. Those advocates frequently justify their work by claiming that it advances free speech or viewpoint diversity while demonstrating a courage to question so-called political correctness.[55]

The popular online magazine *Quillette* was founded in 2015 in this spirit.[56] This publication markets itself with the slogan "Free Thought Lives" as a haven for worthy intellectual positions unfairly censored in academia. Such positions frequently involve unscientific premises about inherent differences in intelligence between "races," the false contention that Black people are more genetically predisposed to criminal behavior than white people, and the bigoted assertion that feminism and transgender identity pervert natural law.[57] The notion that *Quillette* offers even greater freedom to explore ideas than allegedly censorious universities, however, has attracted some credentialed researchers themselves.[58]

Institutions of higher education should welcome the development of new and potentially transformative ideas or modes of expression. Resurgent race science hinders those goals. So-called science of this sort promotes old and regressive ideas hostile to a diversity of evidence-based argument. The racist core of renascent arguments for allegedly inherent racial differences is time-worn: the idea of "polygenesis," or separate racial origins for white and Black people, dates back centuries. The conceit of genetically distinct "races" is also scientifically erroneous: the Human Genome Project proved that the genetic code for white and Black people—for all human beings—is 99.9 percent the same.[59] The minor genetic variations that do exist among human populations are evidence of general human diversity, not fundamentally distinct races.[60] Race is not a biological category. It is a political category.

Many self-identified conservative thinkers retort that such minor genomic differences can nonetheless explain differences in intelligence or achievement based on supposedly categorical racial differences. Such claims are scientifically false. Minor genomic differences that explain differences in skin color (or sexual differences) do not determine intelligence or achievement. Greater genetic diversity can be observed *within* so-called racial groups than between them.[61]

Renewed citations of arguments for inherent racial differences in media commentary and on university campuses descend from early modern founts of prejudice, regardless of whatever political affiliation supporters of those arguments claim. In the name of viewpoint diversity, however, some members of universities are now entertaining this faux science as a seemingly illuminating scientific and political perspective. Here, a commitment to viewpoint diversity based on the idea of ideological balance has not led to valuable new ideas, much less to truth. In the case of resurgent race science, the conceit of ideological balance has led to the opposite of substantive intellectual diversity and scholarly truth: enhanced public legitimacy for scientific falsehoods that political and religious authorities have used to justify systemic discrimination throughout Western modernity.

Giving equal weight to antiscientific viewpoints in university teaching and research undermines that teaching and research. Giving equal weight in higher education to viewpoints about historical persons and events that most professional historians reject distorts the work of evidence-based history. I do not propose excluding such viewpoints from university classrooms altogether or for censuring students who espouse them. Evidence-based teaching and research consist precisely in open dialogue and sustained investigation about the relative merits of differing ideas. Evidence-based explanations for why certain viewpoints lack substantive merit do not signify knee-jerk disengagement, much less censorship. Meritorious academic ideas can withstand informed academic scrutiny. Independent thought means being able to collect data, information, and testimony for your own purposes and judge the validity of particular arguments—not being forced to directly debate someone who espouses a disproven view. A standard of viewpoint parity among stereotypical political orientations, however, can threaten freedom of independent judgment and substantive intellectual exchanges by disguising discredited and bigoted views as seemingly meritorious academic viewpoints.

Conclusion

Understanding that viewpoint diversity polemics promote circumscribed definitions of diversity—or viewpoint *parity*—is essential to understanding how they have inspired an increasingly popular and seemingly new intellectual doctrine. That doctrine did not emerge ex nihilo, but in direct response to periodic movements for greater social and intellectual diversity in public institutions. The dangers that the cleverly repackaged philosophy of viewpoint diversity pose to such institutions are apparent in a variety of past and present forms. Examples include partisan pressures on journalists to reduce political information to a competition among stereotypical viewpoints, recently passed education policies that claim to protect viewpoint diversity through enhanced monitoring or restriction of educational content, and unscientific racial prejudices disguised as seemingly fresh and meritorious viewpoints in universities. The following chapters progressively show how polemics about allegedly poor viewpoint diversity and so-called liberal indoctrination in higher education have evolved into threats to truly diverse academic perspectives and First Amendment freedoms. That story begins, in Chapter 2, by examining manufactured outrage about two concepts in particular during the mid-2010s: trigger warnings and safe spaces.

2
Trigger Warnings and Safe Spaces

During the 2013–2014 academic school year, the Oberlin College Sexual Offense Policy Task Force published a now-infamous resource guide. It advised Oberlin professors to adhere to a policy of including trigger warnings on their syllabi in cases of potentially disturbing course materials.[1] These warnings would inform students that portions of course content might "trigger" strong emotional reactions or feelings of discomfort, especially for survivors of trauma required to study graphic depictions of violence or sexual assault.

Word of this policy recommendation circulated throughout mainstream journalism and social media. The *Los Angeles Times* editorial board acknowledged that the Oberlin College resolution was advisory in nature, not official policy, but still likened it to "a parody of political correctness." The editorial board called the recommendation an "attack on academic freedom" and chided universities that allegedly aspire to "bubble-wrap students against everything that might be frightening or offensive to them."[2] "Safe spaces," another columnist opined in the *New York Times*, "are an expression of the conviction, increasingly prevalent among college students, that their schools should keep them from being 'bombarded' by discomfiting or distressing viewpoints."[3] Such commentaries inspired scores of articles and blog posts that lampooned ostensibly fragile, naïve, and easily triggered college students as well as their supposedly feckless, politically correct professors. Those plentiful articles and blog posts overwhelmingly presented badly distorted yet addictively entertaining narratives about the realities of teaching and administration in higher education.

A series of troubling incidents at the University of Missouri from 2015 to 2016, soon after the reports about trigger warnings at Oberlin College, inspired on-campus student protests. Those protests attracted, in turn, prolonged national media attention. A student group known as Concerned Student 1950 protested a host of issues with the support of some faculty and administrators. Points of conflict included racism on campus, workplace benefits, and insufficient administrative responses to concerns about the treatment of students of color. A hunger strike by graduate student Jonathan

Butler and, eventually, a strike by the university football team (refusing to play scheduled games until student concerns were addressed) became the most widely reported forms of protest. Increased national focus on these episodes eventually hastened the resignations of top university leadership, including the president and chancellor.[4]

Articles in mainstream publications and ideologically slanted forums alike derided University of Missouri student protesters for their alleged entitlement and intolerance. Conor Friedersdorf, a columnist at *The Atlantic*, opined that student protesters had "weaponized the concept of 'safe spaces,'" referring to their "behavior" as "safe-baiting: using intimidation or initiating physical aggression to violate someone's rights, then acting like your target is making you unsafe."[5] Friedersdorf offered this sweeping assessment based only on secondhand reports in social media or from other journalists. His wording illustrates the journalistic tendency to interpret the social activism of Black people in criminal terms—with descriptions of mobs, "aggression," and weaponry.[6] This kind of subjective and prejudicial condemnation of predominantly Black student protests at the University of Missouri typified what passed for journalism about those protests in many mainstream outlets.

In the event, news reports about protests at the University of Missouri imitated historically dated partisan narratives about college campuses. Conservative media, as the previous chapter noted, have long claimed that US institutions of higher education are bastions of dangerous liberal political correctness that promote breakdowns in civil order.[7] After all, William F. Buckley helped to define the intellectual ethos of the modern conservative movement in the early 1950s with *God and Man at Yale: The Superstitions of "Academic Freedom,"* which described his encounters with alleged liberal indoctrination as an undergraduate student.[8] However, advocacy for so-called viewpoint diversity in its increasingly popular form—a polemical doctrine about higher education disguised as an allegedly centrist intellectual philosophy—gained traction *after* national reporting about the incidents at Oberlin College and the University of Missouri.

This chapter examines an essential phase in the development of contemporary campus misinformation, including viewpoint diversity arguments: the simultaneous popularization and apparent intellectual legitimation of obsessions with trigger warnings and safe spaces on university campuses. Prevalent reports about these academic innovations from the mid-2010s forward helped dated arguments about liberal, anticonservative college campuses become seemingly new, centrist, and scientific perspectives on free speech in higher education. The popular appeal of viewpoint diversity as an apparently new model of intellectual diversity in universities could not have emerged as it did without widespread hyperbole about these key terms in particular—trigger warnings and safe spaces. Sensational news coverage as well as apparently intellectual commentary about the alarming significance of trigger warnings and safe spaces at Oberlin College and the University of Missouri established a now-common playbook of campus misinformation: take the unfamiliar language of select university policies or student behaviors out of context, claim that they represent most policies or students, then proclaim that higher education is in peril.

Appearances of the phrases "trigger warnings" and "safe spaces" spiked dramatically in public discourse following the incidents at Oberlin College and the University of Missouri.[9] A variety of organizations announced their mission to combat what those incidents allegedly revealed about free speech on college campuses. *Quillette*, the online magazine that describes itself as "a platform for free thought"[10] and routinely features viewpoint diversity polemics, was founded in 2015. Heterodox Academy was founded in the same year to counteract "a lack of ideological diversity" that has allegedly "broken" higher education.[11] These developments *seemed* to announce a new movement, with new arguments, in response to an allegedly unprecedented series of university crises. In truth, the conceit of irrational liberal academic hegemonies suppressing viewpoint diversity offered merely new, and politically potent, verbal costuming in which to clothe long-standing arguments against the perceived culture of college campuses.[12] Entertaining and easily recycled narratives in this vein fixated on one central and newly devised character in particular: the coddled student who irrationally craves trigger warnings and safe spaces.

The Trope of the Coddled Student

The assumption that trigger warnings and safe spaces are common on university campuses is central to present-day campus misinformation in general and to viewpoint diversity polemics in particular. Two primary forms of hyperbole feed this assumption: (1) the notion that "coddled" students now demand that faculty use trigger warnings on syllabi to shield them from discomforting material and (2) the conceit that colleges provide safe spaces to which easily "triggered" students can retreat when they encounter people who disagree with them.

Exposés about triggered students who crave safe spaces suggest a melodramatic and easily recycled narrative about the culture of higher education.

Consider, for example, *New York* magazine columnist Jonathan Chait's factually misleading description of these trends at the height of national reporting about Oberlin College and the University of Missouri:

> At a growing number of campuses, professors now attach "trigger warnings" to texts that may upset students, and there is a campaign to eradicate "microaggressions," or small social slights that might cause searing trauma. These newly fashionable terms [suggest] that people should be expected to treat even faintly unpleasant ideas or behaviors as full-scale offenses.[13]

Chait's account is based more on uninformed stereotypes about college campuses than on detailed information. He, or any other opinion writer, cannot know how many students or faculty across literally thousands of universities in individual classrooms use the language of "trigger warnings" or "microaggressions," much less why or how often they do so. We can highlight the strangeness of such fixations on a few isolated terms by remembering that members of many different professions—from professional sports and the US military to medical organizations and the tech sector—routinely communicate with one another using idioms that seem odd or nonsensical to people outside those professions. Sweeping generalizations based on incidental information therefore suffice in columns like Chait's to create a cynical idea of college campuses rather than a fully informed engagement with their complex realities. Here, too, is Greg Lukianoff's and Jonathan Haidt's sweeping and factually questionable assessment of the same scenarios: "The ultimate aim, it seems, is to turn campuses into 'safe spaces' where young adults are shielded from words and ideas that make some uncomfortable. . . . This movement seeks to punish anyone who interferes with that aim, even accidentally."[14] The authors' description also reflects a simplistic narrative devoid of substantive context, not a realistic account of university affairs in their full diversity across thousands of institutions. Such a melodramatic narrative is likely more entertaining and intuitively understandable for general readers compared to investigative journalism focused on specific issues in higher education.

The imagery of coddled and ideologically rigid undergraduate students has quickly become synonymous with campus culture itself. This development is due, in large part, to a chorus of opinion writers, bloggers, and pundits who promote fear-based appeals about trigger warnings and safe spaces based on atypical campus incidents. The spillover effects of such misinformation on civic discourse in the United States undermine the cause of constructive deliberation. Phrases like "trigger warnings" and "safe spaces" have entered national debates as all-purpose denigrations of social and political groups dedicated to principles of equality and social justice. Americans now routinely mock one another, in the traditional media and on social media alike, for being easily "triggered" (meaning fragile, irrational, or emotionally unstable) and for craving a "safe space" (an allegedly cowardly show of weakness or fear). New terms of denigration in popular discourse, not substantive public deliberation, are some of the most obvious results of the viewpoint diversity movement in higher education to date. The following sections show how rampant hyperbole about trigger warnings and safe spaces on college campuses drove the earliest phases of such misinformation.

Trigger Warnings

Suddenly plentiful calls for viewpoint diversity on college campuses in 2015 and 2016 were never based on full and accurate information or peer-reviewed research about higher education—especially concerning tales of trigger warnings and safe spaces. Those calls were the first waves of contemporary misinformation about college campuses that continues to negatively influence public perceptions of higher education. Oberlin College never adopted a policy requiring professors to use trigger warnings on syllabi. The resource guide produced by the Sexual Offense Policy Task Force strongly advised such warnings, but apparently before thoroughly consulting Oberlin faculty. The proposal language was tabled due to deliberations between faculty and administration. Oberlin College never officially required faculty to use trigger warnings on syllabi and does not require them to do so now.[15] Vague reports about other universities that apparently considered trigger warning policies nonetheless circulated in the wake of the proposed Oberlin College policy.

Trigger warnings first appeared in online communities. Those warnings advised users with a history of personal trauma, such as sexual assault, that they might encounter content on specific websites that could trigger symptoms of posttraumatic stress disorder. Miscellaneous university instructors later adapted this practice in their syllabi or other course materials. Such academic equivalents advised students that specific class content could conceivably affect students with various past traumatic experiences.[16] Instructors who occasionally invoke trigger warnings do so customarily to signify support for students with experiences of trauma, not to shield them from class activities or discussions.

Attempting to quantify how many professors use trigger warnings is difficult because definitions of trigger warnings are inherently subjective or impressionistic. What specific words or phrases qualify as a trigger warning? Is a one-sentence trigger warning the same as a trigger warning composed of several paragraphs? Is an instructor's preview about specific course content a trigger warning even if the instructor never uses that term? The notion of an official count, let alone sweeping claims about university teaching based on any such tally, introduces more abstraction than clarity into discussions about classroom content. Some of the available data, however, strongly indicate that trigger warnings were rarely used on campuses in 2013 and 2014, during initial waves of public derision about them, including at so-called elite liberal arts institutions.[17]

On-campus resource centers for diversity groups or offices of student affairs at some institutions might occasionally *recommend* versions of trigger warnings to faculty and provide guidance for usage. Yet those entities do not, by themselves, make and enforce university policy. Such entities tend to be far less powerful offices compared to other, more traditional elements of university hierarchies.

I neither endorse nor oppose the use of trigger warnings in university classrooms. I oppose, rather, spreading misinformation about the nature and extent of trigger warning use on college campuses to foment cynicism about higher education. Many faculty from coast to coast are essentially free to use trigger warnings, or not, at their professional discretion—precisely in the name of academic freedom. Undergraduate students are free to enroll, by choice, in the occasional courses where professors use trigger warnings on syllabi. Those students are equally free to either avoid or withdraw from a course, by choice, if an instructor happens to use trigger warnings on the syllabus. Furthermore, resources like motion picture ratings systems, parental guides for popular media or young adult fiction, and broadcasters' warnings that a news segment might be inappropriate for young viewers have been socially ubiquitous for decades. The presence of those messages underscores the unscientific and contrived nature of fixations with trigger warnings among journalists and pundits.

Trigger warnings are just one of many teaching devices that a given university instructor *might* use in a classroom situation, from syllabus composition and personal communication styles to audiovisual materials and classroom seating configurations. Such warnings are just one device among many that professors may use to perform a necessary instructional task: previewing course content to encourage the most constructive kind of learning experience—that is, preparing students to *engage* with course material as best fits their specific needs, not excusing them from doing so. Consulting responsible data about the use of trigger warnings in higher education can be useful, but assuming that such data reveal something conclusive about the mental health of students or the quality of teaching in universities mistakes the proverbial forest for the trees. Teaching requires instructors to manage myriad situational factors—some predictable, some unpredictable—on a continually changing basis. The presence of a written trigger warning on a syllabus reveals little about how a professor may or may not use it as a tool of communication or interaction in the classroom (or even if every student read the syllabus, and thus the trigger warning, at all). If the occasional presence of ill-defined trigger warnings on specific campuses raises such alarm, then the potential effects of numerous other teaching tools like PowerPoint slides, online audio-visual materials, or structured seating arrangements in classroom spaces deserve equal, if not greater, scrutiny. Yet other sections of university syllabi or consciously designed elements of learning environments have inspired none of the mockery, invective, and melodrama that the idea of trigger warnings on university campuses has inspired.

Prominent advocates for viewpoint diversity on college campuses have unintentionally proven that their initial denunciations of trigger warnings were polemics unsupported by professional research. In the summer of 2018, advocates of viewpoint diversity and other agents of campus misinformation enthusiastically publicized what they described as the first peer-reviewed social scientific study of trigger warnings. The findings from a team of psychologists at Harvard University were inconclusive. "Trigger warnings," the authors concluded, "may inadvertently undermine some aspects of emotional resilience. Further research is needed on the generalizability of our findings."[18] (I address this study and the growing body of social scientific research on trigger warnings in Chapter 4.) Advocates of viewpoint diversity and other sources of campus misinformation, however, claimed that this single study *proved* that condemnations of trigger warnings had been prophetic and scientifically valid all along. Pamela Paresky, a senior scholar in human development and psychology at the Foundation for Individual Rights in Education (FIRE), reported that the "new study out of Harvard—the first randomized controlled experiment designed to examine the effects of trigger warnings on individual resilience—may indicate that" arguments about the serious psychological harms of trigger warnings "were right."[19] This interpretation is a creative way of verbally managing the fact that previously broad descriptions and strident critiques of trigger warnings prior to 2018 were based on hyperbole and hearsay, not scientific evidence or informed scholarly investigations.

Trigger warnings were, and are, rarely used on college syllabi. University policies do not generally mandate their use. Now-common arguments that cite the allegedly increasing use of trigger warnings, mandated by institutions that coddle rather than educate close-minded students, began as a collection of subjective and poorly informed claims about teaching practices and university policy-making. Trigger warnings, however, were not the only target of popular invective against college students and university campuses in the mid-2010s. Manufactured outrage about safe spaces at that time also helped to affix the trope of the coddled student in public discourse about higher education.

Safe Spaces

Misinformation about safe spaces on college campuses proliferated in the wake of protests at the University of Missouri. The incidents at that university were connected to widely reported unrest in Ferguson, Missouri (part of the nearby St. Louis metropolitan area) following the now-infamous fatal shooting of Mike Brown. A white policer officer fatally shot Brown, an unarmed Black teenager, amid suspicious circumstances in August 2014.[20] Black Lives Matter, a nonviolent activist movement that seeks to counteract systemic violence and discrimination against Black people, gained national visibility in the wake of this tragedy.[21] A wave of protests and riots in Ferguson in late 2014 also fueled national controversy over racial inequalities in the criminal justice system and the dangers of a militarized police force, as evident in aggressive police responses to predominantly Black protesters in Ferguson.[22]

   The Ferguson unrest in 2014 and rising conflicts over racism on the University of Missouri campus beginning in 2015 were meaningfully connected. The Black Lives Matter movement was already growing, to a large extent, on college campuses at the time. (Part of continuing opposition to that movement in self-described conservative circles thus rests on the assumption that universities nurture dangerous leftist ideas.) Many Black undergraduate students at the University of Missouri, especially members of Concerned Student 1950, argued that the case of Ferguson demonstrated how excessive police force disproportionately affects young Black people. Events in Ferguson also demonstrated, to those same students, the urgent need to protest structures of systemic racism that enabled such violence and inequality.[23]

   In historical terms, however, the roots of predominantly Black student protests at the University of Missouri from 2015 to 2016 run far deeper than the conflicts in Ferguson that preceded them. A longer historical perspective concerning the segregationist legacies of many institutions of higher education reveals the severity of misinformation about university campuses—especially the idea of "safe spaces"—that those protests inspired. Numerous campuses served as havens for pro–Lost Cause symbolism, historiography, and culture throughout the late nineteenth and early twentieth centuries. Defenders of the so-called Old South from organizations like the United Confederate Veterans and United Daughters of the Confederacy successfully lobbied universities to dedicate vast portions of both public and private campuses to Confederate leaders, from monuments and statuary to the names of classroom buildings and residence halls.[24] Extensive areas of state university campuses like the University of Mississippi, the University of Alabama, and the University of North Carolina became, to a large extent, living shrines to antidemocratic Confederate memory based on blatant historical falsehoods.[25] Southern university administrations in the early 2020s continued to explore proposals for renaming campus facilities that still bore the names of Ku Klux Klan leaders—often in the face of notable resistance to those proposals.[26]

Some pundits today claim that these forms of Lost Cause nostalgia are innocuous markers of history. The proud words of Confederate nostalgists who worked hard to establish such memorials and Old South rituals on college campuses disprove those claims. Julian S. Carr, an industrialist and former private in the Confederate Army, presided over a dedication ceremony for the "Silent Sam" Confederate Monument at the University of North Carolina in 1913. In addition to honoring Confederate soldiers, he said, the monument would remind the "present generation . . . of what the Confederate soldier meant to the welfare of the Anglo Saxon race" and that "the purist strain of the Anglo-Saxon" should remain superior.[27] Carr's dedication address was typical. Confederate nostalgists like him wanted to be remembered and celebrated for establishing Lost Cause narratives, rituals, and memorials in southern colleges and universities as symbols of school pride and communal belonging.[28] Every such narrative, ritual, and memorial sought to justify racial inequality, false history, and opposition to democracy.[29]

Institutions of higher education in other parts of the nation, including Ivy League campuses, also frequently embraced such culturally conservative and exclusionary narratives, rites, or symbols. John W. Burgess of Columbia University, one of the founders of political science in the United States, taught that Black people were intellectually inferior and uncivilized compared to white people. Academic arguments of this kind supported growing sentiment among white communities in the early twentieth century that recognizing the right of Black people to vote after the Civil War had been a mistake. As a Princeton University professor of political science, future US president Woodrow Wilson recycled antebellum tropes when he opined that formerly enslaved people and their descendants could not understand the concept of freedom and were not ready for full citizenship.[30] Lost Cause narratives became thoroughly institutionalized in the school symbolism and classroom content of many universities—throughout the nation, not only in southern states—over the course of the twentieth century.

The work of making those institutions less exclusionary and more naturally diverse continues today. Administrators at historically segregated state schools, including the University of Missouri, now frequently embrace the goals of diversity and inclusivity in the name of both social justice and quality education regardless of their individual political affiliations.[31] Yet the physical and ideological architecture of the Old South associated with numerous institutions of higher education never fully collapsed. The late twentieth century witnessed two mass movements around racism and inequality in the United States: a movement for lawful desegregation of public facilities and a movement that proudly embraced the cause of massive resistance in response. The ideology of massive resistance used every conceivable legal tactic to delay federal desegregation in higher education throughout the 1950s and 1960s. Members of that movement also engaged in civil disobedience and periodic mob violence to prevent even a single admitted Black student from attending classes at institutions like the University of Mississippi and the University of Alabama. Mass resistance to lawful desegregation was, in many respects, successful; immediate and full desegregation never occurred after *Brown v. Board of Education* in 1954.[32] Gradual desegregation arguably continues today insofar as hate speech against Black people and other displays of intimidation or hostility toward them persist on historically segregated campuses.[33] Black History Month in 2022, for instance, commenced with a series of bomb threats against historically Black colleges and universities across the United States.[34]

The University of Missouri was a case study in lingering antebellum-style racism among an increasingly diverse academic community prior to both the events at Ferguson in 2014 and on-campus conflicts that erupted in 2015. Late one night in 2010, during Black History Month, two white students placed hundreds of cotton balls on the lawn in front of the University of Missouri Black culture center. The symbolism of this vandalism was clear: it was well-established code for slavery (antebellum slavery depended on cotton) and for terror against Black people in the dead of night during Reconstruction.[35] For many Black people on university campuses, such incidents of hate and intimidation are merely the latest additions to historically recent familial or generational memories of organized mass resistance to their presence on college campuses.

Indeed, some University of Missouri Black students subsequently testified to less visible forms of attempted intimidation, such as racist epithets, that they experienced on campus.[36] University administrators acknowledged

evidence of such discrimination, but also persistently understated its significance in hopes of maintaining positive school spirit or a favorable institutional
reputation. Discriminatory displays continued at University of Missouri in
2015 after Black student protests began in earnest. Some white participants
in university activities reportedly turned the MIZZOU cheer, a call-and-re-
sponse ritual of school pride, into an angry chant directed at Black student
protesters.[37] This verbal tactic was consistent with segregationist rhetoric: an
assertion of university symbolism to communicate to Black students that they
were not full members of the university or did not belong at all. Historically
disenfranchised groups who advocate for equality, justice, and public accountability often receive threats and intimidations in response. The case was
no different for activist students on the University of Missouri campus. They
reported harassment by other students who allegedly used racist language and
symbols. In one case, a swastika was drawn on a dormitory wall with feces.
Student activists also reported additional threats of violence on social media,
frequently accompanied with Confederate symbols. Yet university leadership
was slow to respond.[38]

These incidents at the University of Missouri during the 2010s were
not isolated. Such episodes formed an institutional pattern that university
administrators acknowledged, even if they failed to sufficiently address it.
Those episodes were consistent with documented histories of racist intimidation on predominantly white campuses. Understanding this dynamic is essential to understanding student protests at the University of Missouri from
2015 to 2016.[39] Many pundits or intellectual commentators, however, ignored
the need for such a historically informed perspective in favor of campus
misinformation.

Students from historically disenfranchised communities who occupied
university grounds in protest were not feebly retreating from dissenting
viewpoints. They were standing in the gap, so to speak, as many nonviolent
civil rights protesters have done before them. Those students refused to cede
university space to racist intimidation, refused to stop protesting when faced
with repeated threats to their safety, and thereby put their bodies on the line
in public. The students involved gathered for purposes of safety and solidarity in numbers. They publicly protested—at a time of heightened threats
to students of color—in the spirit of classic nonviolent disruptions and civil
disobedience: to draw attention to inequalities and abuses of power seldom
investigated in national media. Such students engaged in a classic assertion of
First Amendment rights—not only of speech, but also assembly—in the face
of racist intimidation and potential violence. Tropes of campus misinformation about trigger warnings, safe spaces, and insufficient viewpoint diversity,

however, erroneously depicted those assertions of First Amendment rights and voluntary political organization as *suppressions* of free speech and the free exercise of political liberties.

I oppose shutdowns or destructive organized actions for allegedly controversial campus speakers. Escalating conflict with these tactics seldom, if ever, offers a constructive way to resolve conflict. Intensifying dispute for its own sake is a dubious way to ensure inclusive academic climates or protect student rights and dignity. Sensationalizing incidents of campus conflict, however, to stereotype undergraduate students in general—characterizing them as predominantly violent and unthinking protesters—is also unconstructive and irresponsible. I equally oppose attempts to sensationalize incidents of campus conflict in ways that suggest student protest and dissent in general are illegitimate and hostile to free speech rather than legitimate forms of free speech themselves.

Selectively sensationalized incidents at the University of Missouri nevertheless played a large role in popularizing the idea of safe spaces as a common smear against college students specifically and nonviolent protesters in general. Campus misinformation proliferated over the course of 2015, helping to normalize the notion that narcissistic delusions of trauma plague many, if not most, university student groups. This type of vocabulary additionally fixed in public discourse the idea that socially and politically active students—especially those who represent historically disenfranchised groups—were gutlessly protesting for a space of learning and discussion free from ideas and arguments that might conflict with their own.

National reports about events at the University of Missouri legitimated such assumptions by focusing on groups of students who occupied university grounds as a form of protest. Some of them used signs to designate safe spaces where they could publicly gather and organize while asking the media not to intrude and sensationalize their cause.[40] These safe-space signs, a relatively marginal aspect of dramatic and prolonged on-campus events, were prominently featured in news reports about the University of Missouri. Media fixations with this comparatively superficial element of the campus protests overlooked the documented fact that members of many historically disenfranchised communities know how frequently the press portrays them in negative, and often criminal, terms—including when they organize democratically for social justice and equality. Empirical studies even indicate that some news organizations feature Black people *only* as criminals.[41] Protesters of color at the University of Missouri did not retreat from differing ideas; they sought to resist familiar and well-documented patterns of racist depiction in the news media.

The concerns of those students, backed by empirical studies of journalism, turned out to be well founded. News reports and after-the-fact commentaries overwhelmingly depicted University of Missouri student protesters as the chief sources of conflict and their actions as symptoms of strange obsessions with trigger warnings or safe spaces. *Washington Post* columnist Ruth Marcus cited those protesters as proof of "overreaction to offensive episodes" or instincts to throw a "tantrum," allegedly common among the latest generation of college students. Marcus claimed that student protests against racist displays at the University of Missouri and ineffective administrative responses to them were instances of "coddling."[42] Columnist Kathleen Parker, also of the *Washington Post*, quoted Purdue University president Mitch Daniels's opinion of students' allegedly excessive sensitivities: "If universities want to embarrass themselves with their behavior, allowing people to be shouted down or disinvited, that's their problem. But if they're spawning a bunch of little authoritarians with an inverted view of our basic freedoms, that's everybody's problem." Parker quipped that "the obvious next book" on this topic—the apparent oversensitivity of what she called "the 'Swaddled Generation'"—should be titled "'Dictators in Diapers.'"[43] Recall here that the University of Missouri football program staged a boycott in support of the student protesters and top university leaders resigned amid growing calls for institutional accountability. Yet the urge to scapegoat and deride students from historically disenfranchised communities, whose political activities formed only one dimension of prolonged campus controversies, was apparent in the words of public figures like Marcus, Daniels, and Parker.

The published opinions of those figures generally omitted extensive and well-documented institutional as well as national histories of racist harassment and intimidation that deeply informed the University of Missouri protests. Fixating on the conceit of safe spaces and triggered, coddled, or fragile student protesters did not lead to widespread appreciation for greater viewpoint diversity at the University of Missouri. Rather, such fixations served as pretext for disregarding a spectrum of insights about the history of race, power, and inequality in higher education as well as many Black students' testimony to that lingering history in suddenly prevalent mockery of their cause. Effective conflict resolution does not require everyone to agree with the arguments or tactics of all contributing parties to institutional conflict, but it does require us to recognize all contributing factors to that discord in an informed manner.

The timeline in the popularization of public ridicule about safe spaces in universities—especially as a feature of viewpoint diversity arguments—is clear. The notion that students routinely and impetuously demand safe spaces on college campuses rapidly became, after the events in Missouri, an oft-cited justification for deriding undergraduate students in general and for claiming that free speech and intellectual diversity in higher education is imperiled.[44] Campus misinformation distorted the reality of students from historically disenfranchised communities freely organizing in the name of equality, against patterns of racist intimidation, to validate the specious assumption that coddled or easily triggered undergraduate students cannot stand to encounter differing ideas.

A New Vocabulary

Misinformation about trigger warnings and safe spaces appeared to justify a quickly expanding and increasingly popular vocabulary in the wake of alarmist public discourse about Oberlin College and the University of Missouri. A wave of headlines across mainstream publications beginning in 2015 illustrates the early flourishing of this vocabulary:

"In College and Hiding from Scary Ideas," *New York Times* (March 21, 2015)

"A Plague of Hypersensitivity," *Chronicle of Higher Education* (May 11, 2015)

"Trigger Warnings, Colleges, and the 'Swaddled Generation,'" *Washington Post* (May 19, 2015)

"The Coddling of the American Mind," *The Atlantic* (September 2015)

"The Rise of Victimhood Culture," *The Atlantic* (September 11, 2015)

"Students' Requests for Trigger Warnings Grow More Varied," *Chronicle of Higher Education* (September 14, 2015)

"The Gravest Threat to Colleges Comes from Within," *Chronicle of Higher Education* (September 28, 2015)

"A Faculty's Stand on Trigger Warnings Stirs Fears among Students," *Chronicle of Higher Education* (October 6, 2015)

"College Is Not for Coddling," *Washington Post* (November 10, 2015)

"What's Happening to College Students Today?," *Psychology Today* (November 30, 2015)

"Young Fogies: Modern Illiberalism Is Led by Students," *Washington Post* (November 30, 2015)

"College President: 'This Is Not a Day Care. It's a University!,'" *Chronicle of Higher Education* (November 30, 2015)

"Speaker Beware," *Chronicle of Higher Education* (February 29, 2016)

"Wondering Whether Today's College Students Have Become Too Fragile?," *Washington Post* (May 13, 2016)

"The Chilling Effect of Fear at America's Colleges," *The Atlantic* (June 9, 2016)

"How Trigger Warnings Silence Religious Students," *The Atlantic* (August 30, 2016)

This representative sample of headlines in mainstream articles over the course of little more than a year does not even include myriad examples from explicitly partisan periodicals or websites. The list is a telling snapshot of the degree to which public discourse about the largely invented dangers of trigger warnings and safe spaces introduced an entire terminology of ridicule as an allegedly truthful assessment of the state of higher education. Terms like *hiding, hypersensitivity, fears, victimhood, fragility*—formulaic descriptors of allegedly coddled students—typify the early emergence of this larger vocabulary from 2015 forward.

Subsequent parts of this book show how such terms and the pejorative ideas behind them became the standard vocabulary for a cottage industry of pseudoscientific or pseudo-intellectual commentary about the troubling psychological state of most college students. In order to reach that point, however, the larger vocabulary of ridicule and condemnation that alarmist narratives about trigger warnings and safe spaces inspired required a degree of intellectual legitimation. One of the most influential sources of that legitimation appeared prior to the start of the fall 2016 academic semester.

The University of Chicago Letter

Incoming University of Chicago students received an atypical welcome letter from the dean of students in August 2016. The letter proudly announced the institution's "commitment to freedom of inquiry and expression" and issued this proviso to new students:

> Our commitment to academic freedom means that we do not support so-called "trigger warnings," we do not cancel invited speakers because their topics might prove controversial, and we do not condone the creation of intellectual "safe spaces" where individuals can retreat from ideas and perspectives at odds with their own.[45]

Mainstream media and partisan outlets widely publicized the letter; growing ranks of viewpoint diversity advocates enthusiastically affirmed it. *New York Times* columnist Bret Stephens hailed University of Chicago president Robert Zimmer as "Our Best University President"[46] for his ostensible willingness to defend free speech, open inquiry, and democracy from the stultifying effects of trigger warnings and safe spaces on campuses. Organizations like the Cato Institute and FIRE similarly praised the institution.[47]

Thousands of colleges issue welcome letters to incoming students annually—without widespread notice. The August 2016 University of Chicago letter was designed to generate publicity. With this letter, the leadership of an influential and elite university, long associated with innovative teaching methods and distinguished scholarship, intellectually laundered misinformation about trigger warnings and safe spaces. The letter to first-year University of Chicago students suggested, without evidence, that such forms of alleged coddling were prevalent on other university campuses while describing them as antithetical to free speech and diverse viewpoints.[48] This customary welcoming document more likely responded to pejorative and increasingly popular *ideas* about trigger warnings and safe spaces that permeated reporting about events at Oberlin College and the University of Missouri. Conservative candidates for office frequently encourage outrage about out-of-touch university campuses to increase support among voters; the University of Chicago letter potentially illustrated how higher education leaders may now use an analogous tactic to burnish their support among donors, boards of trustees, alumni groups, and others.[49]

The message to incoming students, moreover, appeared in connection with the university's Report of the Committee on University Discipline for Disruptive Conduct.[50] Together, the documents reflect a disciplinary or punitive approach to matters of free speech and dissent—a commitment to *regulating* speech in the interests of order or civility rather than a more open-minded commitment to viewing speech and dissent as matters of both educational and social exploration.[51] Strangely enough, portions of the letter that prominent commentators praised as defenses of free speech explicitly announced that certain kinds of speech would not be allowed (specifically, references to trigger warnings and safe spaces or petitions to university leadership regarding outside speakers). In sum, the University of Chicago public statements not only helped to legitimate campus misinformation but also expressed a willingness to *prohibit* certain forms of free speech or academic instruction instead of fully addressing actual threats to academic freedom and open debate.

The esteem in which the University of Chicago letter is now held among viewpoint diversity advocates suggests another form of campus misinformation: specifically, misleading ideas about how universities may best protect free speech or academic freedom among students and faculty. Organizations like FIRE and Heterodox Academy advise universities to adopt the University of Chicago letter (or related statements from its special committee on freedom of expression) as an administrative model.[52] Doing so would allegedly signify that a given college or university is seriously committed to defending free speech and open debate on its campus.

The University of Chicago letter, however, was a symbolic gesture, not a binding policy document. Contemporaneous documents—like the one from the University of Chicago committee on disruptive conduct, which its senate later approved—suggest a disciplinary or punitive approach to issues of campus expression. Expressing solidarity with the University of Chicago letter or related documents from late 2016 does not demonstrate that a college or university protects free speech any better or worse than other campuses do. That expression of solidarity indicates approval, instead, with a patently disciplinary, hierarchical, and potentially prohibitive attitude toward matters of free speech and academic freedom. Such a mentality contrasts sharply with the collaborative, experimental, pluralistic, and empathic theory of education in democratic society that famed philosopher of education John Dewey advocated as one of the University of Chicago's most influential faculty members.[53]

Chapter 6 shows how powerful federal officials cited the University of Chicago letter to justify potential restrictions on traditionally protected First Amendment freedoms. Suffice it to say for the purposes of this chapter, the University of Chicago letter emerged at an important turning point amid overwhelmingly sensationalized accounts of trigger warnings and safe spaces overtaking college and university campuses. The institution's flurry of public statements in the mid-2010s lent intellectual legitimacy to a prejudicial vocabulary about occasional and poorly understood aspects of university teaching or administration.

Conclusion

From the beginning, agents of campus misinformation cited trigger warnings and safe spaces on college campuses not simply to debate the merits of those devices in academic environments but to create a comprehensive and disturbing narrative. This chapter showed how exaggerations about trigger warnings and safe spaces in the mid-2010s quickly became allegedly convincing signs of ominous developments in higher education that miscellaneous reports about such warnings or spaces could never hope to prove in an empirically responsible way. Reports about trigger warnings and safe spaces seldom presented fair and accurate accounts of university teaching. Yet broadsides about trigger warnings and safe spaces, personified in the figure of the pathologically coddled student, generated popular new stereotypes about students from historically disenfranchised communities.

The next chapter shows how such symbolic narratives became even more elaborate in successive iterations. Opinion writers and scholarly figures transformed hyperbole about trigger warnings and safe spaces into recurrent warnings about something even more sensational and empirically suspect: warnings about a free speech crisis sweeping higher education. In a matter of mere months, teaching devices that much of the public had never heard about—which many professors and students never used or encountered themselves—became the unquestioned causes of a profound emergency that had already debilitated many university systems, according to numerous opinion writers and scholarly figures. Such rapid rhetorical escalation, from slim and inconsequential data to alarmism about large impending calamities, is a typical feature of intensifying misinformation.

3

Declarations of Emergency

Campus misinformation includes repeated declarations of alleged crisis. Such misinformation embraces dramatic hyperbole about intermittent controversies at a small number of universities. A chorus of seemingly disconnected sources, including mainstream news outlets, public intellectuals, and hyperpartisan pundits, routinely raise common alarm about those miscellaneous controversies. Their uniformly similar narratives distinguish campus misinformation from professional journalism that specializes in reporting about higher education. The ostensible purpose of campus misinformation is not to publicize the results of investigative reporting into specific educational issues or events, but to continually assert the idea that college campuses have descended into a state of emergency.

The previous chapter illustrated how the popular impulse to declare crises on university campuses frequently overrides meaningful considerations of fact and context—a telltale characteristic of misinformation. Yet initial declarations of emergency can pose an eventual problem for sponsors of misinformation. If the proverbial sky does not fall after the first round of dire public warnings, then those sponsors must find new ways to plausibly *re*declare alleged states of emergency. Agents of campus misinformation, including advocates for viewpoint diversity, for several years now have promoted the idea that universities are at a dangerous and chaotic tipping point. The edifice of higher education, however, still stands. The demand for education in myriad programs at thousands of universities across the nation remains high. Those institutions continue to provide essential credentials for entry into numerous professions and civic offices.

This chapter shows how contributors to initial forms of sensationalism about safe spaces and trigger warnings in the mid-2010s attempted to sustain increasingly hyperbolic portrayals of college campuses as a regular feature of public discourse—and continue to do so today. Maintaining cycles of campus misinformation required contributors to find new ways of declaring imminent emergency, meaning new ways to warn about the supposed widespread dangers of specific incidents on a small number of campuses. The examples of campus misinformation examined in this chapter demonstrate how loosely connected reports about trigger warnings, safe spaces, and the like became normalized as a regular feature of social and political commentary across a variety of media platforms.

Easily recycled reports about the systemic collapse of higher education benefit different adherents to campus misinformation. Such misinformation helps public figures to gain large public followings and the appearance of expertise from these continual expressions of alarm; it also provides consumers of news and information with an addictively entertaining narrative that allows them to feel part of an important movement. Campus misinformation illustrates a powerful pattern that many manipulative campaigns exploit in advertising, politics, and more: arouse uncertainty or even fear about an allegedly dire problem, then proffer a solution that promises to efficiently resolve that problem. Neither the description of the problem nor the posited solution need to be empirically valid to persuade vast numbers of people.

Frightening and melodramatic depictions of college environments common to outlets of campus misinformation exemplify such standard manipulative cycles. The increasingly influential messages that comprise those cycles suggest a media campaign rather than a consistently responsible, evidence-based debate. Claims about liberal indoctrination on college campuses dating back to the 1950s thrive anew in contemporary media networks because, according to lawyer and journalist Frank LoMonte, "online news organizations and social media (and especially ideologically aligned media)" can now "amplify and prolong" fixations with miscellaneous controversies on a small number of campuses.[1] The following sections of this chapter explain in detail how various figures thus amplified and prolonged campus misinformation as a semipermanent media campaign. I focus on recurrent language choices and narrative frameworks, which contributors to this kind of discourse use to normalize the idea that university students, faculty, or administrators are responsible for an alleged state of emergency in higher education.

Ultimately, I show that this hyperbolic premise originated in an ideological echo chamber shaped by circular metadiscourse (or an abstract, unempirical style of discussion) about free speech on college campuses. Such metadiscourse reflects elitist cynicism about the state of universities rather than consistently responsible evidence-based research into its complexities. Understanding how dominant patterns of informational distortion about higher education thrive in present-day media environments and ideological echo chambers promotes constructive, and not only critical, goals. That understanding can help members of college campuses and members of the public alike initiate more informed and constructive dialogues about the real challenges that higher education faces as well as its indispensable importance to democratic society.

Normalizing the State of Emergency

From late 2017 through early 2018, the *New York Times* opinion section published numerous columns that decried the rise of an intolerant left and an attendant free speech crisis on university campuses. The opinion page seemed to be sounding an alarm. The logic of these columns about higher education, which claimed to detail how coddled and violent undergraduate students had precipitated a free speech crisis, was echoed in still more *New York Times* columns on separate topics over the same period. Numerous articles reflexively alluded to "Trumpism" and "liberal intolerance," presumably nurtured on college campuses, as equally pernicious forms of extremism tearing the country apart. Such messages closely paralleled conservative rhetoric from the 1950s and 1960s by identifying liberal intolerance as an existential threat to critical civic institutions—particularly institutions of higher learning. Arguments consistent with viewpoint diversity polemics, which sought to repackage those dated conservative appeals, occupied a considerable amount of real estate in the nation's paper of record in a relatively short amount of time. The inflection point was noticeable enough that *Slate* published an article on the subject with this headline: "Sweet Jesus, Will the NYT's Conservatives Ever Write about Anything but the 'Intolerant Left' Ever Again?"[2]

Claims about coddled students and an alleged free speech crisis in universities became prominent in national media beyond fixations in the opinion section of the *New York Times*. The newspaper functioned as a key point of influence and legitimation in a larger, evolving network of misinformation. Similar polemics appeared in popular outlets like *Time*, the *Chronicle of Higher Education*, the *Wall Street Journal*, and the *Washington Post*. The *Atlantic* featured regular articles about alleged free speech crises on college campuses and the fragility of students, in addition to magazines like *National Review*, *The Federalist*, and others.[3]

Polemics about alleged crises of intolerance in higher education also created sustained attention and escalating outrage in social media. This vigorous social media uptake of campus misinformation was a logical outcome: initial narratives about trigger warnings, safe spaces, and coddled students established relatively simplistic and easily recirculated melodramas. Sharply increased amounts of campus misinformation circulated in conventional news sources and on social media, creating feedback loops or ideological echo chambers among journalists, social media users, and intellectual figures with large online followings. Several prominent university faculty and administrators have published books in recent years devoted to the idea that the sociopolitical views of some students and faculty are threats to free speech and open inquiry.[4] Moreover, powerful elected officials allied themselves with the cause of viewpoint diversity, becoming agents of campus misinformation themselves (a claim that I illustrate at length in Chapter 6). Proliferating public commentary on alleged free speech crises in universities from late 2017 through early 2018 helped turn periodically disparaging descriptions of campus culture into a veritable media sub-industry suited to sustaining tales of that supposed crisis indefinitely.

Influential figures in national media amplified and prolonged campus misinformation at this time with increasingly elaborate and vastly exaggerated narrative conceits. Many of them helped to transform specific campus incidents into alleged signs of uniform sociological or psychological flaws among college students writ large. In a March 2018 column titled "Understanding Student Mobbists," *New York Times* columnist David Brooks falsely claimed that "students across the country continue to attack and shut down speakers at a steady pace." A mob mentality, he posited, characterizes the general mentality of most college communities. Brooks dubiously claimed to explain how undergraduate students in general, hundreds of thousands of them, now understand issues like racism as a homogeneous group: "progress is less about understanding and liking each other and more about smashing structures that others defend." At some point, "reason, apparently, ceased to matter" for contemporary college students.[5] In contrast to people who "grow up in a progressive middle-class home, go to a liberal arts college and then move to a hipster neighborhood," Brooks opined in yet another column, we should aspire to emulate "a social type" that he described as "the Amphibians—people who can thrive in radically different environments."[6] Brooks's commentary on the contemporary culture of universities consisted almost entirely of unempirical stereotypes, which he promoted as representative descriptions of innumerable students and professors. Broad generalizations about where people grow up, go to college, and ultimately live support reductive narratives about large parts of society, but not substantive analyses of the behaviors or motivations of actual people within diverse demographic groups. We should always welcome constructive deliberations over systemic problems in higher education based on a cross-section of evidence and expertise. Brooks's columns promoted, instead, a substantially invented narrative full of clumsy stereotypes, blatant exaggerations, and the mere appearance of social scientific terminology ("mobbists," "Amphibians") designed to elevate campus misinformation to the status of seemingly refined social commentary. The overriding purpose of campus misinformation in this vein is not to report about events or simply offer an opinion about them, but to categorize enormous numbers of people as one abstractly defined social type.

Brooks, however, was only one of several figures in this period at the *New York Times* alone who successfully sustained and legitimized campus misinformation. In September 2017, *New York Times* columnist Bret Stephens published a column titled "The Dying Art of Disagreement." Like Brooks, Stephens proved expert in semantically costuming large amounts of exaggeration and speculation as ostensibly elevated reflection. For example, Stephens described college campuses as the foremost personification of "the age of protected feelings purchased at the cost of permanent infantilization." In "college," he proposed, "the dominant mode of politics is identity politics . . . in which the primary test of an argument isn't the quality of the thinking but the cultural, racial, or sexual standing of the person making it."[7] For writers like Stephens, tropes of campus misinformation signified a degree of intellectual expertise. He refashioned those tropes into a mode of commentary that imitated classical philosophical reflection—a treatise on the concept and practice of disagreement as an art—instead of more conventional opinion writing.

Stephens's assessment was specious not only because his claim to know the uniform way that most students and faculty members think, across thousands of different institutions, is dubious on its face. His underlying thesis about the dying art of disagreement in higher education was also false. Universities are major sources of both practical and theoretical training in conflict analysis and dispute resolution. Various offices at many different institutions maintain resources for managing difficult discussions of enormously sensitive topics.[8] Thousands of students in thousands of classrooms on any given day study principles of constructive disagreement in numerous disciplines. Such fields include argumentation and debate, analytic philosophy, democratic theory, sociology, conflict resolution, and more. Recognizing these facts does not require specialized research; it requires merely browsing available online course offerings for myriad colleges and universities. By these measures, the so-called dying art of disagreement is more alive now on university campuses, more democratically accessible across a greater diversity of viewpoints, than at any prior point in history. Commentaries from figures like Stephens illustrate how pundits sought to enhance their reputations as thought leaders by disguising cynical campus misinformation as alleged intellectual reflection.

Then–fellow *New York Times* columnist Bari Weiss illustrated, around the same time, how useful campus misinformation could be to pundits who seek to promote themselves as incisive political analysts. In March 2018, Bari Weiss published a column titled "We're All Fascists Now." The column was inspired, in part, by disruptive but nonviolent student protests at Lewis and Clark University Law School during a lecture from Christina Hoff Sommers, an author and resident scholar of the American Enterprise Institute.[9] For Weiss, this incident was prime evidence that "we live in a world in which politically fascistic behavior, if not the actual philosophy, is unquestionably on the rise." Such incidents, she insisted, have become "routine."[10] Weiss's tremendous hyperbole dramatically upped the ante as to what campus misinformation allegedly revealed. Her columns went beyond speculations about the alleged social or psychological frailties of college students to promote the false premise that universities are now nothing less than engines of fascism. Tropes of campus misinformation, in this case, supported a provocative new kind of political commentary.

We should always welcome thorough and fair assessments of any on-campus conflict, like the one at Lewis and Clark University that inspired Weiss's column. A small number of such randomly assembled examples of campus conflict does not support the conclusion that colleges are havens of fascism. Basic rules of logic and evidence caution against this extremely hasty generalization; a wealth of historical evidence also contradicts it. Totalitarian regimes throughout modern history, from Nazi Germany to the Soviet Union and beyond, almost always depicted independent universities as bastions of allegedly dangerous ideas or behaviors. Diatribes against the alleged cultural dangers of liberal arts institutions or scientific experts in research universities are consistent features of present-day authoritarian movements in countries like Russia, Hungary, and Brazil. The conduct of a limited number of students within a large campus population on one occasion at a single university, or even a small number of institutions, may well deserve scrutiny and condemnation—as is true for irresponsible and disruptive members of various workplaces on any given day. The notion that such a single incident, or a statistically small number of incidents, in specific pockets of larger university communities demonstrates a nationwide wave of fascism is illogical and ahistorical. Beginning with this framework for debate over the state of US higher education does not indicate a meaningful, evidence-based effort to understand the real-world problems and complexities that affect some college campuses; it indicates a partially imagined fable meant to maintain popular cycles of outrage. Yet this unsubstantiated premise generated significant amounts of public attention for the pundits who energetically promoted it in 2017 and 2018, thereby extending the scope of campus misinformation into a semipermanent fixture of political commentary.

Such reports have become op-ed staples in mainstream journalism and partisan media outlets. Self-described liberal and conservative writers now regularly churn them out in response to the latest sensationalized incident at a given institution of higher education. Context and proportion are dramatically flattened. Random incidents that depict a sliver of the reality on a given college campus are taken as proof that most members of those institutions are irrational and intolerant. News about higher education during the summer of 2019, for instance, caused the machinery of campus misinformation to go into overdrive yet again. The relevant reports concerned two controversial campus episodes: a court filed a multimillion-dollar ruling against Oberlin College because of student protests that targeted a local business, and Harvard University removed law professor Ronald Sullivan from his secondary position as faculty dean of a student residence because of concerns over his role on the legal defense team for accused (and eventually convicted) sexual assailant Harvey Weinstein. Notice the significant prima facie differences between these two incidents: different institutions, different legal situations, different timelines of relevant events. Reporting about these episodes nevertheless lumped them together as one kind of evidence in a new round of dire warnings about intolerant, out-of-control college students and feckless university administrators. Nicholas Kristoff's concerns in the *New York Times* about the "prickly intolerance" of undergraduate students rehearsed all of the now-standard tropes of this genre. Those tropes included sweeping conclusions about campus culture drawn from one or two easily sensationalized controversies, the unempirical premise that students embrace "every kind of diversity except one: ideological diversity," and the unsubstantiated claim that students protest trifling matters instead of combating "actual injustice."[11] Members of a democracy, we should remember, do not have to pass a sociopolitical litmus test to exercise their First Amendment freedoms.

Fear of student activists, like those at the University of Missouri, has become a regular element not only of op-eds about higher education but also intellectual commentaries that examine civic discord in general. Authors of such commentaries across a spectrum of ideological perspectives go out of their way to insert cherry-picked anecdotes from higher education as convenient all-purpose explanations for numerous social maladies. In 2018, *The Atlantic* announced a yearlong series of special events and commentaries labeled "The Speech Wars." (Notice how the theme of *wars* in this case imitates uses of military terminology in political journalism to sensationalize electoral cycles.) *The Atlantic* published a rationale for this free speech project that repurposed characteristic conceits of campus misinformation into a default assessment of ideological intolerance throughout US society: "We need to understand why so many factions and individuals across America have traded dissent and useful argument for intolerance and illiberalism."[12] Columnist Andrew Sullivan made the same assertion in even more ominous tones designed to evoke totalitarian imagery: "What matters most of all in these colleges—your membership in a group that is embedded in a hierarchy of oppression—will soon enough be what matters in the society as a whole."[13] These polemics illustrate how commentators in a cluster of privileged positions adopted hyperbole about campus speech crises as an easily recycled but seldom questioned lens for understanding multifarious sociopolitical problems. In August 2021, journalist and historian Anne Applebaum further prolonged the media lifespan of such hasty generalizations. She recycled unempirical tropes about coddled students, overprotective administrators, and campuses operating under the rule of "mob justice" in an article about the corrosive influences of social media.[14] These examples illustrate how periodic reflections from influential commentators combine to sustain the false premise that universities are prime sources of democratic erosion.

Ample evidence and common sense contradict these all-encompassing representations. They do not accurately reflect the demonstrable realities of US higher education across thousands of diverse campus communities or student populations. Those representations reflect, instead, a cynical fashion among pundits in relatively privileged positions for questioning whether college students as a group are mature and informed enough to freely use their constitutionally guaranteed First Amendment rights. Commentaries of this sort propose a broad defense of free speech and open inquiry only to identify the specific exercise of free speech and freely chosen ideas among college students as sources of debilitating civic breakdown.

Columnists have significantly extended the public influence of those narratives by including them as thematic pillars of popular books. Political commentator Noah Rothman's *Unjust: Social Justice and the Unmaking of America* laments that college campuses foment radical commitments to social justice sponsored by the "identity-obsessed left." He describes such radicalism—movements for "social justice"—as the "vicious progeny of identity politics," a kind of "paranoia" that profoundly threatens multiple aspects of American life.[15] Robby Soave, associate editor at *Reason*, projects a veneer of even-handedness in *Panic Attack: Young Radicals in the Age of Trump*, when he concedes that not all college students are hostile to free speech; but Soave nevertheless endorses the now-familiar canard that a majority of college students have adopted that hostility.[16] A variety of popular sociopolitical commentaries, marketed for their ostensibly bold insights, therefore share a dubious and unoriginal premise: university students and faculty are responsible for the worst ills of society. Basic rules of logic and evidence caution against positing the same simple explanation as the source of many different social or political developments. Commentaries that do so fail to engage with the full and complex realities of higher education today, but they succeed in generating public cynicism about the First Amendment rights of certain student groups based largely on stereotypes. Messages of this kind appear to be highly marketable and entertaining for popular audiences—a reliable way to promote oneself as an ostensibly incisive public thinker.

In sum, pundits with large media platforms like those mentioned in this chapter have created a de facto news beat devoted to the latest apparent outrages, often without context or meaningful evidence, at miscellaneous college campuses. The overlap between these commentaries and professional journalism in matters of higher education is slight. This disparity parallels the results of prior advocacy for viewpoint diversity in political journalism—or obligatory viewpoint parity, as I described it in Chapter 1. Sensational narratives about allegedly fierce ideological clashes in universities closely resemble the evolution of mainstream political journalism into a form of political theatre that features staged ideological clashes among telegenic personalities. Each form of distorted information promotes entertaining storylines and cycles of outrage about their respective subject matters while failing to substantively inform the public about how vital institutions function. Yet opinion writers and ideological firebrands alike appear to be dedicated for the foreseeable future to sustaining sensational narratives about campuses gone wild and, thus, continued misinformation about universities.

The Viewpoint Diversity Echo Chamber

The formulaic quality of storytelling in prominent examples of campus misinformation deserves closer scrutiny. By-the-numbers narratives in this polemical genre suggest a central tale fashioned in ideological echo chambers rather than fair, deeply informed, and ethically responsible commentaries. The basic story about coddled and triggered undergraduate students who desire safe spaces and ideological conformity stays the same from one popular account to the next—as a seemingly universal explanation for many different social or political problems. Standard polemical conceits and well-worn stereotypes about those students and their campus communities have assumed the *appearance* of fact through sheer circulation among elite pundits while remaining factually specious on substance.

The examples in this chapter further show that agents of campus misinformation not only tell the same basic story repeatedly, but they tell it in common idiosyncratic terms. All-encompassing descriptions of allegedly intolerant student groups and their ideological overseers among faculty and administrators—with seemingly obligatory mentions of coddling, trigger warnings, safe spaces, and the like—typify the essentially uniform hyperbole of this descriptive terminology. Campus misinformation promotes frightening descriptions of university campuses consistently on the brink of chaos or violence. The language of such misinformation portrays students in particular as strange creatures indeed: coddled and fragile, yet intimidating and violent; thuggish and punishing, yet passive, unthinking, and easily indoctrinated. Contributors to the genre of campus misinformation depict the personal characteristics and behaviors of college students in negative terms to create all-purpose scapegoats for any number of social or political problems. Such depictions are not designed to make logical or empirically verifiable sense; they are designed to confirm and perpetuate existing ideological prejudices.

Standard narrative turns and language choices of this sort are often essential to the formation of ideological echo chambers that popularize misinformation. Ritually repeating the same basic story in the same terms allows members of a social group to *feel* that they have discovered a proven and simple explanation for complex and distressing problems. This kind of echo chamber has influenced public debate over the state of higher education by popularizing dubious claims that rely on what scholars of propaganda call "glittering generalities": words "used to stir up our emotions and befog our thinking," thus moving us to "form a judgment to accept or condemn, without examining the evidence."[17] Campus misinformation shows how strategically vague terms can powerfully move audiences to either accept or condemn ideas, people, and groups, often at a considerable distance from actual events, without critically examining evidence and context.

The glittering generalities of campus misinformation also merit scrutiny for what they *omit* from sensational narratives about higher education. Almost without exception, the strident commentaries that I cite in this chapter fail to quote students, faculty, and administrators who populate universities as their places of work and study.[18] Selectively quoting students from prior sources as stand-ins for entire student populations instead of soliciting a meaningful cross-section of student perspectives in context is common in viewpoint diversity assessments of higher education.[19] Hence, those arguments often begin in an empirically specious and ideologically undiverse way: by occluding faculty, student, or administrator perspectives that would complicate sensationalized narratives about free speech wars and crises of intimidation on college campuses. Sources of campus misinformation typically describe faculty or students who advocate for social justice, political equality, and robust institutional diversity through the lens of prior reports and recurrent stereotypes about miscellaneous campus incidents—not in direct and substantive conversation with a cross-section of such student or faculty communities.

As a professor myself, this kind of noticeably un-diverse selectivity in the case of student viewpoints is particularly glaring. Professors interact with anywhere from dozens to hundreds of undergraduate students in classrooms multiple times a week, not to mention in numerous other on-campus activities, throughout any given academic term. Understanding how diverse even a small group of students can be, in ways that social or political stereotypes cannot describe, is essential to effective teaching. A major source of animus in campus misinformation appears to be the fact that current university administrators often regard undergraduate communities as meaningful stakeholders in campus policies or as collaborative participants in learning environments—precisely because of the diverse perspectives that they can provide. Granted, many institutions of higher education continue to function as inflexible hierarchies based on entrenched executive models; these proverbial leviathans are slow to turn due to the weight of tradition and bureaucracy. However, student groups on many campuses today are more meaningfully incorporated into institutional decision-making, often by the choice of the institutions in question, than they were even a few decades ago. Such solicitation of some student views in the formation of university policies may explain why commentators in privileged positions, whose own projections of expertise might depend on the appearance of elite credentials from exclusive institutions, describe those practices as "coddling" or "infantilization." Claiming to diagnose the allegedly broad ills of most universities without either featuring a diverse cross-section of student perspectives or attempting to understand student participation in campus affairs reflects not just any kind of echo chamber, but an elitist one.

This elitist aspect is consistent with my overriding claim that viewpoint diversity polemics suggest a reactionary metadiscourse. A metadiscourse is a way of speaking about the speech of other people in broad and speculative terms, prone to glittering generalities and somewhat removed from worldly realities. Advocates of viewpoint diversity *describe* the speech of students, faculty, and administrators without significantly consulting people who work, study, and live on campuses allegedly plagued with regimes of intolerance and disorder. Moira Weigel, a scholar of media, technology, and literature, aptly observes that such metadiscourse suggests an exercise in style over argument. The style in question "wants above all to be reasonable," in contrast to supposed "partisans of identity who are too emotional to think clearly," and engages in "elaborate syntactic balancing acts" that border on "meaninglessness" to do so.[20]

One of the most elaborate demonstrations of this metadiscourse in action, which indicates an ongoing media campaign rather than substantively informed debate about higher education, is the University of Austin. The university announced its formation in August 2021 with alarmist tropes lifted directly from numerous op-eds on campus speech crises: "We are alarmed by the illiberalism and censoriousness prevalent in America's most prestigious universities and what it augurs for the country."[21] This announcement, in other words, was not an educational mission statement so much as an op-ed in its own right that conflated public discourse about higher education with sensationalist media narratives. Former op-ed writer Bari Weiss was the university's foremost founding trustee; its board of advisers included other opinion writers, corporate leaders, and impressively credentialed scholars who also frequently act as pundits in national media. The University of Austin was unaccredited, with no curriculum, upon its announcement in the fall of 2021 (its website promised programs in coming academic terms). The organization was an immediate cause célèbre among viewpoint diversity advocates. Yet it appeared to exist, to a large degree, as a media site devoted to polemics about the alleged failings of other universities and as a fundraising vehicle that used such phrases as "academic freedom" and "the pursuit of truth" like advertising slogans.[22]

The labeling of this institution as a "university," which did not resemble a university in any meaningful way upon its founding, exemplified the reactionary metadiscourse that typifies campus misinformation. University of Austin boosters declared, only days after its founding was announced, that it "puts the rest of academia to shame," might inspire "a revolution" or "a new Renaissance," and could "spark a new Enlightenment."[23] This metadiscourse reflects coordinated efforts among privileged groups not to administer actual academic programs but to restore a nostalgic ideal of higher education. Such an ideal defines university teaching and research as a rarified sphere of unusually bold thinkers who must, allegedly, be freed from the opinions and criticisms of colleagues or the public to pursue truth on our behalf.

The University of Austin might reflect an emergent international trend against more democratic and socially diverse universities. In May 2021, an "ultra-conservative Polish think tank" called Ordo Iuris "inaugurated a university intended to mold future leaders who espouse the conservative

Christian values that the nationalist government champions, and push back against Western liberalism."[24] Political supporters of the Ordo Iuris International Academy[25] described the university, at the time of its founding, as "a bulwark against human rights fundamentalism and political correctness."[26] Both the International Academy and the University of Austin thus evince a reactionary nostalgia for universities led by intellectual, financial, and political elites rather than a commitment to egalitarian models of higher education.

Fortunately, there are both more historically informed and democratically inclusive ways to debate the state of higher education. Including a meaningful cross-section of perspectives from student groups, faculty, and administrators would complicate abstract metadiscourses about allegedly disturbing trends on college campuses endemic to campus misinformation. Thousands of students, faculty, and administrators collaborate daily to maintain positive and inclusive university climates based on the free and respectful expression of competing views. Many of them do so voluntarily in addition to their formal studies or teaching and research obligations. Working to maintain an academically constructive and socially inclusive campus environment is even a crucial part of many administrators' jobs, such as deans of student affairs or professional staff in student support offices. Viewpoint diversity advocates and other purveyors of campus misinformation, however, rarely seek out the professional experience or expertise of diverse students, faculty, and administrators.

Ideological echo chambers that frequently sponsor misinformation sustain alarm with abstractions and airy metadiscourse because they distract from internal contradictions at the heart of such misinformation. Identifying the nature of these contradictions in the case of campus misinformation further illustrates the reactionary strains of such messages about higher education. Agents of campus misinformation contend that universities are now hostile to viewpoint diversity, defined according to political stereotypes, because campuses allegedly coddle easily triggered students who crave safe spaces and emotionally erupt in the face of dissenting views. Warnings about free speech emergencies on college campuses do not rest content with condemning instances of unsanctioned disruptive protests or even statistically rare instances of violent disruptions (incidents that the proper offices should address on a case-by-case basis). Such declarations of emergency claim to diagnose something ominous about *the majority* of college students.

The stock examples of dangerous student thought and behavior that agents of campus misinformation emphasize, however, do not concern the majority of college students at all. Such stock examples focus tightly, in an intellectually and empirically un-diverse manner, on specific kinds of students: those who vocally oppose forms of structural discrimination that target historically disenfranchised groups in higher education and society at large. Sources of campus misinformation seldom use the language of coddling, infantilization, and liberal intolerance to characterize the thought and behavior of many kinds of students across a meaningful spectrum of different identity categories. These terms never apply to the ideas or behaviors of, say, students with passionate views about astronomy, medieval history, nanotechnology, Chinese archaeology, or myriad other academic and cultural interests. The language of coddling, infantilization, and intolerance is typically reserved for people of color, women, LGBTQ students, and students from other historically marginalized communities who question persisting university hierarchies. Formulaically describing only specific kinds of students in this way, according to stereotypes about allegedly homogeneous groups, is not consistent with the goal of a centrist, scientific, or truly constructive debate about higher education. Such descriptions are consistent with an implicitly prejudicial code useful for promoting negative public perceptions of students from historically disenfranchised communities.

Some basic work in translation, out of explicitly negative terminology into more constructive and plausible descriptions, might further reveal the function of those warnings as a reactionary code predicated on irresolvable internal contradictions. The fact that students, faculty, and administrators successfully collaborate as a regular part of university affairs on many campuses might be one paradoxical source of viewpoint diversity ire about how servile administrators coddle and infantilize liberally intolerant students. Many campuses are now *more* democratic and *more* openly solicitous of traditionally overlooked student views—at least compared to previous eras of higher education dominated by elitist values and exclusionary policies. Once again, much work remains to be done in making colleges and universities more democratically inclusive, economically affordable, and socially diverse, but institutional reforms in that direction have been a pronounced trend in contemporary higher education.[27]

In this context, the hyperbolic conceit that university administrators coddle students portrays significantly positive developments in needlessly negative terms. Many institutions of higher education solicit student input or participation in decision-making (admittedly with varying degrees of genuineness and success) as an exercise in academic and civic development. Complaining that colleges infantilize undergraduate students is misleading and derisive. Teachers and administrators increasingly recognize that individual learning experiences can be improved by understanding how students' personal histories of trauma, economic insecurity, and other hardships influence their in-class performance. The sweeping trope of liberal intolerance substitutes an unnecessary stereotype for a more responsible explanation of crucial transitions in the culture of higher education. Some students from historically disenfranchised groups insist on institutional equality without ceremonial deference to traditional or exclusionary university hierarchies—as they are free to do in the name of academic freedom and First Amendment liberties.

Translating the glittering generalities on which campus misinformation depends into more constructive terms thus reveals serious internal contradictions in claims about alleged free speech crises on college campuses. Those claims indicate a confused and reactionary response to generally positive trends in higher education: administrators who solicit student opinions, professors who recognize that supportive learning environments can lead to better-quality academic exchanges, and students from traditionally excluded communities who use their free speech to raise questions about institutional norms and authority. To acknowledge that certain administrators, professors, and students sometimes err or abuse their institutional roles in such pursuits does not invalidate the reality that, on balance, universities protect First Amendment rights and model democratic debate better than most other parts of society. The notions that increased campus diversity hinders ideological diversity, that more student speech presages a free speech crisis, or that more democratic campus norms threaten democracy are fundamentally paradoxical. Yet those notions appear to represent coherent argumentative premises for members of echo chambers who presume that universities should remain exclusive and that norms of civility should circumscribe free speech.

Conclusion

This chapter demonstrated how waves of misinformation about trigger warnings, safe spaces, and the coddled college students who allegedly crave them rapidly evolved into a regular feature of national media commentary. This kind of commentary served other purposes than those of investigative journalism about higher education in the late 2010s. Formulaic warnings about the disturbing opinions of college students from historically disenfranchised communities allowed opinion writers and intellectual commentators to increase their public stature. Routine warnings about free speech crises, in which the freely held ideological views of some students seemed to endanger not only higher education but democratic society writ large, emerged as the rhetorical signature of this empirically deceptive mode of popular commentary. That rhetorical signature is also indicative of misinformation. Sponsors of misinformation frequently extend its lifespan and public influence by finding new ways to raise alarm after initial predictions of doom do not come to pass.

Especially dramatic claims—like those of an alleged free speech crisis in scores of colleges and universities—require particularly convincing evidence, or at least the appearance of such evidence. Pundits and intellectual commentators who claimed an endemic lack of viewpoint diversity in higher education throughout the late 2010s not only cited sensationalized media reports about trigger warnings, safe spaces, and the like to support those claims. Viewpoint diversity advocates, I previously noted, also argued that the pro-diversity and pro-inclusion behaviors of students, faculty, or administrators reflected potentially deep-seated psychological and sociological problems within those groups. The trope of the *emotionally fragile* and *coddled* student who *irrationally demands* trigger warnings and safe spaces suggests basic elements of a larger psychological and sociological profile. Adherents to the viewpoint diversity philosophy thereby claimed to promote not only a new and politically centrist perspective on diversity in higher education, but a scientific one. Wider networks of campus misinformation amplified such pretenses of scientific commentary to further popularize narratives about a supposed systemic crisis in higher education—a simultaneous free speech *and* mental health crisis.

The conceit of scientific evidence within campus misinformation therefore deserves focused examination. In the next chapter, I demonstrate how such appeals to scientific evidence promoted significant amounts of pseudoscience about college students and campus culture during the late 2010s. My goal in that chapter is not only to illustrate the dangers of such pseudoscience as a putative form of evidence in popular debates about higher education. I also suggest more responsible ways to use and interpret scientific evidence in democratic decision-making about many critical issues.

4

Pseudoscience

Understanding common uses and abuses of scientific evidence in public argument is a vital part of democratic decision-making. Healthy democratic deliberation presupposes that communities should make decisions about crucial issues informed by shared empirical understandings of the world as much, or more, than simple ideological differences or competing beliefs. Scientific evidence should not dictate public policies; collaborative human judgment involves persuasion based on many kinds of qualitative and quantitative evidence as well as subjective values and interests. Acknowledging the findings of sound scientific research whenever appropriate, however, can help to focus public deliberation on empirically grounded interpretations of real-world problems and a range of evidence-based solutions to them.

Actual public debates, however, often fail to manifest this ideal deliberative scenario. People frequently abuse the ideal function of scientific evidence in democratic argument. Agents of misinformation do so with a variety of techniques, from distorting existing research to fabricating dangerous pseudoscience that many people mistake for the real thing. Misinformation campaigns do not lack "data." They *proliferate* it.

Even the most ideologically extreme conspiracy theorists or propagandists insist that their demonstrably false claims are scientifically valid. Those who contend that people of color are genetically inferior to white people, for example, have inaccurately defended such bigotry as enlightened scientific fact for centuries. During the COVID-19 pandemic, antivaccination advocates inaccurately argued that they understood vaccination science better than credentialed and publicly accountable medical experts. Political factions who undemocratically sought to overturn the results of the 2020 presidential election falsely claimed that "the media" had suppressed allegedly voluminous proof of electoral fraud. These examples indicate that misinformation backed by pseudoscience is a recurrent social and political problem. Recognizing differences between sound scientific argument and pseudoscience is therefore an important facet of constructive democratic participation.

Disingenuous uses of language are central to deceptive uses of scientific evidence. I illustrate this claim in the present chapter by examining how campus misinformation, including arguments for viewpoint diversity on college campuses, promotes pseudoscientific discourse about higher education. Misinformation often relies on members of the public not to recognize the difference between a fog of pseudoscientific terms and careful scientific arguments based on responsible analyses of data. The most information-rich age in human history presents a proverbial double-edged sword. Contemporary communication technologies allow more people than ever to access scientific research on any given topic (although historically marginalized communities continue to experience unequal access to those technologies). Relatively easy access to abundant sources of scientific information, however, also means that more people than ever can successfully manipulate the language of scientific research and promote specious claims across a variety of mass media.

My analyses of questionable scientific claims in this chapter, including flawed interpretations of quantitative data, support my central argument about the *language* of campus misinformation. In his classic *Statistics as Principled Argument*, psychologist and political scientist Robert Abelson wrote that the "field of statistics is misunderstood by students and nonstudents alike."[1] Statistical researchers and members of the public both often fail to recognize that the process of justifying inferences drawn from quantitative data involves degrees of rhetoric: "there are analogous features between the claims of a statistical analyst and a case presented by a lawyer—the case can be persuasive or flimsy (even fishy), the style of inference may be loose or tight, prior conventions and rules of evidence may be invoked or flouted, and so on."[2] The standards of persuasiveness in statistics, by this logic, should be as rigorously applied as any other facet of the field, including efforts to identify the best possible data points for comparison, better or worse models with which to explain their relative significance, and criteria for distinguishing between systematic and chance explanations of research outcomes.[3]

Campus misinformation contains numerous examples of misleading appeals to scientific evidence, including distortions of statistical data. I showed, in previous chapters, how historically dated partisan arguments for viewpoint diversity assumed seemingly new and centrist form in campus misinformation beginning in the mid-2010s. The appearance of this allegedly new philosophy of education lent a semblance of intellectual legitimacy to sensationalism about trigger warnings, safe spaces, and an alleged free speech crisis in higher education. The pretense of data-driven scientific argument played a crucial role in elevating campus misinformation to a semipermanent form of punditry and intellectual commentary, and therefore deserves focused examination unto itself.

Advocates of viewpoint diversity often claim that their arguments about diversity and ideological openness in higher education reflect scientific data. Those advocates, I mentioned in Chapter 1, often appropriate the language of scientific methods from fields like political science and social psychology to polemically encourage preferred formulas of viewpoint diversity rather than studying levels of viewpoint diversity within different organizations from a more traditional academic perspective. In this chapter, I show how such appeals to seemingly conclusive data involve verbally assembled facsimiles of scientific argument rather than sound scientific claims. This demonstration is a necessary step in promoting more constructive public debate about the state of higher education and its role in US democracy given the prevalence of pseudoscientific tropes in popular arguments about college campuses today.

My claims in this chapter call into question misuses or distortions of research in the behavioral sciences, not ethical and learned versions of it. Academic and private-sector researchers alike conduct massive amounts of methodologically careful and responsible survey research. They do so by seeking training in research ethics, requesting input from colleagues during the course of research, following institutional policies for research on human subjects, and submitting work for peer review to ensure quality and accuracy. I also seek in this chapter to promote a practical knowledge of standards and principles that distinguish such sound scientific argument from specious approximations of it.

Encouraging more responsible uses of scientific evidence in response to misleading popular discourse about higher education is thematically apt. Preparing students to construct persuasive arguments based on many sources of credible evidence, rather than viewpoints alone, is one of the overriding goals of higher education. Pursuing that goal as democratic citizens requires us to recognize the following common misuses and abuses of scientific evidence: (1) confusions of correlation with causation, (2) news reports that distort the results of scientific studies, (3) poorly worded survey questions that generate suspect data, and (4) spurious statements of research methods. I demonstrate, in the following sections, how each of these pseudoscientific techniques helped campus misinformation to grow in popularity and putative intellectual legitimacy during the late 2010s. In doing so, I simultaneously indicate more empirically sound and ethically responsible ways to use or interpret scientific evidence, whether in debates over the state of higher education or in other arenas of democratic argument.

Question the Causation

Our modern information environment is rife with a specific kind of logical error. Healthy consumers of news and information might have previously encountered versions of the following claims: Regularly drinking coffee either helps or hinders some facet of our health. A president's economic policies led to either a robust economy or an economic recession. The stock market either rose or fell because of an electoral outcome. Such common storylines indicate potential confusions of *correlation* with *causation*, or perceptions of a cause-and-effect linkage between distinct and broadly related phenomena. Mistaking correlation with causation leads to potentially erroneous arguments in which people assert that if two things happen at the same time, then one of them must cause the other.[4]

Confusions of correlation with causation are common in present-day misinformation about college-age young people. Hyperpartisan agents of campus misinformation gleefully stereotype contemporary undergraduate students for their alleged generation-wide emotional or psychological instabilities. This kind of invective, which thrives on social media, characterizes the source of those perceived frailties as not simply generational, but political: college-age young people are weak and coddled because they are more liberal or progressive than other groups.

Such hyperpartisan invective, however, represents a toxic extension of seemingly scientific claims about viewpoint diversity. A variety of academic figures, predominantly from social scientific fields, claim that deep-seated cognitive explanations exist for why college students allegedly exhibit disconcerting levels of frailty and intolerance when confronted with differing ideas or challenging circumstances.[5] Advocates of viewpoint diversity propose two core explanations for this lack of personal resilience and psychological balance among college-age young people: social media and a culture of coddling.

First, advocates of viewpoint diversity contend that social media wreaked cognitive and emotional havoc on young people born from approximately the mid-1990s to the early 2000s. Members of this generation were both different and troubled relative to previous generations, according to this logic, because they belonged to the first generation to grow up with social media. *Gen Z* has emerged as the dominant label for this group in popular discourse (along with alternatives like *iGen*) to symbolize the ostensible influence of social media in its maturation.

The broad correlation of generational status with social media that labels like "Gen Z" symbolize have inspired forms of popular psychology and sociology devoted to probing that correlation. Psychologist Jean Twenge argues that the effects of social media on contemporary college-age young people are dire. Consider the following summary from one of her popular books on the subject:

> They are the first generation for whom Internet access has been constantly available, right there in their hands. . . . iGen is distinct from every previous generation in how its members spend their time, how they behave, and their attitudes toward religion, sexuality, and politics. . . . They are obsessed with safety and fearful of their economic futures, and they have no patience for inequality based on gender, race, or sexual orientation. They are at the forefront of the worst mental health crisis in decades.[6]

According to this argument, scientific studies prove that social media has changed how young people understand reality, process ideas, and view themselves in relation to others in society—all for the worse. The ostensible media immersion of Gen Z or iGen, Twenge posits, is not only generationally unique; it also indicates a generation-wide pathology.

The mode of discourse about Gen Z that Twenge exemplifies turns a broad correlation between social media and generational diversity or moderation into a default causal principle. If members of Gen Z grew up with social media, according to this perspective, then that media must explain their social, political, and economic views. Figures like Twenge not only mistake correlation with causation as such. Her research goes beyond maintaining that social media causes the sociopolitical views of Gen Z to further suggest that those views warrant clinically based concerns about the well-being of younger adults. Expressing concern for inequalities based on "gender, race, or sexual orientation" might not, in Twenge's analysis, reflect a freely chosen and rational position. Rather, she describes such concerns as a sign of irrational obsessions—an indicator of allegedly inherent narcissism or maladaptation to real-world affairs among members of Gen Z or iGen. The apparently representative sociopolitical views of college-age young people, in this analysis, symptomize "the worst mental health crisis in decades."

Second, advocates of viewpoint diversity in higher education contend that college-age students today exhibit cognitive or emotional deficiencies when faced with dissenting views because parents and communities have raised them in a culture of coddling. The previously cited passage from Twenge hints at this increasingly accepted line of reasoning: the lifelong immersion of Gen Z in social media technologies and its members' alleged obsessions with safety reputedly go hand in hand. Agents of campus misinformation cite putative scientific evidence that our culture overly validates the instinctive emotional reactions of children by rewarding them for dependence rather than resilience and preparing them to expect safety rather than adversity. Such perceived psychological issues overlap with questions of free speech in viewpoint diversity arguments: those arguments posit that free speech in general is eroding because maturing generations of young people allegedly perceive new and different ideas as threats to their safety.

Beginning in the late twentieth century, the story goes, fearful parents obsessed with keeping their children safe from the slightest harm or even the most casual slight from others created young adults used to existing in a protective bubble. Greg Lukianoff and Jonathan Haidt call this "safetyism" and draw heavily from Twenge's arguments about iGen to make their case. "Gradually," they write, "in the twenty-first century, on some college campuses, the meaning of 'safety' underwent a process of 'concept creep' and expanded to include 'emotional safety.' "[7] This narrative of concept creep applied to college campuses indicates another instance of correlation accepted as causation: "The preoccupation with safetyism is the clearest in the generation that began to enter college around 2013,"[8] meaning Gen Z.

Authors like Twenge or Lukianoff and Haidt cite statistically higher rates of self-reported anxiety, depression, or mental health struggles among young people to support their stated concerns about the well-being of Gen Z.[9] Ample data verify such increasing rates of diagnoses, and evidence indicates that the COVID-19 pandemic contributed to even further increases.[10] Yet attributing such increases to either a uniform cause (like social media or parenting) or claiming that those increases point to a uniformly negative outcome (such as fragile young people) is scientifically questionable. Decreased social stigma surrounding those diagnoses and refined diagnostic techniques are equally if not more relevant contributing factors. The premise that increased mental health diagnoses among young people signify a psychologically damaged or troubled generation suggests a degree of mental health stigma itself. Conclusions that public figures like Twenge or Lukianoff and Haidt draw about college-age young people raised in a culture of both social media and "safetyism" thus reflect several faulty confusions of correlation with causation.

Additional research supports my claims about confusions of correlation with causation in popular discourse about Gen Z. University of Oxford psychologists Amy Orben and Andrew Przybylski recently evaluated "statistical methods" used in research like Twenge's while also consulting a broader range of data collected from over 350,000 adolescents. They found that popular arguments about the allegedly negative psychological impact of new technology on young people typically interpret data "with an analytical flexibility that marks small effects as statistically significant, thereby leading to potential false positives and conflicting results." Such arguments, in other words, treat extant data in highly selective ways and often inflate the importance of marginally significant details. In sum, "The association we find between digital technology use and adolescent well-being is negative but small, explaining at most 0.4% of the variation in well-being."[11] A report on Orben and Przybylski's research in *Scientific American* explained the significance of their findings in this way: "Technology use tilts the needle less than half a percent away from feeling emotionally sound. For context, eating potatoes is associated with nearly the same degree of effect and wearing glasses has a more negative impact on adolescent mental health."[12] In isolation, certain factors might *seem* to cause corresponding outcomes. Measuring those factors against a variety of other relevant data, however, often reveals that their significance might be far less substantial than originally thought.

Influential psychologist and statistician Jacob Cohen succinctly explains the essential scientific lesson about correlation and causation in such circumstances. "Causality," he writes, "operates on single instances, not on populations whose members vary."[13] If I want to prove a cause-and-effect relationship in a scientifically sound manner, in other words, then I must demonstrate that relationship in a specific circumstance among a limited number of variables. Claiming that a multifaceted phenomenon like social media creates a predominant effect on an entire generation, which encompasses many different people in myriad social situations, violates that scientific principle.[14]

Technologies affect us as human beings in multifarious social, neurological, and behavioral ways. We should seek to understand and evaluate those changes—but not invoke questionable science to stereotype or scapegoat entire generations for our common, cross-generational problems. Research even suggests that some demographics of *older* US citizens are more likely than younger users to help circulate and amplify scientific or political misinformation online.[15] Disturbing uses of social media in the early 2020s both supported that premise and suggested flaws in prior hypotheses about the allegedly novel relationship between social media and Gen Z. Antivaccination sentiment and medical misinformation flourished on platforms like Facebook and Twitter throughout the COVID-19 pandemic. Ensuing hostility to health and safety measures across numerous social media groups prolonged the severest parts of the pandemic and contributed to medically preventable infections, hospitalizations, and deaths. Moreover, online falsehoods and conspiracy theories about widespread electoral fraud in the 2020 presidential election fueled the January 6, 2021, insurrection at the US Capitol. Social media platforms provided a virtual home for the spread of those falsehoods and conspiracy theories, which contributed to an attempted violent overturning of US popular government.

I agree that we should be concerned with the potential interpersonal and psychological effects of social media on young people. Yet that concern also applies to the effects of social media on the well-being of many different groups—including members of older generations who find themselves caught up in organized hostility to public health measures or political conspiracy theories. The overriding revelation of the Facebook papers, which I mentioned in Chapter 1, was that even Facebook executives understood how extremist groups disproportionately benefit from corporate-regulated social media platforms in their efforts to heighten sociopolitical divisions. Creating pseudoscientific stereotypes about the sociopolitical views or mental health of college-age young people based on sweeping assertions about social media does not substantively address the harmful influences of social media on different demographic groups, including those young people.

Popular cynicism about college-age young people frequently increases in times of sociopolitical division or rising student activism.[16] Recurrent adult beliefs that college students are acutely narcissistic, much more so than previous generations, are seldom scientifically sound.[17] In 2010, a team of psychologists at the University of Illinois responded to reports of an alleged "narcissism epidemic" by comparing data across studies. Their findings indicated that putative evidence of narcissism reflected a recurrent developmental phenomenon, not a new and unprecedented epidemic. The researchers analyzed recent individual studies of allegedly increased narcissism among college students against "preexisting meta-analytic data" and found "no increase in narcissism in college students over the last few decades. . . . Age changes in narcissism are both replicable and comparatively large in comparison to generational changes in narcissism."[18] In 2017, moreover, a team of psychologists concluded that "recent cohorts of college students" do not suffer from a "socalled 'narcissism epidemic'": "extant empirical research . . . is quite mixed with respect to whether narcissism has increased at all among adolescents and emerging adults over recent decades," which contradicts "consistent claims that the cultural climate has shifted fundamentally toward fostering narcissism."[19] College students, both studies inferred, often experiment with forms of personal expression or interpersonal behavior that suggest heightened degrees of narcissism to older generations, yet they do so customarily as a stage of maturation, not as a permanent condition.[20] "Narcissism" in these contexts more accurately describes fairly typical developmental behaviors of not-yet-full adults experiencing rapid life changes.

The pseudoscientific confusions of correlation with causation in this section not only indicate misuses of scientific evidence in public argument. Those misuses also generate allegedly scientific support for stereotyping and scapegoating college-age young people. Such pseudoscientific discourse posits the broad demographic characteristics of young people as compelling causes of numerous social ills rather than one set of meaningful factors within a complex and evolving social fabric. Understanding the empirically demonstrable causes of serious shared problems is important work for democratic citizens as well as scientific specialists. We can all contribute constructively to that work by recognizing faulty interpretations of those causes based on misuses of scientific evidence.

Question the Headlines

Agents of campus misinformation, including prominent viewpoint diversity advocates, often seek to prove their pseudo-diagnoses of college students by relying on public opinion survey research. Such research can appear to distill a spectrum of views about complicated issues into neat categories within a reasonable margin for error. Political journalists rely on poll results from organizations like Gallup, the Pew Research Center, and Rasmussen Reports to explain election cycles and political decision-making to the public at large. Political scientist W. Lance Bennett adds that "communication strategists" commonly use polls "to get their messages into the news to create the impression of broader credibility." For this reason, opinion polls themselves "tend to follow the language of political spin."[21] The degree to which many public opinion polls actively shape public opinion, rather than merely reflect or record it, is subject to debate even among statistical researchers.[22]

Scientifically sound polling can certainly provide rich and indicative data about public views. Much of the public, however, is now accustomed to accepting broad, after-the-fact summaries of survey research from reporters and pundits. Such predispositions suggest why agents of misinformation often rely on polling data: the gap between survey research and the conclusions that public figures use its data to promote can be wide and full of distortions. This section illustrates the value of questioning headlines or secondhand commentaries about individual opinion surveys in two notable cases of campus misinformation: a 2017 Brookings Institution study of college students' First Amendment views and what researchers called in 2018 the first peer-reviewed scientific study of trigger warnings.

One of the central claims of the viewpoint diversity movement—that rampant political correctness now imperils free speech rights on college campuses—gained seemingly powerful scientific support in September 2017. At that time, the Brookings Institution released a survey of college students' views about the First Amendment, conducted by John Villasenor, a Senior Fellow in the institution and a professor at the University of California, Los Angeles. Villasenor surveyed fifteen hundred individuals about the nature of the First Amendment and their opinions on such timely topics as hate speech and controversial speakers on college campuses. Based on survey results, he expressed concern about college students' understanding of the First Amendment and their tolerance for free speech rights.

National media outlets and viewpoint diversity advocates amplified Villasenor's most noteworthy conclusion with alarm. "A surprisingly large fraction of students," he stated, "believe it is acceptable to act—including resorting to violence—to shut down expression they consider offensive."[23] Villasenor offered this general assessment based on results from individual survey questions that asked respondents to consider how they might respond to different speaking situations. Agents of campus misinformation seized on this finding to promote sweeping generalizations about college students that went far beyond the limited data of the study itself. The headline for *Washington Post* columnist Charlotte Rampell's op-ed on the survey was typical: "A Chilling Study Shows How Hostile College Students Are toward Free Speech." Rampell misleadingly reported that "[a] fifth of undergrads"—not only those who Villasenor surveyed, but undergraduate students in general— "now say it's acceptable to use physical force to silence a speaker who makes 'offensive and hurtful statements.'"[24] A headline in the *Weekly Standard* hyperbolically claimed, "Survey Confirms What Many Suspected: Free Speech Is in Trouble."[25] The *Wall Street Journal* editorial board substituted melodrama for measured reporting about the survey: "James Madison Weeps: A Brookings Survey Finds College Students Are Clueless about Free Speech."[26] Purveyors of campus misinformation gamely retweeted such articles, increasing their influence over public opinions of college students.

These dramatic reports about college students' alleged ignorance of the First Amendment or intolerance for competing views rested on what one expert in scientific polling described as "malpractice" and "junk science."[27] Villasenor did not administer his survey to a randomly assembled group of verified college students; he administered it to an opt-in group of fifteen hundred online volunteers who self-identified as college students. The survey results did not reflect, with any degree of certainty, the views of college students. Villasenor did not submit his report for peer review—a standard practice in scientific research to cross-check data and vet interpretations of them.[28] Finally, he administered the survey soon after the horrific Unite the Right event, amid impassioned public controversy over hate speech, resurgent white supremacy, and related episodes of mass violence.

A cross-section of reliable public opinion research, not an isolated poll or two, strongly suggests a dramatically different picture of student support for First Amendment freedoms. Political scientist Jeffrey Sachs compared the results of several reputable research projects concerning free speech attitudes among young people. His analysis of data from sources like the General Social Survey (the results of which span nearly fifty years), a 2018 Gallup–Knight Foundation survey, a separate 2016 Gallup survey, and multiple surveys by academic researchers concluded that surveyed college students are often just as likely, if not more so, to support free speech rights compared to other social or demographic groups. This combined data, Sachs argued, also indicate that "college attendance" itself "may actually bolster a student's support for free speech rather than undermine it."[29] Yet pseudoscientific discourse about free speech crises or growing ideological intolerance on college campuses typically receives far greater public attention than scientific studies that contradict such discourse.

We should think critically about the conclusions we wish to draw even from social scientific research that appears to validate our own positions. Survey results provide *one* kind of data about the opinions or beliefs that some people hold. However, individual surveys or opinion polls do not offer complete portraits, unto themselves, of how different social groups think and behave. "Our ability to generalize is always weaker than we think," Abelson warns. That ability to generalize depends on our ability to replicate research results over time. It is true that the entire goal of scientifically conducted opinion research is to identify generalizable conclusions about social groups, but resisting the urge to generalize beyond the scope of immediate data is always scientifically appropriate.[30] If a reasonable chance exists that future surveys with different protocols or participants would yield contrasting results, then a researcher should exercise caution in offering broad generalizations about entire groups or situations.[31] Asserting broad conclusions about large groups of people based on limited data risks violating an essential principle of data interpretation.

Questionable scientific reports about personal fragility and ideological intolerance among college students based on individual surveys continued to emerge after Villasenor's Brookings Institution report. In July 2018, the self-described first peer-reviewed scientific study of trigger warnings appeared online in the *Journal of Behavior Therapy and Experimental Psychology.*

Lead author Benjamin Bellet, a doctoral candidate in psychology at Harvard University, and his coauthors designed an experiment "to investigate the psychological effects of issuing trigger warnings." They "randomly assigned" trigger warnings to some "online participants" but not to others before "reading literary passages that varied in potentially disturbing content." After analyzing the results, Bellet et al. concluded that trigger warnings "increase people's perceived emotional vulnerability to trauma [and] increase anxiety to written material perceived as harmful."[32] The authors concluded that trigger warnings may decrease emotional resilience in subjects—or, by the same token, *increase* their psychological fragility.

Efforts to promote this experimental study in popular media as the first peer-reviewed research of its kind suggested an attempt to generate publicity regardless of the actual scientific findings involved. Most academic journal articles claim to present new or different contributions to existing research, but less frequently claim to be the first of their kind. Such a claim to newsworthiness parallels the conceit of the August 2016 University of Chicago letter to incoming students—a normally routine document that was written to generate news ledes about trigger warnings and safe spaces. The specific research findings that an individual study generates offer the best evidence of its scientific value, not the claims of researchers or their supporters to have produced the first study of its kind. For example, I could design a first-ever peer-reviewed study to measure how the instructions section of an exam psychologically affected students who took it or a first-ever study to measure how the chairs in which those students sat affected their exam scores. Such claims to first-ever status, however, communicate nothing about whether a study yielded significantly new or different findings measured against existing bodies of knowledge. Asserting scientific achievement in this way indicates a desire to generate headlines as much as academic insights.

Purveyors of campus misinformation accordingly seized on the 2018 trigger warnings study. Bellicose media like *Breitbart*, *National Review*, the *Daily Wire*, and the *College Fix*—which routinely feature polemics against college students and professors—promoted its findings in concert. Many of their headlines were declarative: "Harvard Study: Trigger Warnings Actually Harmful to Students," "STUDY: 'Trigger Warnings' Are Harmful to College Students."[33] *Psychology Today* followed suit: "Harvard Study: Trigger Warnings Might Coddle the Mind."[34] The Foundation for Individual Rights in Education (FIRE) approvingly promoted the Harvard University study.[35] In short order, networks of campus misinformation and advocates for viewpoint diversity claimed that a single experiment proved something that no single experiment can scientifically prove: trigger warnings in university classrooms are psychologically harmful. The researchers themselves, to their credit, made no such claims. From hyperpartisan media to popular psychology journals or blogs, however, headlines and initial reporting sped past the nuances of their research to declare that science had proven the harms of trigger warnings on university syllabi.

Such immediate headlines eclipsed important details about how the experiment worked and who participated in it. Bellet et al. used Amazon Mechanical Turk to survey online participants about their experiences with trigger warnings. Amazon Mechanical Turk is a "crowdsourcing marketplace" designed to make data collection easier for researchers of all types, whether academic or corporate.[36] The number of online participants in Bellet et al.'s study was notably small—270 total—and the average age of those participants was thirty-seven. In other words, the researchers did not administer the survey to college students per se and the experimental conditions did not include classroom environments. The total number of respondents to this experimental survey was smaller than the total number of students in a single large lecture course of the kind that numerous universities offer in multiple academic subjects at any given time.

Bellet and his co-researchers also excluded participants who reported a history of trauma. Trigger warnings, I noted in Chapter 2, were first used in online communities to forewarn users with a history of personal trauma about website content that could trigger symptoms of posttraumatic stress disorder. Miscellaneous university instructors later adapted trigger warnings to portions of their syllabi for analogous reasons.[37] An online survey of respondents who might not have been college students, which excluded participants who reported histories of personal trauma, offers tenuous insight into how a teaching device intended to support college students with histories of personal trauma psychologically affects students in educational environments.

Finally, in statistical terms, the results of Bellet et al.'s study were inconclusive. Their data showed only slight differences in the self-reported effects of trigger warnings on participants who received them compared to the group of participants who did not. The "effect size" between the two groups was small (which co-researcher Payton Jones conceded[38]) and could be explained as a random or chance outcome. News reports about the study, as well as some of the conclusions that Bellet et al. drew from it, hinged on the mere fact of a difference between the trigger warning and non–trigger warning group. Documenting slight differences between experimental groups and control groups, however, is common due to the presence of "sensible experimental manipulations."[39] Researchers can record a difference between two groups, but that difference does not directly indicate a generalizable claim to *significance* about how large classes of human beings think or behave. These caveats are neither exotic nor merely technical; they reflect basic guidelines of accurate and responsible statistical interpretation.

The scientific method allows researchers to responsibly generalize about expansive causes and effects only after generating a large amount of similar experimental results using common protocols. Bellet et al.'s experiment proved, instead, what can happen under the experimental protocols that they used and therefore provides bases for some generalization in similar conditions. Yet their experimental data did not reveal anything substantive about the uses and effects of trigger warnings in other contexts shaped by innumerably different variables. Professional journalists and sources of campus misinformation who reported that Bellet et al.'s initial study proved the harmful effects of trigger warnings on college students vastly overstated the significance of the researchers' actual findings. In doing so, those secondhand reports misinformed the public about available research on this topic.

Other research teams published a spate of subsequent experimental studies on trigger warnings. Synopses of their results from researchers and journalists alike continue to produce disconcerting levels of misinformation about psychological frailties and ideological intolerance among college students. In March 2019, University of Waikato psychologist Mevagh Sanson and her fellow researchers published another widely publicized experiment. The researchers surveyed a combination of nearly fourteen hundred college students and online volunteers.[40] Sanson and her coauthors attained similar results to Bellet et al.: their experiment with a mixed group of volunteers, not exclusively college students, yielded no substantial difference in effect size between participants who did and did not receive a trigger warning prior to viewing disturbing content. "These results," the authors concluded, "suggest a trigger warning is neither meaningfully helpful nor harmful."[41] The central statistical finding of the March 2019 study was that trigger warnings produced *no* meaningful effect on participants in the study itself.[42]

Sanson and her coauthors nevertheless imported assumptions about undergraduate students to redescribe this patently neutral effect as confirmation that trigger warnings *harm* college students. "College students," they wrote, "are increasingly anxious, and widespread adoption of trigger warnings in syllabi may promote this trend, tacitly encouraging students to turn to avoidance, thereby depriving them of opportunities to learn healthier ways to manage potential distress."[43] Sanson et al. did not need to design an experiment to reach this conclusion, and their data did not lead to it. That conclusion simply reproduces prior polemics about coddled and ideologically intolerant students.

Sanson and her coauthors' unsubstantiated claims marked an important turning point in pseudoscientific discourse about trigger warnings. Experiments designed to assess the effects of trigger warnings on research participants now commonly embrace a problematically circular form of interpretation. Without being able to measure significant effects on participants from those warnings, much less demonstrate harm, some researchers inevitably argue that trigger warnings are harmful *because* they have no effect. The same Harvard University psychologists who produced the much-sensationalized 2018 study of trigger warnings, for example, designed a subsequent experiment to address the fact that their prior data excluded subjects who reported personal traumas. Payton et al. concluded, with this alteration, that trigger warnings "are not helpful for trauma survivors." Trigger warnings, they reported, did not positively impact participants' self-reported PTSD. This assessment is not surprising; a one-time exposure to a written trigger warning is unlikely to therapeutically address PTSD symptoms. "It is less clear," the authors conceded, "whether trigger warnings are explicitly harmful." Payton et al. nevertheless resolved this potential contradiction—the fact that being "unhelpful" is not the same as being "harmful"—by concluding that "because trigger warnings are consistently unhelpful, there is no evidence-based reason to use them." The authors not only admitted that their second study showed no harm from trigger warnings, they warned against ever using them because they are, allegedly, "unhelpful."[44] Like Sanson et al., Payton and his co-researchers imposed a headline-ready conclusion onto data that did not support that conclusion as a research finding.

Such conclusions represent significant linguistic goalpost-shifting from prior arguments about the perceived effects of trigger warnings. Lukianoff and Haidt's 2015 article in *The Atlantic*, which inspired the experimental research cited in this chapter, posited that devices like trigger warnings and safe spaces *actively harm* the education and mental health of young people.[45] Widely publicized statements like the University of Chicago's letter to first-year students in August 2016 reinforced the premise that trigger warnings and safe spaces in educational institutions impede, or actively harm, the academic development of college students.

The most consistent finding of the scientific studies cited in this chapter, however, is that trigger warnings produced little effect, if any, on participants in experimental conditions—no demonstrable harm. Agents of campus misinformation, including advocates for viewpoint diversity, have responded to such findings by counterintuitively claiming that trigger warnings *are* actively harmful because they have little, if any, effect on users. That counterintuitive premise relies on a semantic shell game in which the observed *minimal* and *neutral* effects of trigger warnings become evidence of their allegedly *significant* and *harmful* effect.

The examples of misleading headlines and dubious after-the-fact summaries of scientific data examined in this section demonstrate why we should receive simplified reports about statistical research into complicated realities with a degree of healthy skepticism. Such secondhand reporting is prone to hyperbole and sensationalism; these tendencies frequently distort or misrepresent scientific data in ways that help to popularize pseudoscience. Questioning whether headlines and media summaries accurately report the specific findings of scientific studies in their original research context, however, can help us to see through frequently spurious assertions of empirical fact in critical public debates.

Question the Questions

Examining the language of the individual questions that make up public opinion surveys can also indicate pseudoscientific discourse in the guise of credible research. Survey teams can easily write questions to manufacture desired results, not to document opinions or beliefs in scientifically responsible ways. The wording of survey questions in many opinion polls that viewpoint diversity advocates cite illustrates this claim. Widely publicized polls from the late 2010s *appeared* to offer nonpartisan scientific evidence of political biases, psychologically fragile students, and poor free speech climates on college campuses. The wording of individual questions in those polls, however, raises concerns about their scientific merits.

Long-standing research in the behavioral sciences shows that even small differences in the wording of survey questions can affect the nature of respondents' answers.[46] The effects of question wording can be subtle enough that "different question wordings may influence responses even" when "the wordings seem semantically equivalent."[47] Two questions that convey the same meaning with slightly different words can yield substantially different results.

Consumers of news and information do not have to consult academic research to judge for themselves the scientific merits of survey questions. Survey Monkey, a popular and convenient online survey tool, offers short summaries of common mistakes in question wording likely to corrupt data; those summaries comport well with established social scientific research methods.[48]

This online resource is one of many convenient, publicly available tools that can help anyone spot the difference between scientifically sound interpretations of data and pseudoscientific claims.

Identifying faulty question wording in Villasenor's survey of college student attitudes toward free speech did not require specialized training. For example, his repeated use of the word "all" in a question about on-campus learning environments (highlighted in bold here) required respondents to answer with *absolute preferences*:

> If you had to choose one of the options below, which do you think it is more important for colleges to do?
> Option 1: create a positive learning environment for **all** students by prohibiting certain speech or expression of viewpoints that are offensive or biased against certain groups of people
>
> Option 2: create an open learning environment where students are exposed to **all** types of speech and viewpoints, even if it means allowing speech that is offensive or biased against certain groups of people? (Italics in original.)

Survey Monkey explains that "absolutes in questions force respondents into a corner where they can't give useful feedback. These questions usually have the options Yes/No and include wording such as 'always,' 'all,' 'every,' 'ever,' etc." The options provided to respondents in such question wording often include an either-or choice between an unrealistic option (see "Option 1") and one that seems more reasonable or intuitively "correct" in the context of the question as written. Survey questions of this sort generate suspect data because they nudge respondents toward a favored response.

"Option 2" in the quoted example from the Brookings Institution survey illustrated another serious problem in question wording: *double-barreled questions*. The query asks respondents to assess the level of harm in learning environments created by *"speech that is offensive or biased against certain groups of people."* Offensive speech and biased speech may refer to distinct forms of expression, depending on the circumstance (offensive speech causes anger or offense in general; biased speech is prejudiced against specific groups). Villasenor's cited question is double-barreled because it requires respondents to answer two questions with a single response. "Survey questions," Survey Monkey advises, "should always be written in a way that only one thing is being measured. If a single question has two subjects, it's impossible to tell how the respondent is weighing the different elements involved." The unclear responses that double-barreled questions generate provide researchers with some degree of latitude to infer what they think those responses mean in potentially specious ways.

I previously noted that experts in opinion polling criticized Villasenor's Brookings Institution report. However, the question wording in some comparatively uncontroversial surveys of college students from the late 2010s was similarly problematic. In March 2018, for instance, the Knight Foundation published a widely anticipated report based on a survey of college students' views about First Amendment issues. Consider the problematic wording of this heavily loaded question: "Do you think colleges *should or should not* be able to establish policies that restrict each of the following types of speech or expression on campus?" [emphasis mine]. This wording asks respondents to indicate whether they either *support* or *do not support* two diametrically opposed scenarios—restricting speech *and* not restricting speech—with a single answer. Respondents might think that they answered the question in one way, but a researcher could interpret their responses to mean something different from that original intent.

Question wording in this part of the Knight Foundation survey also forced respondents to render a single opinion on many different scenarios by including a catch-all list of dissimilar "types of speech or expression." That list ranged from controversial political views to offensive slurs and costumes based on racial or ethnic stereotypes. Such wording reduces the ability of respondents to offer appropriately nuanced answers, prompting them to record absolute stances on dissimilar forms of expression that might warrant case-by-case judgments in actual situations.

Other questions from the March 2018 Knight Foundation survey of college students illustrated needlessly complicated or elaborate question wording. The following item, for example, asked respondents to register degrees of agreement and disagreement to a single premise at once: "Do you strongly agree, somewhat agree, somewhat disagree, or strongly disagree with the following statement: the climate on my campus prevents some people from saying things they believe because others might find them offensive."[49] The purpose of an opinion survey like this one is, indeed, to document respondents' degrees of agreement or disagreement to different scenarios. The most scientific way to do so is to provide respondents with opportunities to record those degrees of agreement or disagreement as distinct answers, not in the form of a single lengthy question. Stringing so many potential responses together in a single query begs questions about the consistency or representativeness of the responses in total. Unfortunately, widely consulted polling organizations like the Knight Foundation and Gallup frequently use such problematic question wording in their research on a host of issues.

The *ordering* of survey questions, in addition to their individual wording, can also influence respondents' answers in undetected but significant ways. Psychologists Fritz Strack and Norbert Schwarz explain that researchers sometimes order individual questions to suggest norms of reciprocal conversation between survey writers and respondents: "asking and answering questions is a type of conversation and has properties of a natural discourse in which two (or more) people engage in a purposeful interaction." Yet the degree to which such aspects of conversational sequencing may impact survey responses "tends to be overlooked."[50]

Elements of question ordering that mimic conversational discourse can result in a phenomenon known as *priming*. Priming occurs when the ordering of several survey questions psychologically primes respondents to provide certain kinds of answers. Imagine surveying regular patrons of a particularly busy coffee shop about different facets of their customer experience. A survey could ask customers about their average wait times, then in-store noise levels as they waited, then the quality of the coffee, and finally overall customer satisfaction, in that order. If the first questions reminds respondents of frustratingly long wait times and irritating levels of ambient noise, then such negative impressions could carry over and result in less positive evaluations of coffee quality or overall satisfaction in later answers. A different question order might produce qualitatively different results. This example illustrates how priming can influence opinion survey answers in subtle and occasionally inevitable ways. Priming in survey research is, for this reason, not a blatant error in wording or arrangement so much as an element that experienced researchers often expect to manage even in the most scientifically rigorous studies.[51]

In contrast, purveyors of pseudoscientific discourse skillfully but irresponsibly prime survey respondents to produce data that confirm preconceived judgments or narratives about specific issues. Survey results that *appear* to decisively confirm broad conceits about higher education (such as the alleged psychological frailty of college students or uniform political bias across thousands of institutions) provide viewpoint diversity advocates with allegedly scientific evidence that exploits popular tendencies to accept opinion poll results at face value. For example, the ordering of questions in the Campus Expression Survey,[52] which Heterodox Academy developed, indicates significant amounts of priming. The organization maintains this survey online so that members of universities can use it to supposedly measure the quality of the climate for free speech and academic inquiry at their home institutions, thereby generating data for Heterodox Academy and allied organizations.

The "core module" of the Campus Expression Survey attempts to assess respondents' comfort levels about expressing their views in classroom discussions of potentially controversial topics. A lengthy sequence of similarly worded queries constitutes that core module. Each question in this sequence asks respondents how they would feel about participating in a distinct hypothetical discussion about "<u>GENDER</u>," then "<u>RACE</u>," then a "<u>POLITICAL ISSUE</u>," then "<u>SEXUALITY</u>," and so forth [emphases in original].[53]

Behavioral science research explains that such a sequencing of questions, even involving "rather innocuous variations" or "formal features of the questionnaires," can "have enormous effects on respondents' answers."[54] Respondents commonly adhere to a tendency known as the *cooperative principle*: voluntary survey participants ordinarily try to be helpful by providing desired information instead of answering questions with minimal thoughtfulness. Respondents of standardized questionnaires like the Campus Expression Survey often use "contextual cues that help determine the communicative intention of the questioner," meaning the "particular response format, the order in which questions are asked, and the wording of questions."[55] The cooperative principle can lead voluntary research participants to draw inferences about how they should answer particular queries from those cues.[56] Recall here that Heterodox Academy was founded on the belief that diversity and inclusion programs pertaining to race, sex, and gender had created ideologically hostile environments for open expression on college campuses. The likelihood that many survey respondents understand the organization's stated reactionary position as such, and that it forms potential subtext for their interpretation of survey questions, is also significant.

Question ordering in the Campus Expression Survey thus exhibits a high potential for priming. The survey simply presumes in-class *controversy* over gender, race, politics, and the like. It reinforces that impression several times by devoting individual questions to automatic levels of controversy and personal discomfort that a class discussion of every such topic might generate.[57] This powerful assumption may prime respondents to assess each imagined scenario and, thus, the "speech climate" of their universities with heightened degrees of concern. Tools like the Campus Expression Survey, which are popular among self-described advocates of viewpoint diversity, arguably *shape* respondents' opinions or perceptions of college campuses more than they generate definitive data about actual on-campus exchanges.

Effectively worded and ordered survey questions can mean the difference between responsibly collected social scientific data and distorted survey results. Citing the latter kind of data to support broad conclusions about entire social groups, such as the psychological wellbeing of college students or their supposed intolerance for dissenting viewpoints, is a hallmark of pseudo-scientific discourse. The examples of faulty question wording and sequencing in this section indicate a larger pattern among seemingly scientific arguments about the state of college campuses today. Some of the most widely publicized opinion research about alleged free speech crises or coddled college students in the late 2010s effectively reinforced preexisting polemical views on those topics rather than generating credible scientific analyses about the state of higher education. Understanding basic and effective criteria for evaluating either the wording or ordering of survey questions can empower anyone to judge the results of opinion polls for themselves, whether those polls concern aspects of higher education or numerous other social and political issues.

Question the Methods

Learning how to identify problems in the stated research methods of news-worthy scientific studies can also help people to distinguish between pseu-doscience that supports misinformation and credible contributions to scientific knowledge. Attaining a functional understanding of the basic principles that all written research methods should follow is a relatively easy task for nonscientists or daily consumers of news and information. The Purdue University Online Writing Lab is merely one of many university-based resources that efficiently explains the main purpose of a written research methodology: "Because your study methods form a large part of your credibility as a researcher and writer, it is imperative that you be clear about what you did to gather information from participants in your study."[58] Consumers of news and information may therefore begin by asking whether explanations of scientific evidence clearly and succinctly explain how researchers attained their results. This question, moreover, can apply to any scientific effort to collect and interpret data—even ones that aggregate data from other sources instead of directly surveying research participants.

A written summary of research methods establishes a contract with readers, from fellow scientists to members of the general public. This contract should be based on *trust* and *choice*. A well-written statement of research methods should trust readers enough to explain clearly what researchers wanted to accomplish, who was involved, and the step-by-step procedures they followed. Trusting readers with these details invites them to examine how well researchers designed and executed the study. Such information allows readers to ask if researchers effectively and responsibly defined the goals of their study in the first place, included the most representative subjects, and followed logical steps in data collection and analysis. Basic methodological information therefore enables readers to make an important choice: to decide for themselves whether they agree with the conclusions that the authors of a particular study reached instead of uncritically receiving research results. Pseudoscientific discourse often occludes such methodological information to exploit widespread popular acceptance of scientific results as seemingly self-evident representations of complicated realities.

Some of the most important databases in the viewpoint diversity movement illustrate obfuscating and exploitative statements of research methods. FIRE maintains a much-publicized "Disinvitation Database." This database lists hundreds of incidents, sorted by year and institution, in which an invited speaker was somehow "disinvited" from speaking on a campus. The purpose of the database, FIRE says, is to document a "worrisome trend undermining open discourse in the academy": an "increased push by some students and faculty to 'disinvite' speakers with whom they disagree from campus appearances." FIRE contends that its data show steady increases in overall rates of disinvitations for more than a decade.

Journalists, advocates of viewpoint diversity, and ideological firebrands reflexively cite data from the FIRE database as supposed empirical evidence of their claims about alleged regimes of censorship in higher education. Frequent mentions of this database on numerous media platforms performed a notable rhetorical function in rampant sensationalism about miscellaneous campus controversies throughout the late 2010s. Labeling an aggregation of information from numerous and often randomly assembled sources as a "database" logically implies that such data are empirically sound and broadly representative as a set unto itself.

The explanation of research methods that accompanies the Disinvitation Database, however, raises concerns about its evidentiary merit. Scrutinizing this methodological statement is crucial because many media figures and academic commentators cite this database as alleged proof of an extremely serious charge: widespread censorship among hundreds of colleges and universities. FIRE explains its methods to database users as follows:

> FIRE researched disinvitation efforts at public and private American institutions . . . by collecting data from a number of sources, including news accounts and case submissions to FIRE and other organizations.
>
>   It is important to note that this research is not exhaustive. It would be nearly impossible to compile information on every disinvitation attempt. However, FIRE is confident that this data accurately documents a culture of censorship on college campuses.[59]

A statement of research methods should answer pragmatic questions about how data were compiled and why. The quoted FIRE research methods are written to provide the appearance of answering those questions while nevertheless omitting vital information. FIRE says that it collected "data from a number of courses," but does not specify which ones. FIRE explains that it included "news accounts and case submissions to FIRE and other organizations," but does not name or enumerate those sources. FIRE thus gives users of this database little information about where the data came from and how they were analyzed—a methodology in name only.

Based on this description of methods, the Disinvitation Database ultimately wants to have it two ways at once. Its authors admit that their research is far from "exhaustive" and that compiling a fully accurate record of disinvitation attempts on college campuses would be "nearly impossible." Yet FIRE nonetheless claims, in one and the same voice, to "accurately document[] a culture of censorship" on college campuses in a way that suggests something close to an exhaustive analysis of available data. The language of the methodology expresses confidence in a research goal that it admits is potentially unattainable in the first place.

The language of FIRE's own methodology raises doubts about the Disinvitation Database as alleged scientific evidence of widespread censorship. That language does not exhibit trust in users regarding how, specifically, its data were selected. Neither does it provide users with necessary information to choose for themselves—to thoughtfully agree or disagree that the database accurately proves a culture of censorship on college campuses. The database functions, more realistically, to publicize a preconceived notion (that a culture of censorship exists on college campuses) through sheer aggregation of online content, not to make a systematic, evidence-based case for that contention.

Crucial explanatory elements of the FIRE Disinvitation Database's methodology—like criteria for defining a "disinvitation incident"—only create more analytic confusion. FIRE offers three primary categories of such incidents: "Formal disinvitation," "Withdrawal by the speaker in the face of disinvitation demands," and " 'Heckler's vetoes.' " Each definition is not a scientific measurement in and of itself, but an impressionistic category that encompasses secondhand reports or miscellaneous anecdotes about various campus incidents. Some scientific researchers warn against treating anecdotal evidence as substantive data because anecdotes typically rely on easily distorted, after-the-fact narration (a topic I examine at length in the next chapter).[60] The FIRE Disinvitation Database is, more accurately, an *anecdote*base.

Additional explanations of research methodology from FIRE's other databases indicate similar grounds for concern. Such databases claim to rank different institutions for their protection of free speech rights. For instance, the organization presents an annual Spotlight on Speech Codes. Conor Friedersdorf, a columnist for *The Atlantic*, relied on this resource in a 2016 article titled "The Glaring Evidence That Free Speech Is Threatened on Campus."[61] FIRE lists key features of the methodology that it uses to compile such information:

> FIRE surveyed publicly available policies at 345 four-year public institutions and 104 of the nation's largest and/or most prestigious private institutions. . . . FIRE rates colleges and universities as "red light," "yellow light," or "green light" based on how much, if any, protected speech their written policies restrict.[62]

Thousands of colleges and universities exist in the United States. *Which* 345 four-year public institutions did FIRE choose, and *why*? The methodology is vague on this crucial point. FIRE lists selected schools by rating, but those schools vary widely in size and type of institution. "The nation's largest and/or most prestigious private institutions" is a similarly imprecise category.

FIRE's definitions of what constitutes a "red light," "yellow light," or "green light" rating, moreover, are blatantly subjective. "A red light institution," for example, "has at least one policy both clearly and substantially restricting freedom of speech." The definition for this rating includes the fact that the institution "bars public access to its speech-related policies by requiring a university login and password for access" or bans "offensive speech." The criteria for these ratings, in other words, are both vague and potentially arbitrary; such definitions only beg more unanswered definitional questions. These methodological criteria suggest strategically flexible conceits useful for pulling data out of their original context—some of which might be relatively innocuous, like needing a password to access university information—and transforming them into "evidence" of allegedly serious and pervasive free speech violations.

The language of these methodologies indicates an unwillingness to communicate trust and choice to readers, as a credible research methodology should. Research statements of this sort withhold a full view behind the proverbial curtain of research processes, which would allow consumers of news and information to decide for themselves whether everything adds up as it should. Casually adopting the language of scientific research while adhering to dubious research methods is a hallmark of misinformation. This technique allows sources of misleading claims to project the image of scientific authority while promoting, in truth, deceptive pseudoscience.

The language that FIRE uses to describe the import of this now-widely consulted online resource obscures more than it reveals in another crucial manner. In principle, nothing is wrong with student or faculty groups asking, even passionately demanding, that an invited speaker not appear on a given campus at a given time. Making demands of power holders and staging non-violent protests are legitimate exercises of First Amendment freedoms. Members of campus communities can engage in those forms of expression while still adhering to both campus policy and First Amendment law.

Freely petitioning university administrators to reconsider invitations to specific outside speakers is not censorship. Those petitions stimulate institutional deliberation over "a value judgment"—the relative value, in other words, of particular words, ideas, and arguments to the educational climate of the institution in question.[63] (Violent demonstrations are unacceptable and ineffective ways to stimulate such deliberation and judgments.) Some student and faculty petitions to university administrators may be inadvisable or poorly executed. Yet such petitions, and even passionate demands, illustrate an important element of campus self-governance and academic freedoms: the ability to openly debate which kind of invited speakers do and do not contribute desirably to the educational mission of a given academic community. This observation applies equally to social and religious groups that frequently exercise their constitutional freedoms by protesting scientific facts about evolution or histories of racism, sexism, and homophobia in universities as well as public schools. Members of academic communities always have the right to request that certain speakers not appear on their campuses or to voice their views about educational content without broaching censorship.

None of these claims contradict the core legal standards that protect free speech while prohibiting censorship on college campuses. Law professors Erwin Chemerinsky and Howard Gillman conveniently summarize those standards: "*A campus can't censor or punish speech merely because a person or group considers it offensive or hateful* [italics in original]."[64] *Censorship* in such a case would occur if administrators at a publicly funded university unilaterally determined which speakers could and could not be invited to campus based on the invalid ground of perceived offense. Saying that members of academic communities who exercise their democratic rights to petition powerholders engage in censorship, however, is inconsistent with a defense of civil liberties. *Counter-speech*, I explain in Chapter 6, is an important democratic safety valve against threats of official censorship.[65] Event organizers and university administrators, working in collaboration, can always choose to entertain petitions or protests against particular speakers and events—or decide not to entertain them at all.

The issue at the heart of the free speech crisis on campus is not whether one thinks that such requests and demands are politically sensible, or if students and faculty express them in consistently civil and emotionally temperate ways. The issue is whether members of campus communities have the First Amendment right to freely make those requests and demands. They do. Instead of reflexively pathologizing or criminalizing such requests and demands, we can treat them as opportunities for practicing constructive democratic deliberation about interrelated issues of educational climate, First Amendment rights, ethical judgment, public safety, and more. The ability to petition power holders is essential to democracy, whatever the merits of the petitions in question.

The language of the Disinvitation Database illustrates how advocates of viewpoint diversity have coined a pseudoscientific vocabulary to insinuate that some democratically articulated requests or demands automatically constitute censorship. *Disinvitation. De-platforming. De-recognizing. Canceling.* Every such term communicates strong negative connotations. Semantically, those terms not only suggest that some inherent right is being taken away when other people exercise competing rights. Presented in the format of a database, this terminology also claims to provide empirical proof of such infringements. In principle, neither inference is true.

Universities can freely invite or not invite speakers so long as they abide by institutional policies and the law—just like many other kinds of institutions. Receiving an invitation to speak is a privilege, not a right. Invented terms like "disinvitation" or "de-platforming," moreover, do not refer to widely agreed-upon or precise empirical categories. Increases in what some people choose to call, with heavily pejorative connotations, disinvitations or de-platforming do not directly indicate censorship of any kind, much less pervasive anti–free speech attitudes. The conceit that organizations can measure or rank institutional obligations to free speech and intellectual diversity in narrowly statistical ways is neither scientifically nor democratically responsible. Remembering to ask whether organizations that compile resources like the Disinvitation Database trust the public with clear explanations of their methodologies can help anyone to recognize suspect forms of data collection and the faulty narratives that they support.

Conclusion

Misinformation based on the simple appearance of scientific evidence promotes faulty information in two primary ways. First, such misinformation manipulates scientific evidence to mislead the public about expert research findings and interpretations of specific issues. Remembering to ask simple questions—about the difference between correlation and causation, how research results are described in secondhand reports, and the wording of survey queries—can equip us to distinguish between pseudoscientific discourse and sound scientific arguments. This chapter has demonstrated that the need to ask such questions is particularly acute in the case of public discourse about higher education.

Second, distorted uses of scientific evidence also misinform the public about sound scientific practices in general. The examples in this chapter of pseudoscientific discourse about college-age young people and higher education not only contained suspect data or specious interpretations of them unto themselves. Networks of campus misinformation also cited those isolated opinion polls and research experiments throughout the late 2010s to publicize allegedly significant revelations about the quality of academic environments or intellectual exchange. The pretense of such supposedly data-driven revelations obscured an important empirical reality: universities employ layers of qualitative and quantitative measurements to assess campus climate and learning experiences as a basic part of their daily functioning. Those continual measurements typically generate deeper, more reliable, and more representative information about campus environments than periodic and randomly administered studies from outside groups can generate.

Institutions of higher education operate, to a large extent, by consistently measuring teaching effectiveness, learning outcomes, and constructive debate according to a variety of substantive indices. College administrations set standards for curricular content and typically require different programs to verify their compliance with those standards. Many institutions are legally obligated to regularly document how their programs deliver educational content fairly and equitably to all students. Numerous universities have established offices of educational equity to investigate student complaints about biases or unfair treatment (a positive entailment of pro-diversity and pro-inclusion policies in higher education). Universities evaluate the quality of teaching through such tools as student course evaluations, peer observation of teaching practices, and required reports from professors about their course content. Evidence of effective teaching—entailing the ability to maintain positive and inclusive classroom environments—is a requirement for promotion and tenure in most institutions. In-class instruction provides weekly face-to-face opportunities to observe and interact with students as to the quality of their learning experience. Regular course assignments are, in essence, devices for assessing the effectiveness of learning environments;

instructor evaluations of those assignments provide repeated opportunities for dialogue about educational progress in context. Many universities are, by these measurements and others, data-generating machines that persistently seek to document the quality of academic climate at specific institutions at many levels.

I do not claim that such efforts are always effective or evince uniformly positive teaching and intellectual debates. I contend, rather, that such combined measurements offer far better empirical evidence about climates of campus expression or the merits of specific educational practices than periodic surveys based on random respondents. Quantitatively, the data from the studies examined in this chapter represent a sliver of the data that a given university administration regularly compiles about those matters. Qualitatively, the preponderance of continually amassed and institutionally specific information in different colleges offers much richer evidence of campus affairs than headline-ready opinion polls or arbitrarily assembled databases. The notion that such individual tools, unto themselves, offer empirically deep or revelatory information about multifaceted learning environments reflects a pseudoscientific approach to the critical task of documenting effective teaching and debate on university campuses. We can promote more constructive public debate about the state of higher education by featuring richer and more representative sources of evidence pertaining to the quality of specific academic environments. Doing so may better inform the public about how universities tend to function as complex but vital institutions.

Unfortunately, persistent appeals to alleged scientific evidence of crises in higher education lent additional credence to proliferating tropes of campus misinformation in the late 2010s. Agents of campus misinformation not only declared a putative free speech crisis in universities. Their passionate claims to this effect, which employed questionable scientific studies for validation, helped to popularize an alternate reality of life and work on college campuses. Dystopian descriptions of various social and political realities are consistent with the spread of misinformation. The projection of such a reality allows agents of misinformation to assert that a calamitous state of affairs exists even if many people remain unconvinced as a factual matter. Narratives of student mobs that shut down or cancel most invited speakers to college campuses, or rule many universities with force, was integral to producing this sort of alternate reality in the late 2010s. I devote special attention to these hyperbolic tropes in the next chapter because they produced the most heated debate and lasting false impressions about the state of higher education out of any mode of discourse analyzed in this book.

5
Mobs and Shutdowns

Eddie Glaude, professor of religion and African American studies at Princeton University, appeared as one of the weekly guests on HBO's *Real Time with Bill Maher* in October 2018. During a panel discussion on current events, Maher asked Glaude disdainfully about "free speech" being "stifled on campus with students protesting controversial speakers" as a troubling symptom of "political correctness." Glaude answered that such descriptions were "overstated." He offered a relatively obvious observation: "There are thousands of lectures on college campuses across the ideological spectrum that happen every day without these incidents." Maher responded incredulously, "You read about it a lot. A lot." Glaude explained, accurately, that such reports are a form of sensationalism about universities.[1]

This telling exchange between Maher and Glaude handily illustrates how campus misinformation had successfully popularized an alternative reality about college campuses by late 2018. That misinformation, I showed in previous chapters, originated with hyperbolic fixations on the idea of trigger warnings and safe spaces on college campuses. A sustained, sensationalized media operation subsequently made warnings about campus speech crises a semipermanent form of polemical entertainment disguised as intellectual commentary. Contributors to this media campaign frequently sought to substantiate their claims about dangerously coddled young people and ideological rigidity on college campuses with pseudoscientific discourse. In this chapter, I explain how such individual strains of discourse combined in the late 2010s to popularize an alternative reality of enraged student mobs that routinely shut down or cancel a wide variety of outside speakers on most university campuses. This alternative reality warrants scrutiny because it hinders constructive, evidence-based debates about free speech on college campuses by conflating nonviolent forms of protest and civil disobedience with violent and psychologically unhealthy activities.

Maher was correct, at least, that people read about this alternative campus reality a lot during 2018. Violent events at a statistically small number of institutions in 2017 inspired an apparent competition among some journalists and well-known academic figures for who could draw the hastiest generalizations about higher education based on a limited number of anecdotes. A steady supply of publications in the months prior to Maher's October 2018 broadcast went beyond sustaining alarm about free speech emergencies on college campuses to elaborately depicting a dystopian reality that had befallen most universities. According to this version of reality, "Faculty and student activists have taken to objecting to even mainstream, substantive speakers who do not fit within the narrow confines of their preferred orthodoxy."[2] The alleged power of "an increasingly common response by an increasingly leftist professoriate" was so insidious, according to some commentators, that "real life is beginning to mimic college tribunals."[3] Authors of magazine articles and books claimed that college protesters "have embraced the idea that America is so profoundly corrupt in so many ways that free speech is nothing more than another 'tool of oppression.' In its place, they have put their peculiar idea of 'social justice,' to be obtained by collective use of force."[4] The overall situation in higher education was allegedly so dire that "this year [2017] may become a turning point in the annals of higher education. It may be remembered as the year that political violence and police escorts became ordinary parts of campus life."[5] These wildly inflated claims tell us more about the reductive and sensationalist lens through which some commentators in privileged positions prefer to view contemporary higher education than they do about its multifaceted and comparatively unexciting realities. Understanding how violent conflicts over ideological disagreements may arise on university campuses is necessary to maintaining positive learning environments and social climates. Sensationalizing those rare clashes on college campuses by raising the specter, for instance, of the Chinese Cultural Revolution—a brutal totalitarian era that lasted a decade, involving the state persecution and murder of millions—hinders sober analyses and collaborative resolutions of conflicts where and when appropriate.[6]

Approximately five thousand postsecondary institutions (colleges and universities as well as trade and vocational schools) exist in the United States.[7] A single small liberal arts college holds hundreds of classes a day as well as campus events throughout the week, every one of which is a protected First Amendment forum. Glaude's statement is baseline fact: colleges and universities uneventfully host thousands of lectures "across the political spectrum" every day. Rioting on college campuses most commonly occurs after sporting events. Those periodic riots exemplify what one commentator calls "a long, destructive sports tradition" in North America, encompassing professional and collegiate events, that involves "thousands of people arrested, hundreds injured, more than a dozen killed."[8] Aside from initial condemnations among sports journalists, however, those violent episodes do not inspire sustained intellectual commentary about campuses under siege.

Dramatic narratives of campus tribunals, leftist professoriates, and widespread student uses of force are wild and largely inaccurate overgeneralizations. The manifest purpose of such narratives is not to understand and genuinely engage a spectrum of diverse viewpoints in a spirit of constructive disagreement. Those narratives depict an alternative reality of life on college campuses rooted in stereotypes about fundamentally dangerous and psychologically deluded student or faculty viewpoints. Addressing incidents of violence and concerns over First Amendment freedoms on college campuses wherever they occur is essential to the mission of higher education. Sensationalizing those incidents to falsely portray most institutions of higher education in a state of siege is an ineffective and ethically suspect way to do so.

Cable news programs popularized the idea that pundits hired to stage on-air disagreements yield substantive political information. Reality television popularized the idea that carefully edited petty conflicts among people who knowingly playact for cameras offer unfiltered depictions of ordinary life. Campus misinformation around the time of Maher's broadcast assumed the form of a broadly analogous alternative reality—a dark and frightening depiction of most universities under violent siege based on disturbing incidents at a statistically small number of campuses. Inaccurate claims that unhinged radical student groups now prevent *nearly all* outside speakers from appearing on *the majority* of college campuses were central to the creation of a reality that bore little resemblance to the daily affairs of most campuses. Those claims nevertheless proliferated in online spaces and popular entertainment. Campus misinformation attracts the largest audience when it gives people reasons to feel outraged about specific personalities engaged in an ongoing melodrama—much like cable news, reality television, and social media controversies.

This chapter explains how a cluster of hyperpartisan figures and ideological extremists in 2017 and 2018 especially used social media to market their upcoming appearances at various universities. Promises to intimidate or humiliate students and faculty members suffused pre-event messaging for speakers like Ben Shapiro, Richard Spencer, and Milo Yiannopolous (to name just a few). After their appearances, the same media personalities disseminated social media content that appeared to make good on their promises of intimidation and humiliation, further sensationalizing the confrontations that they helped to orchestrate.[9] Such agents of campus misinformation exploited a statistically small number of atypical violent incidents on specific campuses at this time to normalize an alternative reality of higher education in which most, if not all, universities had turned into hotbeds of intolerance and persecution. Incidents of violence at Middlebury University, Evergreen State University, and the University of California at Berkeley were legitimate causes of concern; extremist groups also helped to foment conflict in online spaces, outside of campus communities, prior to such events. The ensuing brand of sensationalism—portraying college campuses as scenes of showdowns or battles—still thrives in social media alongside numerous other forms of misinformation. Many credulous journalists, or celebrities like Maher, accepted this sensationalized content as a complete story unto itself, seldom asking how or why it was manufactured and disseminated.

Provocateurs and propagandists are free to irresponsibly sensationalize episodes of campus debate as caustic spectator sport. Yet those activities evince dubious commitment to protecting free speech and academic freedom for everyone. Hyperbolic terms dating to this phase of campus misinformation now circulate widely in public discourse as all-purpose denigrations of movements for social justice or democratic equality: *shutdowns*, *canceling*, and *mobs*. Such terms not only project a misleading alternative reality of higher education; they also help to popularize a deeply cynical way of talking about and defining freely exercised rights of protest and social advocacy on behalf of historically disenfranchised communities—first on college campuses, then in society at large.

The alternative reality that terms like "mobs," "canceling," and "shutdowns" evoke portrays freely exercised rights of protest or assembly among relatively disempowered groups as forms of violence and censorship. Maher's language at the beginning of this chapter exemplifies such specious portrayals: he raised the topic of college students who protest controversial speakers *as a form of censorship*, never mentioning that protest is not anti–free speech but a form of free speech itself. Campus misinformation thus promotes an alternative reality that validates privileged views of higher education and democratic society while normalizing default suspicion about whether some social groups may legitimately or safely exercise their protected rights of protest. That alternative reality illustrates the power—and danger—of misinformation rooted in anecdotal evidence.

Anecdotes

Anecdotes are brief and suggestive stories about real persons or events. Those stories necessarily reflect subjective points of view on reality. An individual anecdote about a specific incident may or may not provide meaningful information about similar incidents at other times and places. An anecdote about corruption in a single corporation, for instance, does not mean that all corporations are corrupt. An anecdote about a single politician who badly misquotes economic data in one speech does not mean that the politician knowingly misinforms constituents in all official remarks. Anecdotes are most persuasive as evidence when people use them to illustrate complicated realities and dramatize either real or potential problems in human affairs. This general rule, however, implies that we should assess the evidentiary value of specific anecdotes in relation to other credible and relevant evidence (such as statistical data, historical fact, or expert opinion). For ethical and evidentiary purposes, anecdotes should seldom stand on their own as seemingly self-evident demonstrations of broad claims about the world.

Adhering to these guidelines when employing or evaluating anecdotal evidence is useful because people can easily distort the meaning of individual anecdotes or use them in an unrepresentative manner in public argument. Short narratives told from subjective and potentially inconsistent points of view provide generous opportunities for sources of misinformation to adjust the original story to suit their purposes or assert isolated incidents as broadly representative facts. I cite anecdotes myself throughout this book. I do so, however, for two primary purposes: to show how other people have used anecdotes in misleading ways and to offer additional anecdotes that point to a larger array of relevant information and context. The key issue with anecdotal evidence is not whether people can or should use them to support particular claims, but *how*.[10]

This guideline can be valuable not only for academic discussions of anecdotal evidence but also in our daily consumption of media and information. Especially alarming, sympathetic, or vividly told anecdotes can overwhelm critical thinking in the absence of other compelling and credible information. Researchers who examined how anecdotal evidence affects medical decisions, for instance, found that a negative anecdote that conveys seemingly worrisome medical information may cause people to discount "strong statistical information" that supports a generally positive outlook.[11] A single disturbing and memorable story can move people to disregard complicating or contradictory evidence from other sources, thereby affecting all kinds of personal opinions and decisions.

Campus misinformation consists, to a large degree, in cycles of manufactured outrage based on miscellaneous anecdotes taken out of their original context, making them appear to be more significant and provocative than they often are. Prolonged controversy at the University of Missouri throughout the 2010s, which I discussed in Chapter 2, featured an especially notable exploitation of anecdotal evidence. Viral video of what has become known as the Melissa Click incident inspired outrage about campus safe spaces like few others.[12] Click, an assistant professor of communication at the University of Missouri at the time, hostilely confronted an alleged student videographer[13] who attempted to document the student protests. The video circulated widely, fueling ire across traditional and online media about seemingly coddled, entitled, and irrational college communities. To this day, some media personalities and figures in academia continue to cite the Melissa Click incident as compelling proof that campus safe spaces erode viewpoint diversity and sociopolitical tolerance.

The University of Missouri terminated Click's contract, and her much-publicized actions triggered initial prosecutorial charges. The momentary incident did not materially affect multiple campus controversies that transpired over months, if not years, at the University of Missouri. The videographer whom Click confronted used his Twitter account to criticize media fixations with this isolated incident for overshadowing substantive journalism about the student protests; he encouraged media organizations to "focus some more reporting on systemic racism in higher ed institutions" instead. The very student who Click confronted, that is, explained that media outlets had sensationalized this encounter into an unrepresentative, out-of-context anecdote that failed to capture the full complexity and substance of the campus protests.

Other misuses of anecdotal evidence in campus misinformation further underscore how effectively it can produce an alternative reality of higher education. Consider the much-lampooned Delaware State University policy on snowball fights and water guns. In August 2018, the *Daily Wire*, *National Review*, and other hyperpartisan media outlets gleefully seized on word that the university had banned snowball fights and water guns from campus. Yet another opportunity proved irresistible to ridicule college students for craving safe spaces and bemoan the administrators who coddle them.[14] These reports grossly distorted easily attained facts. Delaware State University included its anti-snowball-and-water-gun policy in the university code of student conduct approximately twenty years prior to the August 2018 media reports. This policy also banned fighting, harassment, and wearing masks except for authorized functions or winter weather. Delaware State University has "no record of any student ever being cited for violating the rules pertaining to snowballs, masks or water guns." Many university administrators were not aware that the policy language even existed prior to externally manufactured outrage about it.[15] Instead of verifying easily researched matters of fact, many media personalities and intellectual commentators rushed to amplify false claims about the state of higher education based on one selectively reported, out-of-context anecdote.

These examples indicate how anecdotes, like misinformation itself, contain *some* fact or truth. They are based on something real in the world (like an actual encounter on the University of Missouri campus or an actual entry in Delaware State University policies). People use anecdotes manipulatively, however, by taking them out of their original or most indicative context so that they appear to prove claims that other, less intuitively engaging forms of evidence disprove. Manipulative uses of individual anecdotes in this manner suggest a microcosm of how misinformation operates in general: by focusing selectively on pieces of information and distorting or inflating their meaning to support specious claims. Climate change deniers cite anecdotes about periods of unusually cold weather during spring or summer months without conceding that the vast majority of credible climate scientists attest to alarming levels of global warming. Organizations that promote election fraud myths cite anecdotes of people attempting to vote who are not qualified to do so without acknowledging that those incidents constitute a miniscule portion of all voting activity and do not impact electoral outcomes. *Mis*information, then, is not a complete fabrication, but a specious *misuse* of information.

Acknowledging that anecdotes relate at least some fact, or that misinformation does contain some legitimate information, is important in the case of claims about allegedly widespread violent mobs who shut down or cancel invited speakers on most college campuses. Those claims began as responses to actual outbreaks of condemnable violence or other unacceptable behaviors in and around specific institutions. Such atypical events corresponded to a national increase in sociopolitical hostilities following the divisive 2016 presidential election. I refer here to some of the most frequently cited incidents in continuing cycles of outrage about college campuses, all of which occurred during the spring of 2017:

- February 1, 2017: Alt-right polemicist Milo Yiannopoulos was scheduled to speak at the University of California–Berkeley campus during a college speaking tour. Many faculty members petitioned to cancel the event. Fifteen hundred people turned out to protest Yiannopoulos. The protests were peaceful until 150 Black Bloc protesters—members of a militant left-wing group—arrived and lit fires, threw rocks at police, set off fireworks, pepper sprayed bystanders, and damaged property. The Black Bloc riot injured six people, and the Yiannopoulos event was canceled.[16]

- March 2, 2017: Political scientist Charles Murray was set to speak on the Middlebury University campus in Middlebury, Vermont. Some students in attendance turned their backs on Murray and chanted slogans for twenty minutes, preventing him from speaking. Organizers moved Murray to a secondary location and established a livestream connection, which broadcasted his conversation with a faculty member to the original lecture site. A group of students later attempted to prevent him from leaving campus by car. Protesters also injured Murray's academic escort, political scientist Allison Stanger, during the confrontation (she suffered a concussion).[17]

- April–June 2017: Controversy erupted over an annual "Day of Absence" at Evergreen State University in Olympia, Washington. The occasion traditionally symbolized support for students of color involved in community-building activities. Prior to the 2017 Day of Absence, Rashida Love, campus director of First Peoples Multicultural Advising Services, disseminated an email that suggested white students should participate in the occasion in a "show of solidarity." Biology professor Bret Weinstein sent a lengthy email reply, or self-described "formal protest." He described Love's recommendation as a form of race-based oppression and an assault on free speech. Weinstein's publicly circulated response led some students to call on him to resign; students also petitioned the university to terminate his employment if he did not do so. Student protesters confronted Weinstein and disrupted his classes, then occupied campus offices and blocked building exits. The situation became unsafe enough that Weinstein held his biology class in a nearby public park. The university eventually shut down temporarily because it received an "execution" threat.[18]

These events were unequivocally reprehensible. Nothing like them should ever occur on a college campus. Such incidents suggest hallmarks of institutional failures to anticipate or manage conflict among many different parties, from event organizers to students and administrators—not the automatic domination of one stereotypical political affiliation over another. This type of conflict cycle can occur in many different communal or institutional environments, no matter what matrix of political views may be involved.[19] The case of Evergreen State University is an especially concerning example[20]—and, thankfully, an atypical one in higher education. Interpreting cycles of conflict escalation according to political stereotypes resembles political journalism that sensationalizes clashes among telegenic personalities instead of informing the public about all contributing factors to institutional breakdowns.

Inaccurately claiming that the cited incidents represent the norm in US universities is a dubious way to learn from specific institutional cycles of conflict. Selectively sensationalizing incidents of campus violence is a specious way to examine the grave issue of violence where it does occur in learning environments. None of my claims in this chapter entail an effort to minimize the seriousness and significance of such incidents, much less claim that media figures fabricated reports about them. My goal, rather, is to take those incidents as seriously as possible by assessing their significance in context, measured against other kinds of pertinent evidence.

The National Center for Education Statistics (NCES), an office of the US federal government, publishes annual crime statistics at postsecondary institutions. The center organizes statistics according to the most common categories of criminal behavior on campuses, such as burglaries, sexual assaults, robberies, aggravated assaults, and motor vehicle theft. No category exists for violent shutdowns of invited speakers. Federal data show that forcible sex offenses and forms of theft account for the sizable majority of on-campus violence.

Moreover, the statistical trend for total crime in postsecondary institutions was mostly downward from 2009 to 2018. NCES records an 8 percent rise in total crime between 2014 and 2017, but that total figure decreased by 16 percent in 2018. In general, crime statistics fell across postsecondary institutions throughout the 2010s[21]—precisely as agents of campus misinformation announced that many or most universities were increasingly violent and dangerous.

In the following section, I examine recent claims about violent student mobs and shutdowns on most university campuses according to a richer and more illuminating sense of historical and sociopolitical context. I do so not simply to establish a more accurate and nuanced portrait of higher education. I also aim to introduce a more constructive framework of debate about free speech and diversity on college campuses—one less indebted to sensationalized, out-of-context anecdotes as primary sources of evidence and the problematic vocabulary of mobs, shutdowns, and cancellation that they inspire.

Context: Massive Resistance to Desegregation

James Howard Meredith graduated from high school in 1951 and subsequently served in the US Air Force for several years. After completing his military service, Meredith intended to become the first African American to attend the University of Mississippi. He matriculated at Jackson State

College to establish his academic credentials and applied to the University of Mississippi in January 1961. The university did not decline his application based on academic merit; it refused to consider his application at all. Meredith sued the university for illegal discrimination—a case that the Supreme Court ultimately decided in September 1962 when it ruled that the University of Mississippi must admit him.

The Supreme Court ruling, however, did not end campus and community resistance to the enrollment of even one Black student—meaning discrimination against *all* qualified Black applicants. Mississippi governor Ross Barnett appointed himself registrar of the university to further prevent Meredith's admission. When Barnett eventually negotiated with federal authorities, allowing Meredith to enroll, segregationist mobs assembled on the University of Mississippi campus and staged a series of violent riots. Thousands of white undergraduate students and regional members of White Citizens Councils or other pro-segregation groups made up the mobs. This violent takeover of the university, in which mobs clashed repeatedly with only a small number of federal marshals, led President John F. Kennedy to deploy over twenty thousand federal troops to quell the insurrection. Two people died in the violence, over two hundred marshals and soldiers were injured, and approximately two hundred rioters were arrested.[22]

Meredith officially registered as a University of Mississippi student in October 1962. Even then, resistance to his presence on campus continued—and would continue for years to come. Meredith was the target of a sustained campus-wide campaign of "Rebel Resistance" intended to continually isolate, harass, and threaten him. Simply attending classes was dangerous enough for Meredith that federal troops remained on campus for more than a year to protect him. Meredith earned his undergraduate degree in August 1963 and graduated from Columbia University Law School in 1968.[23] Yet he sustained violent pro-segregationist attacks, at a cost to his personal health and safety, for years to come. Organized resistance to his enrollment at the University of Mississippi never fully ended.

James Meredith is still alive at the time of this writing. What some authors call a historic insurrection at the University of Mississippi is well within living memory for many Americans. Pro-segregationist state officials who opposed lawful, court-ordered desegregation remained in place. Moreover, the University of Mississippi was only one university campus that refused to enroll even a single qualified Black student. Organized resistance to desegregation and mob violence also characterized events at the University of Alabama in the same era. Autherine Lucy was the first Black student to desegregate the University of Alabama. A "white mob," which quickly "grew to 1200 people," threatened Lucy's safety on campus, "burned a cross, marched through town singing Dixie," and "terrorized any African Americans it encountered."[24] The case of James Meredith, in other words, is far from isolated. His experience is consistent with well-documented regimes of massive resistance to desegregation throughout higher education.[25]

In addition to segregated universities, some state governments authorized entire school systems to close rather than desegregate. They often did so in association with White Citizens Councils and other pro-segregationist groups.[26] Large white mobs demonstrating on college campuses and in front of school buildings became common during the earliest waves of desegregation. Photographs of such mobs harassing and threatening the first Black elementary school students to desegregate school systems in cities like Little Rock, Arkansas, offer some of the most enduring imagery from this era.[27] Ruby Ridges, the first African American student to desegregate a Louisiana elementary school, is one of the most famous such students. She is also, at the time of this writing, still alive.

Massive resistance to desegregation in both higher education and K–12 education throughout the country never fully ended, meaning that the work of desegregation never fully succeeded. The Unite the Right Rally at the University of Virginia (UVA) in August 2017 vividly demonstrates this fact. White supremacist and neo-Confederate groups organized that mass demonstration, which featured slogans about racial superiority and burning torches that recalled nighttime Ku Klux Klan rallies, as a purposeful form of mob intimidation on a university campus.[28] The choice of UVA as the "rally" site was intentional: early in the twentieth century, the university became "a center of an emerging new strain of racism—eugenics—that would create and perpetuate myths created under the guise of scientific research, but ultimately was intended to demonstrate white racial superiority."[29] The white supremacist mob that staged a symbolic occupation of the UVA campus and incited widespread violence throughout the university community is convincing proof that pro-segregation campaigns continue. Recognition of this fact forces the conclusion that the difficult work of desegregation must continue. Such competing forces shaped, and continue to shape, US educational systems in profound ways. Members of many Black communities have never known anything but layered forms of social and institutional resistance to their historically recent presence on predominantly white college campuses—frequently including mob violence.

Mobs. Riots. Intimidation. Harassment. Ideological indoctrination. These words carry historically informed meaning. They are not abstract concepts or theoretical premises. We know what mob violence, student riots, and ideological indoctrination look like on college and university campuses. The most virulent forms of those evils in US history are historically recent and vividly remembered—lingering influences in higher education today. The structural denial of access for Black people, women, sexual minorities, and impoverished communities, which never completely ended, is an essential starting point for any discussion about infringements on free speech in current higher education. This well-documented historical context—of universities proudly declaring themselves to be elite institutions *because of* structural discrimination—is a crucial, evidence-based resource for evaluating claims about mob violence, riots, ideological indoctrination, and free speech crises in universities today.

Violent protests like those that transpired at Berkeley, Middlebury, or Evergreen State in the spring of 2017 warrant appropriate investigation, disciplinary measures, and effective institutional strategies to prevent their recurrence. Scapegoating only some parties involved in those conflicts based on stereotypes about political affiliation and mental health, or claiming that those atypical incidents reveal mob rule on most university campuses, does little to substantively address the root causes of such conflicts. Scapegoating large student and faculty groups in that manner also eclipses vast portions of desegregation-era history as a critical source of information about the dynamically changing state of higher education in the present.

Context: Coordinated Anti-university Campaigns in the Present

An informed historical perspective on patterns of systemic discrimination and mob violence in higher education is directly pertinent to current claims about free speech crises and allegedly widespread student mobs on college campuses. Forms of bigotry and dehumanization consistent with that history helped to foment conflicts on some university campuses following the divisive 2016 presidential election. Extremist groups have, in recent years, initiated anti-university campaigns in countries like Russia, Poland, Hungary, and Brazil. Such campaigns warn that universities have become centers of leftist ideological indoctrination insofar as the topics of gender or sexual diversity and multiculturalism threaten the traditional heteronormative, masculine, and Christian hierarchy of those nations. In the prejudicial terms of these anti-university campaigns, liberal arts institutions make society weaker and more effeminate while diluting its so-called heritage.[30]

Appearances of white supremacist propaganda on US college and university campuses nearly doubled during the 2017–2018 academic year. The Anti-Defamation League reports that this conscious targeting of hundreds of college campuses began in January 2016, intensified in the fall of that year, and "steadily increased" afterward.[31] In the summer of 2017, the Southern Poverty Law Center advised that "extremist speakers are touring colleges and universities across the country," aided by "heavy use of social media and memes," in order "to recruit students to their brand of bigotry, often igniting protests and making national headlines."[32] The Unite the Right Rally occurred that same summer. Online and on-campus propaganda efforts in 2017 and 2018 were consistent with twentieth-century pro-segregationist intimidation campaigns: both campaigns promoted false ideas about human inequality and attempted to normalize those ideas in universities as meritorious academic viewpoints.

Online dimensions of contemporary anti-university campaigns also indicate why the small number of violent incidents on specific campuses frequently involved ideologically opposed extremist groups from outside those academic communities. Some University of California–Berkeley faculty and student groups peacefully protested Milo Yiannopolous's scheduled February 1, 2017, appearance; no students or faculty were arrested because Black Bloc protesters reportedly initiated the violence.[33] The same dynamic occurred on a much smaller scale the very next day (February 2, 2017) when self-described "Western chauvinist" and founder of Vice Media Gavin McInnes spoke at New York University. Non-university protesters gathered prior to the speech and reportedly clashed with McInnes's supporters once he arrived at the speaking venue.[34] Throughout the remainder of 2017 and into 2018, sources of campus misinformation decried these incidents while sensationalizing nonviolent but occasionally disruptive protests of speakers like white supremacist Richard Spencer, political commentator Ben Shapiro, and philosopher Christina Hoff Sommers.[35] Conflating incidents of campus violence with nonviolent protest implied a dystopian reality in which most invited university speakers were victims of mob-enforced shutdowns. Agents of campus misinformation coined an entire vocabulary for this purpose, filled with vague but suggestive terms like *de-platforming*, *canceling*, and *dis-invitations*.

Nonviolent protest, however, is protected free speech. Many kinds of institutions make routine judgments as to which public figures they wish to host without engaging in censorship. In fairness, organizations like the Foundation for Individual Rights in Education (FIRE) compile databases of dis-invitations or cancellations for invited speakers on college campuses to try to demonstrate a quantitatively significant intolerance for diverse viewpoints in higher education.[36] Yet as I explained in Chapter 4, such databases typically feature unscientifically compiled anecdotal evidence devoid of explanatory context.

Most incidents of violence on a small number of campuses from 2017 to 2018 thus conformed to a pattern seldom acknowledged in campus misinformation. Extremist figures with large online followings and a history of anti-university rhetoric advertised their upcoming speaking appearances as showdowns or battles among conflicting ideologies in locations where non-university extremists might show up. Yiannopoulos, for example, generated publicity for one of his college speaking tours by publishing an article on *Breitbart* titled "How to Beat Me (Spoiler: You Won't)." He mockingly instructed college students on how they should respond to his upcoming appearances: "1) Don't act like a rabid animal . . . 2) Do your homework . . . 3) Stump me in the Q&A, not during my speech . . . 4) Whichever side resorts to violence, intimidation or aggression, loses . . . 5) Your university's reputation is in your hands. Remember that."[37] Consistent with popular ridicule of triggered college students who desire safe spaces, propagandists promoted their upcoming speaking tours as voyeuristic exercises in emotionally triggering members of university communities with opposing views. Many self-described conservative politicians now seek, in the relevant slang, to "own" liberals as a political strategy.[38] Hackers originally coined the term: "owning" someone meant to make a fool of someone and defeat them in online activity. Gaming communities adopted variants like "pwned" to typographically emphasize this connotation of defeat and humiliation. The term evolved into a political mantra over the late 2010s via conservative or alt-right speaking tours during which self-styled provocateurs promised, in the spirit of Yiannopolous's article, to "own" college students at their campus appearances.

These kinds of dual online and on-campus intimidation campaigns continued in remote learning environments during the COVID-19 pandemic. Many universities were forced to deliver classes through online teaching throughout much of 2020 and 2021, which provided ample opportunities for online extremist groups to disrupt virtual classes and events at numerous institutions with graphic expressions of hate, bigotry, and obscenity. White supremacist groups reportedly executed many of the "Zoom bombings" (named for a popular video platform in remote learning) and frequently targeted students of color and diversity-themed college events hosted online. The Anti-Defamation League recorded even higher levels of white supremacist propaganda aimed at university students in this context than during the rapid rise of such propaganda in the late 2010s.[39] These expressions of hate and interference with academic freedom became distressingly common in the pandemic era of remote learning—a virtual approximation of pro-segregationist campaigns designed to shut down or forcibly cancel (if one wants to use that terminology) scores of individual remote class sessions and university events for months on end. The fact that this nationwide wave of online harassment failed to inspire meaningful commentary about the dire state of free speech and academic freedom on college campuses additionally indicates how selectively journalists and intellectual commentators focused on atypical incidents of speaker shutdowns in the late 2010s.

Responding violently to anti-university campaigns aids the efforts of extremists to normalize anti-university sentiment. Such responses do not serve the democratic pursuit of social justice. However, ignoring the fact that anti-university campaigns helped to foment conflict surrounding invited speakers in the 2010s—and resembled historically recent massive resistance to university desegregation—shows a selective commitment to understanding all threats to open debate and academic freedom in higher education.

Extremist speakers invited to college campuses are free to engage in the disingenuous and tactics I have described. Protecting their rights of personal expression contributes to protecting First Amendment freedoms as broadly as possible. Yet speakers who transparently attempt to antagonize and humiliate certain social groups bear proportional responsibility for the predictable effects of their speech. Intentionally sowing discord and division intended to make open and reasonable debate impossible—as part of a campaign to limit the rights of others, no less—is a recipe for undermining First Amendment rights at large, not for protecting them. Speakers in this mold who met organized protests on college campuses leading up to and soon after the presidential election of 2016 were not *deprived* of First Amendment rights; they used those rights skillfully to produce the easily sensationalized outcomes that they desired.

Anecdotal evidence, moreover, does *not* show that intentionally provocative speakers routinely overcame large obstacles to speak on college campuses during the late 2010s. Speakers featured in the much-publicized anecdotes cited throughout this chapter spoke on college campuses *routinely* from 2017 to 2018 and continue to do so. Media personalities and extremist figures now increase their public profiles with well-funded college speaking tours during which they paradoxically complain, before large audiences in university venues, that college campuses will not tolerate their speech. The rapid political ascent of Turning Point USA (TPUSA) is one of the most elaborate examples of this paradox. The stated mission of "TPUSA activists" is to "promote and re-brand conservative values on their campus" based on the premise that most universities are hostile to those values.[40] TPUSA advertises hundreds of college speaking events across the nation, which have helped it to reportedly generate tens of millions of dollars in revenue while becoming a leading force in national Republican Party campaigning.[41] Promoting the alternative reality of mobs who shut down or cancel most invited speakers on most university campuses is now a manifestly effective publicity tool for generating organizational revenues and political capital from college speaking tours.

In most cases, universities in the late 2010s hosted the antidemocratic or pro-inequality speaking tours of provocateurs and propagandists without violent incidents or disruptions (nonviolent protest, of course, is protected speech). On the whole, universities even hosted propagandists who promoted their upcoming appearances as forms of confrontation with and denigration of on-campus student and faculty groups. This fact further demonstrates the degree to which agents of campus misinformation promoted selectively narrated anecdotes about only some on-campus appearances to popularize an entire alternative reality. Violent demonstrations against invited speakers, or any other kind of speaker, should never occur on college campuses—and members of those campuses may freely exercise their First Amendment rights to vigorously and nonviolently protest invited speakers.

Agents of campus misinformation who claim that such incidents of on-campus dissent reveal broad student and faculty intolerance to diverse viewpoints overlook yet another obvious fact to the contrary. The speakers in question met organized protests in a statistically small number of circumstances not because those speakers represented an array of diverse viewpoints. Rather, such speakers advocated contemporary versions on a *single*, old, and disproven worldview: that some human beings are inherently unequal to others. No violent demonstrations apparently occurred on campuses in response to lectures on sports kinesiology, astrophysics, late-nineteenth-century Scandinavian literature, the presidential election of 1860, hotel management, differences among Native American religious rituals, early-twentieth-century theories of mass communication, European parliamentary systems, ethnomusicology, the mating cycles of fruit flies—or potentially innumerable other topics discussed without incident on any given day in tens of thousands of university classrooms and lecture halls.

The notion that invited speakers with extremist views represent a coherent conservative viewpoint is a misnomer. They advocate disproven ideas about alleged human hierarchy. The speakers in this chapter encountered vehement opposition in select university settings not because of their formal political affiliations but because their ideas about cultural, racial, sexual, or religious superiority are empirically false and hostile to historically disenfranchised communities. The respective arguments of McInnes,

Shapiro, Spencer, Yiannopolous, Murray, and Sommers all contain versions of the same basic idea: some things about human beings are immutable (like race, sex, and gender), and apparent differences among them show that one kind of human being is superior to another. This critical reality—a coordinated anti-university campaign to normalize one kind of unempirical viewpoint, not promote greater ideological diversity and open debate—disappears from campus misinformation about those speaking appearances.

I make these claims in support of conservative faculty and students on university campuses as much as any other group. Well-funded efforts to hijack the label of conservatism and turn it into a tool for normalizing antidemocratic ideas about long-disproven cultural hierarchies do not enhance the academic experiences of self-identified conservative faculty and students. Associating conservatism with advocates for scientifically disproven ideas about why one culture, race, sex, or religion is allegedly superior to others undermines the cause of principled political conservatism.

In sum, the alternative reality of widespread students mobs who shut down or cancel most invited speakers because they refuse to consider diverse viewpoints is a false one. When considered in its full context, frequently recycled anecdotal evidence used to support that faulty premise leads to an opposite conclusion. A small number of university campuses demonstrated hostility to *one* kind of viewpoint during a coordinated anti-university push that recalled segregation-era campaigns of campus harassment and intimidation. The clearest rhetorical and ideological thread that these figures shared was not a coherent conservative philosophy. They collectively argued that differences among human beings are inherent and that such differences justify classifying human beings into a fixed hierarchy of value based on race, sex, gender, or religion.[42] This core idea is not only empirically false, but also antidemocratic: no popular vote is supposed to change or affect notions of cultural hierarchy as the basis of decision-making and value judgments. Natural or biological order, according to this kind of worldview, conditions the distribution of rights, privileges, or power. Providing an opportunity for figures who espouse this worldview to speak is one thing; asking other people to assume in good faith that their speech contains some degree of commendable truth is quite another.

Conclusion

Throughout this chapter I have sought to place frequently cited anecdotes about student mobs and invited speaker shutdowns on university campuses from 2017 to 2018 in their historical and contemporary contexts. I have done so to model a more constructive framework of debate for addressing those conflicts *as* conflicts, involving a host of contributing factors and collaborative pathways toward resolution, instead of using them as the basis for sensationalist and cynical narratives about higher education writ large. We should certainly be concerned about any outbreaks of politically or ideologically motivated violence surrounding invited speakers on college campuses. An empirically based commitment to addressing violence on those campuses would also center discussion on the commonest forms of on-campus violence across postsecondary institutions—such as epidemic levels of sexual assault, predominantly against women and LGBTQ people. A substantive commitment to addressing ideologically motivated violence on college campuses would acknowledge how multimedia campaigns that attempt to normalize pro-inequality ideas in universities today resemble pro-segregationist campaigns, still within living memory for many Americans, designed to make higher education unlawfully inaccessible to people of color.

Conflating nonviolent protest with violence while praising efforts to transform university debating forums into extensions of social media vitriol is a suspect way to promote principles of free speech and constructive disagreement. In this respect, campus misinformation not only helps to popularize a sensational alternative reality of higher education based on strategically deployed anecdotes. The vocabulary of student mobs, shutdowns, and cancellations that agents of campus misinformation use to popularize that alternative reality also promotes misconceptions about Enlightenment-era legacies of academic freedom and free expression.

Coordinated campaigns in 2017 and 2018 to popularize scientifically disproven ideas about natural order were not only anti-university but also *anti-Enlightenment* in a deeply intertwined way. Efforts to promote individual rights and conditions for rational decision-making freed from cultural dogmas or superstitions form some of the most praiseworthy legacies of the Enlightenment. Some Enlightenment ideals, such as universal human rights and equality, were so radical that many celebrated advocates of those ideals, from Immanuel Kant to Thomas Jefferson, failed to live up to them in all circumstances (most famously in the racist beliefs that many Enlightenment-era luminaries held[43]). The most liberatory dimensions of Enlightenment thought nonetheless provided powerful tools for overcoming cultural hierarchies based on old, unscientific dogmas and superstitions.

Establishing broad-based secular education was a paramount concern of Enlightenment thinkers. Unlearning religious and political dogmas that mandated vast human inequality and prohibited social reform was the essence of education as many Enlightenment thinkers understood it.[44] Leading Enlightenment theories of education directly contradict the contention that universities must choose between truth and social justice, upon which many advocates of viewpoint diversity insist. Michalina Clifford-Vaughan, a member of the London School of Economics and Political Science, wrote in 1963 that "the philosophy of Enlightenment advocated the propagation of knowledge as a means of overcoming social and political evils."[45] Secular universities have been periodic sites of protest in modern times because they protect free expression and uncensored debate relatively well compared to other institutions. Universities thus provide openings for the liberation of truth from dogmatic religious and political authority in pursuit of "freedom and morality in the community."[46]

Signature intellectual ideals of Enlightenment thought like equality, popular government, and scientific reason thus fueled modern movements for human freedom and social justice. Reason, for Enlightenment thinkers, did not mean unflinching civility and credulity before all opinions. Enlightenment thinkers defined reason, according to German philosopher Ernst Cassirer, one of the foremost twentieth-century authorities on Enlightenment thought, as the ability to rigorously question "religious creeds . . . moral maxims and convictions . . . theoretical opinions and judgments"[47] upon which unfit political or religious authorities often relied for their power. In his famous essay "What Is Enlightenment?," Kant accordingly described enlightenment as an ability to end one's "tutelage" to the "statutes and formulas" of police, administrative, or religious authorities and "make use of his [sic] understanding without another's guidance."[48] The speakers named in this chapter seek to promote on college campuses exactly the kind of rule-bound dogmas and superstitions that Enlightenment luminaries rejected in the name of reason. Exploiting anecdotal evidence to promote widespread cynicism about universities while championing such speakers as laudable defenders of free speech and open-mindedness implies a puzzling understand of the First Amendment—one of the most important political outcomes of the Enlightenment.

The alternative reality of higher education examined in this chapter therefore contains dubious versions of important historical and political realities far beyond higher education alone. The distorted worldview of student mobs who instinctively shut down or cancel most invited speakers on most college campuses, based on aggressively sensationalized anecdotal evidence, has helped to popularize questionable interpretations of Enlightenment ideals and the codified First Amendment liberties that those ideals ultimately inspired. In the next chapter, I explain how the language of campus misinformation disseminates misleading ideas about the First Amendment itself. Doing so is a necessary first step toward encouraging more constructive frameworks of debate about free speech in universities and in democratic society writ large.

6

First Amendment Hardball

The concept of constitutional hardball explains how scorched-earth politics and partisan gridlock can lead to the internal breakdown of some modern constitutional republics. Legal scholar Mark Tushnet coined this term to explain how political actors sometimes exploit existing constitutional rules to consolidate power within a narrow political faction instead of preserving a system of power sharing among different political interests.[1] In *How Democracies Die*, political scientists Steven Levitsky and Daniel Ziblatt describe constitutional hardball as "a form of institutional combat aimed at permanently defeating one's partisan rivals—and not caring whether the democratic game continues."[2] Episodes of constitutional hardball illustrate a larger potentiality inherent in popular government: pro-authoritarian movements often corrupt democratic norms and practices by maintaining the mere appearance of adhering to them while transforming those norms and practices into tools of antidemocratic breakdown.

Agents of campus misinformation who justify sensational narratives about higher education by claiming to defend free speech rights engage in what I call *First Amendment hardball*. The language of First Amendment hardball is present when someone advocates for free speech in highly selective and internally inconsistent ways that entail efforts to control conditions of speech in general. This tactic allows practitioners of First Amendment hardball to claim a defense of free speech rights while intimidating others from speaking, finding ways to dominate scenes of public debate, and questioning the legitimacy of others' legitimate rights of speech or assembly.

The previous chapter featured directly relevant examples of First Amendment hardball. Coordinated campaigns among anti-university propaganda outlets in the late 2010s attempted to turn university discussion forums into extensions of social media toxicity through vitriolic speaking tours. Self-styled provocateurs who invoke nebulous definitions of free speech to justify dehumanizing rhetoric on college speaking tours inevitably undermine the goals of open debate and constructive disagreement rather than help to protect First Amendment rights for everyone. Such coordinated campaigns resembled pro-segregation campaigns waged to restrict civil rights for people of color in the civil rights era.

The tactics of anti-university campus speaking tours in the late 2010s also resembled in online spaces a potent form of First Amendment hardball. The philosophy of *cyberlibertarianism* dates from cyberpunk culture associated with early incarnations of the internet. Cyberlibertarianism (sometimes called *technolibertarianism*) holds that government should refrain from regulating the internet in any way so that cyberspace can operate, theoretically, as a semi-utopian domain of unrestricted personal freedom.[3] The influence of cyberlibertarian ideas over internet policy explains much about the state of online discourse today: hate speech, extremist ideas, and interpersonal abuse suffuse that discourse.

This incarnation of the internet, I noted in Chapter 1, is nonetheless heavily regulated—by corporate interests rather than the government. The state of social media increasingly reflects monopolistic ownership of public information networks (not free-market economics) and algorithmic controls that enrich corporations by prioritizing misinformation and abusive speech (not a true marketplace of ideas). Campus speaking tours addressed in the previous chapter suggest conscious efforts to inject principles of cyberlibertarianism into university discussion forums. Cyberlibertarianism has popularized online norms that define "debate" as an exercise in winning at all costs. Appeals to "free speech" in these spaces commonly justify tactics of humiliation and dehumanizing address that make it difficult, if not impossible, for others to freely exercise their own rights of speech and assembly.

The Unite the Right rally in Charlottesville, Virginia, in August 2017 not only exemplified First Amendment hardball in especially elaborate form; it also illustrated the horrific outcomes that such tactics can produce in the nonvirtual world. Neo-Confederates and neo-Nazis exercised their First Amendment rights of assembly and speech by occupying public spaces throughout Charlottesville. Those groups openly advocated white supremacist ideas for weeks on end prior to the rally itself. Unite the Right organizers thus sought to subvert the normal free functioning of civil society in Charlottesville, constituting a common and intimidating presence in public spaces. In the end, those groups also displayed lethal violence in their public demonstrations with frighteningly well-armed militias that threatened rights of political assembly, religious worship, and public speech for other groups—especially members of the local Jewish and Black communities.[4] Organizations that promote bigotry and inequality invoke the mantra of free speech as rhetorical window dressing of a long-term strategy to render public forums unsafe for First Amendment activities among historically disenfranchised groups.

These examples of First Amendment hardball—anti-university campus speaking tours, toxic online discourse, and the Unite the Right violence—suggest that two things can be true at once. First, public institutions should protect the First Amendment rights of everyone, including bigoted and obscene speech as per governing legislation and federal court rulings. Second, civic institutions can and should zealously protect First Amendment rights for all by ensuring that claims of free speech do not serve as a pretext for either dominating free and open spaces of exchange or intimidating others from exercising their own rights. First Amendment hardball is a dubiously asymmetrical way to promote free speech rights for all. Such a mentality claims to protect free speech by favoring specific forms of speech over others—often forms of speech that conform to privileged worldviews and artificial norms of civility or decorum.

First Amendment hardball in the context of campus misinformation additionally classifies some forms of speech as illegitimate according to pseudoscientific narratives about the coddled or mentally fragile nature of college students. In Chapter 4, I examined questionable scientific arguments about Gen Z, which allege that the social and political views of college-age young people symptomatize generation-wide psychological damage from social media and safetyism. Such strategic distortions revise First Amendment principles intended to maintain healthy competition among an array of freely expressed views into justifications for labeling some forms of speech as less psychologically healthy or socially valued compared to other forms. Those justifications frequently apply to the views of people from historically disenfranchised communities.

I do not support censoring or tightly regulating forms of First Amendment hardball in public spaces, including on college campuses. I advocate instead a more accurate and inclusive public discourse about all aspects of the First Amendment. That more accurate and inclusive public discourse should explain the vital role of counter-speech in maintaining democratic spaces of personal expression for everyone.

Learning to recognize and counteract the language of First Amendment hardball is necessary to maintaining truly robust conditions of free speech and assembly. This concern applies to both private and public institutions of higher education. Many private institutions, I previously noted, have codified the benefits of free speech in their governing policies even if they retain greater flexibility than public institutions in abiding by the letter of the First Amendment.[5] Tales of a free speech crisis on college campuses are highly useful to extremist groups that pressure public as well as private universities to accommodate First Amendment hardball (or tactics designed to delegitimize the speech, dignity, and rights of historically marginalized groups while nebulously claiming to defend free speech).

Agents of campus misinformation who disseminate sensational warnings about free speech crises on college campuses count on media outlets and the public to accept their ostensible defenses of free speech at face value. Giving sources of campus misinformation the benefit of the doubt is understandable: that misinformation is crafted to depict a state of seemingly obvious emergency, and popular attention spans can be fleeting. Examining whether habitual appeals to free speech reflect substantive commitments to protecting First Amendment rights for everyone requires some focused consideration of the language and logic behind those appeals and the meaning of the First Amendment itself.

I therefore offer practical and efficient guidelines for distinguishing between substantive defenses of free speech and exercises in First Amendment hardball. These guidelines principally concern implicit definitions of free speech in the context of misinformation about higher education. I show, however, that those definitions also exhibit strong connections with antidemocratic political movements outside of universities.

In the following sections, I not only provide a critical examination of First Amendment hardball in higher education and related sociopolitical forums, but also offer affirmative arguments about the value of the First Amendment itself. That amendment is an essential tool of democratic citizenship and antiauthoritarian society; it rightfully belongs to everyone—without the permission or approval of politicians, pundits, and intellectual figures who attempt to qualify its meaning and provenance. Understanding how to counteract strategically hazy and misleading slogans about free speech that benefit misinformation campaigns is a proactive way to contribute to the ongoing protection of First Amendment freedoms—on college campuses and in society at large.

Freeing the First Amendment from Campus Misinformation

"I disapprove of what you say, but I will defend to the death your right to say it." This famous phrase is commonly misattributed to Voltaire, the French Enlightenment champion of individual rights. In truth, an English writer named Evelyn Beatrice Hall, who published under the pseudonym S. G. Tallentyre, first published the adage in her early-twentieth-century work *The Friends of Voltaire*.[6] Regardless, the phrase is widely accepted as a faithful distillation of Voltaire's ideas on free speech. One of the most quietly revolutionary and radically democratic elements of this pledge to defend free speech is its subtle but important hint of forbearance. Speaking freely, the adage says, does not mean speaking in a manner of which other people approve. Optimal conditions of free speech exist, instead, when social and political institutions empower the most people to speak as they wish—so long as they do not speak to restrict the human rights and dignity of others. Such optimal conditions of speech and conscience imply that members of a community may freely decide for themselves which beliefs, arguments, or ideas they find most persuasive within an ongoing contest of diverse and unregulated voices. The socially and politically revolutionary aspect of this classic Enlightenment ideal lies precisely in its omission of artificial qualifications for speech. Free speech, in the best Enlightenment versions of that ideal, does not need to satisfy subjective standards of civility, moderation, or reason. Speak freely, the adage implies, and I will leave it to *you* to be the best judge of what you want to say and how you want to say it.

Such forbearance is present in the language of the First Amendment from its first words. The text itself is concise yet rich with affirmations of complementary rights:

> Congress shall make no law respecting an establishment of religion, or prohibiting the free exercise thereof; or abridging the freedom of speech, or of the press; or the right of the people peaceably to assemble, and to petition the Government for a redress of grievances.

Government, in other words, should not impose standards on enumerated First Amendment rights—or will only use its power to maintain optimal conditions for exercising those rights if someone or something infringes upon them. This latter proviso is necessary because the freedom of speech listed in the First Amendment is one freedom among several others: freedom of religion, freedom of the press, freedom of peaceable assembly, and freedom to petition the government. People always exercise freedom of speech among other people exercising other freedoms—never in a state of completely unregulated freedom unto itself.

The prime measurement of free speech in this framework is *not* whether that speech adheres to standards of civility, maintains artificial viewpoint parity, reflects an uncoddled mind, or shows deference to tradition. Yet campus misinformation has popularized the dubious notion that speech that does not adhere to these invented qualifications threatens First Amendment freedoms. Campus misinformation is not only a source of false narratives about free speech crises in universities; those messages also constitute a form of misinformation about the First Amendment. Concise and candid information about the nature of free speech rights enshrined in the US Bill of Rights is therefore necessary to counter such influences and reaffirm the richer meaning of First Amendment freedoms.

The First Amendment principally prohibits the *government* from restricting freedom of speech; it does not guarantee that someone can speak at a time and place of their choosing, in any part of society, without opposition.

The First Amendment protects opportunities to speak freely, as anyone wishes, in public settings; it does not allow one to dictate how others should respond. The amendment does not presuppose deference to decorum or authority, expectations of ideological balance, or popular theories of psychological wellness as preconditions for free expression.

The First Amendment protects a person's right to publicly advocate whatever beliefs they choose; it does not require members of the public to listen obediently to whatever is said—or even to listen at all.

In sum, the First Amendment protects opportunities to contest the speech of others—even that of the most powerful political leaders—as much as it protects opportunities to speak for oneself. The amendment enshrines the right to speak back, even uncivilly and disruptively, as much as it enshrines the right to initiate speech. The right to speak back—to question or contest the speech of others—is one of the most patently democratic parts of the First Amendment. Authoritarian regimes work hard to erode this right. The Bill of Rights classifies the freedoms of speech, protest, and assembly as commensurate—not conflictual—liberties.

Arguments for obligatory viewpoint parity present a questionable defense of free speech rights. The notion that those arguments consist of substantive or consistent advocacy for First Amendment rights may, in fact, be a misnomer. Campus misinformation in general promotes a strategically selective version of First Amendment freedoms that champions the rights of speech and protest for some groups at the expense of other groups (most often from historically disenfranchised student and faculty communities). Such misinformation evinces similarities to antidemocratic appeals that invoke nebulous references to free speech as seemingly intellectual justification for limiting free expression and academic freedom.

Authoritarian arguments based on a defense of free speech are common in historical and contemporary pro-authoritarian movements. "In the classic style of demagogic propaganda," philosopher Jason Stanley explains, "the tactic of attacking institutions standing up for public reason and open debate," including universities, "occurs under the cloak of those very ideals."[7] Recent vitriol about liberal intolerance on college campuses claims to identify a new emergency. Those claims, however, evince similarities with old authoritarian diatribes against independent centers of learning. Even people who neither work nor study in universities can help to defend First Amendment freedoms by resisting campus misinformation. That misinformation implicitly endorses hardball tactics that authoritarians use in early-stage efforts to popularize anti-university sentiment as a prelude to undermining democratic freedoms writ large.

I explore similarities between campus misinformation and pro-authoritarian or antidemocratic tactics later in this chapter. First, however, I explain the value of organized protest, civil disobedience, and nonviolent disruptions on college campuses as a vital forms of free expression called *counter-speech* that students from many different sociopolitical backgrounds exercise. Understanding the value of counter-speech to democratic society is necessary to understanding why authoritarian movements seek to curtail it.

The Value of Counter-Speech

Violent intimidation and physical destruction are illegitimate forms of protest on college and university campuses. Violent demonstrations are also exceedingly rare at institutions of higher education in general. For purposes of constructive and accurate debate, we should acknowledge the rarity of such episodes at the outset of any deliberation over the state of First Amendment freedoms on college campuses. Most of those campuses protect First Amendment freedoms better than many other parts of society.

I previously showed that campus misinformation attempts to center deliberations about the state of college campuses on exceptional acts of violent protest and draw broad conclusions about large student or faculty groups as a result. Equating peaceful protesters with more militant and potentially violent groups is a classic technique of misinformation campaigns and a manufactured justification for promoting First Amendment hardball. Portraying peaceful demonstrations as radical and potentially violent actions, thereby undermining the legitimacy of protest in general, is inconsistent with a substantive defense of First Amendment rights.

Once again, I do not support organized efforts to de-platform or shut down controversial campus speakers. On-campus groups that engage in such practices pursue a kind of First Amendment hardball all their own. I oppose, instead, elements of campus misinformation that falsely equate student protest and dissent in general with violent disruption and regimes of censorship. I oppose arguments that provide a potential rationale for defining the First Amendment rights of student protest and dissent as inherently hostile to free speech rather than as legitimate forms of free speech themselves.

Nonviolent campus protests, including acts of civil disobedience, are protected forms of free speech and assembly every bit as much as the speech of a consciously divisive invited speaker. Sources of campus misinformation like those cited throughout this book literalize and strategically distort the language of the First Amendment when they claim that faculty and students who protest controversial campus speakers are hostile to free speech. The phrase "free speech" is a loose shorthand for codified First Amendment freedoms. The idea that free speech rights empower someone to give a speech on a college campus at a time and place of their own choosing is a misleading simplification of First Amendment freedoms.[8]

Universities condition or qualify free speech in several ways, both formal and informal, to function *as* universities.[9] Teaching as a university professor requires a variety of credentials. Peer reviewers and editors evaluate scholarly publications. Poorly constructed arguments will not withstand the criticisms of informed fellow students and faculty. Michael Roth explains the value and purpose of such conditions:

> The classroom has never been an unregulated market, and neither are scientific laboratories or academic journals. They all have procedures to ensure that tools of inquiry are used in a legitimate way to advance work in a particular area, and there are judgments to be made by those with qualifications about what counts as legitimate.[10]

Universities may or may not end up conducting these gatekeeping practices in fair and consistent ways on a case-by-case basis. This reality, however, does not entail some flaw unique to higher education. Bureaucratically structured institutions of all kinds establish governing policies and norms of interaction among their members through some degree of trial and error.

Free and peaceably assembled protests of a controversial speaker do not automatically infringe on that speaker's right to free speech. Freely exercised protest and civil disobedience are not censorship. Expressing strong opposition, even hostility, to a particular viewpoint does not, by itself, indicate unusual amounts of opposition to open discussion and constructive disagreement in general.

Being a thoughtful human does not mean that someone's mind is a perpetually blank slate—a literally open mind—that encounters other people's ideas and arguments as if for the first time. Being a thoughtful human means making judgments about what we like and dislike, what beliefs or arguments we think are persuasive or unpersuasive, what social and political agendas we think are right or wrong. Being engaged citizens in a democracy, moreover, entails two broad imperatives at once: to understand the leading spectrum of social and political arguments as they exist *and* to arrive at personal judgments about which arguments we support and which arguments we oppose. The basic tenets of democracy and free speech do not require us to convince others that such oppositions are rational, civil, or ideologically balanced to qualify as judgments for ourselves.

The disturbingly popular canard of cancel culture portrays counter-speech or petitions for accountability against powerholders as illegitimate and irrational forms of expression.[11] This cynical slogan is an offshoot of campus misinformation—a version of the false premise that college students seek to arbitrarily cancel most invited outside speakers applied to broad social and political commentary. Many invocations of the phrase "cancel culture" indicate a reactionary response to an era of increased pressures for accountability among powerholders, who are often accused of racist, misogynist, or homophobic conduct. Due process for people credibly accused of wrongdoing is essential, and social pressure for accountability based on waves of public opinion does not necessarily reflect well-informed arguments for effectively addressing allegations of individual misconduct. Popular uptake of the cancel-culture premise, however, reveals its highly selective and potentially authoritarian-friendly interpretation of First Amendment freedoms. Republican politicians embraced the idea of cancel culture during the 2020 election cycle, frequently implying that people who criticized or opposed them were engaging in canceling and that freely voting someone out of office manifested this allegedly noxious culture.[12] The erroneous subtext of these messages is that lawful political counter-speech, assembly, and electoral results are forms of censorship.

Colloquial usage of the phrase "cancel culture" rests on an obvious paradox. Public figures in privileged positions regularly claim to be victims of cancel culture while preserving powerful public platforms—remaining conspicuously *un*cancelled and uncensored.[13] The phrase is seldom, if ever, applied to legal and political efforts to restrict freedom of the press or legislative efforts to undermine the right to vote. The conceit of being cancelled, in other words, falsely defines counter-speech as an injustice that unfairly targets people in privileged or powerful stations. This worldview suggests a primary interest in maintaining the influence of a well-insulated status quo rather than defending First Amendment freedoms for all social classes.

Nonviolent protests and acts of civil disobedience on college campuses, or anywhere else, are not assaults on free speech. Such actions *are* forms of free speech and assembly. Those who assert this claim exhibit either an opportunistic understanding of the First Amendment or a shallow commitment to defending it. Yet sources of campus misinformation, aided by some news organizations prone to sensationalized journalism, conflate protected acts of counter-speech with violent campus protests and irrational frenzies of canceling. Agents of campus misinformation amplify the atypical significance of those generally unrepresentative incidents while falsely characterizing petitions for institutional accountability and equality, demonstrations in response to injustices, or calls for economic boycotts as evidence of dangerous radicalism and violent intent.[14] All of these activities are not only constitutionally protected forms of counter-speech but also indications of a healthy democratic society.

The foregoing observations support an even more affirmative principle: counter-speech is an essential sociopolitical antidote to threats of official censorship. Campus misinformation that depicts organized protest as a technique designed to enforce ideological orthodoxies undermines this principle. Freely organized counter-speech that attempts to limit the influence of extremist ideas, even in uncivil ways, is a better symptom of healthy democratic exchange than either state interference in public debate or artificial norms of civility. Counter-speech—nonviolent protests, civil disobedience, boycotts, and the like—help to keep public forums as free as possible for everyone. Nonviolent campus protests provide experience for students and university communities in maintaining the democratic push-and-pull of speech and counter-speech, which reduces the need for government interference in the exercise of First Amendment freedoms.[15] Rights of protest help to systemically protect freedom of speech and prevent official censorship as much as any other expression of First Amendment freedom.

In sum, counter-speech is not censorship; it is an antidote to censorship. Organized nonviolent protests of specific campus speakers, however large and vocal they might be, are not forms of censorship. "Public colleges and universities are free to invite whomever they like to speak at commencement ceremonies or other events," the American Civil Liberties Union explains, "just as students are free to protest speakers they find offensive."[16] Civility and decorum are not required for the exercise of democratic First Amendment rights, whether on campus or off. Democracy requires the freedom to speak and the freedom to speak back.

Conservative Counter-Speech

Self-described conservative student groups illustrate the value and ubiquity of explicitly political student activism in higher education. Young Americans for Freedom (YAF) boasts numerous student chapters on university campuses and organizational partnerships with "the Clare Boothe Luce Policy Institute, the Intercollegiate Studies Institute, the Heritage Foundation, the Foundation for Economic Education (FEE), the *Washington Times*," and others.[17] Since the late 1960s, YAF has trained "conservative student activists" to engage in year-round campus activism, which often consists of protests—counter-speech—against perceived liberal university policies.[18] For generations, YAF members have held demonstrations on college campuses throughout the United States to advocate their beliefs, protest invited speakers, and engage in strategic disruptions of campus events. Conservative political organization on college campuses has been vital to the modern conservative movement writ large, regardless of narratives about widespread university marginalization of conservative students or faculty.[19]

The activist organization Turning Point USA (TPUSA) became a significant force in national political conservatism during the late 2010s. TPUSA helped to dramatically expand already pronounced conservative activism in higher education during those years and contributed substantially to official Republican Party efforts to reelect President Trump in 2020. The organization lists chapters in over twenty-five hundred colleges and high schools in North America at the time of this writing.[20] Like YAF, TPUSA provides funding, training, and other resources to support student chapters in vigorously protesting left-leaning policies while advocating for their own.

Even those examples, however, illustrate only part of the extensive network of on-campus conservative activism and protest in higher education.[21] Other national student organizations support "conservative clubs" on hundreds, if not thousands, of college campuses and sponsor dozens of "field representatives per year to develop new conservative organizations on college campuses."[22] These prominent conservative student organizations demonstrate that conservative activism and protest—often designed to tactically disrupt university events and test the limits of institutional policies—are long-standing and significant presences on numerous college campuses.

Student members of organizations like YAF, TPUSA, and other national conservative groups simply exercise First Amendment rights by engaging in these political activities. This observation is no less true, however, of student and faculty groups that protest nativist, homophobic, anti-Semitic, and Islamophobic speakers on their campuses. Nonviolent protest and civil disobedience are expressions of protected First Amendment freedoms—regardless of social identity, political affiliation, or personal beliefs. I offer these claims to defend the rights of counter-speech for conservative students or faculty as much as students or faculty from any other groups. Placing limits on the counter-speech of one scapegoated social or political group, or normalizing hostilities to constitutionally protected forms of assembly and protest in general, is a first step in undermining the idea of lawful counter-speech for everyone. All student and faculty groups on college campuses should be equally free to engage in constitutionally protected forms of disruptive protest and civil disobedience.

This understanding is crucial in an era of widespread campus misinformation. Abstractions about the allegedly radical ideologies or coddled dispositions of some politically engaged student groups propose artificial and subjective standards for the free exercise of First Amendment freedoms. The same is true for ill-defined standards of civility and decorum. Efforts to popularize distortions about free speech rights and academic freedom in universities based on artificial criteria of ideological balance or viewpoint diversity threaten not only free expression and open debate in higher education. History shows that political interference with university affairs and growing elitist prejudices against specific social groups within academic institutions are also early indicators of rising pro-authoritarian sentiment in society at large.

Campus Misinformation and Rising Authoritarianism

Authoritarianism is not, in my usage, a version of either political conservatism or political liberalism.[23] Authoritarian figures might begin as members of self-described conservative or liberal organizations, but they typically end up propagating similar abuses of power after crossing into patently autocratic territory. Prototypical examples of those abuses include attacks on the free press, state regulation of universities, scapegoating of ethnic or religious minorities, the creation of state police forces, and defenses of cultural heritage. Social and political extremists in this vein, in the United States and abroad, commonly claim to be victims of censorship. Such extremists include claims of censorship and victimization in their propaganda to gain public sympathy and disguise the ultimate goals of their messages: to curb, if not suppress, civil liberties.

Members of contemporary authoritarian movements in Eastern Europe and Russia have used these tactics as part of a larger program to curtail academic freedom and free speech in Western-style universities. Such leaders as Viktor Orbán in Hungary, Recep Tayyip Erdoğan in Turkey, and Vladimir Putin in Russia[24] claim that independent universities threaten free speech.

Those anti-university campaigns abroad, the previous chapter indicated, established a propagandistic template that leaders of anti-university campaigns in the United States have adopted. US propagandists similarly complain about declining tolerance on college campuses for free speech, meaning university opposition to bigoted and discriminatory language.

Appeals to free speech in authoritarian propaganda are strategically deceptive. Pro-authoritarian figures and movements target universities, along with institutions like the free press, because they frustrate authoritarian attempts to establish automatic deference to state power in all parts of society. Independent liberal arts institutions typically promote social and political moderation, cultural pluralism, evidence-based argument, and the value of questioning received wisdom or authority. Such civic and epistemic goods pose obstacles to leaders who seek to rule based on the ideology of one political faction, for the preservation of one allegedly superior cultural hierarchy, or by claiming to possess the authoritative truth of all matters. Disingenuous autocratic claims that universities threaten free speech really mean that those institutions threaten the bigotries and myths of cultural hierarchy upon which antidemocratic leaders, who have no wish to ensure universal free speech, depend for their power. False claims that independent institutions of higher education threaten free speech historically provide pretexts for exerting government control over universities, thereby restructuring curriculums and research programs to promote nationalistic and cultural ideals beneficial to one-party rule.[25]

Distorting the language of free speech rights can provide the appearance of intellectual justification for authoritarian restrictions on individual liberties, academic freedom, and liberal society. Campus misinformation provided the semblance of such intellectual justification during two waves of rising anti-education, pro-authoritarian sentiment in the United States from the late 2010s forward. One of these waves occurred at the highest levels of the federal government, the other in the form of reactionary grassroots politics.

First, a series of federal officials raised the prospect of investigations into free speech controversies and academic content on college campuses in the fall of 2017. The US Senate Health, Education, Labor, and Pensions Committee held a public hearing on threats to free speech on college campuses in October 2017.[26] Connections between ongoing cycles of campus misinformation in the media and coordinated campaigns to foment conflict on university speaking tours were evident. The rationale for the hearing, chaired by Republican senator Lamar Alexander, duplicated the conceit of viewpoint diversity advocates who claimed that a lack of ideological balance (or viewpoint parity) imperiled free speech on college campuses. The hearing prominently featured testimony

from University of Chicago president Robert Zimmer (who helped popularize a punitive approach to campus free speech) and Middlebury University
professor Allison Stanger (who sustained a concussion during violent
demonstrations surrounding Charles Murray's speaking event only months
prior to the hearing). This Senate committee hearing thus added legitimacy to
key tenets of campus misinformation examined in the first three chapters of
this book: questionable claims about ideological diversity in higher education
and exaggerated narratives about substantial increases in ideological violence
on a large number of college campuses.

Other national officials known for their opposition to publicly funded education validated such tenets of campus misinformation in the fall of 2017.
Betsy DeVos, secretary of education in the Trump administration, used her
office to help legitimate melodramatic narratives about trigger warnings,
safe spaces, and ideological orthodoxy. During a 2017 Constitution Day celebration at the National Constitution Center in Philadelphia, Pennsylvania,
DeVos bemoaned "administrators" who "too often attempt to shield students
from ideas they subjectively decide are 'hateful' or 'offensive' or 'injurious'
or ones they just don't like." DeVos's narrative about the dire state of college campuses reflected poorly informed polemics, not extensive data available to her through the federal government: "Today, precious few campuses
can be described as [free and open]. As the purpose of learning is forgotten,
ignored or denied, we are inundated daily with stories of administrators
and faculty manipulating marketplaces of ideas."[27] The daily inundation of
stories to which DeVos refers was, as I previously established, the result of
a cynical campaign to popularize wild overgeneralizations and unempirical
stereotypes about higher education, not consistently sound journalism. She
accordingly praised the University of Chicago letter—which was, itself, a con-
duit of campus misinformation—as a disciplinary model that all universities
should adopt.

US attorney general Jeff Sessions, the most powerful law enforcement official in the nation, promoted campus misinformation only days after DeVos's
remarks. In a speech at Georgetown University Law School, he declared,
"Freedom of thought and speech on the American campus are under attack,"
and blamed "political correctness" as the cause, using tropes taken directly
from widely circulating viewpoint diversity polemics. Sessions made these
assertions about the unwillingness of universities to consider views like his,
of course, as a highly publicized invited speaker at Georgetown University.
The attorney general cited unscientific surveys from organizations like the
Foundation for Individual Rights in Education (FIRE) to claim that the "fragile
egos" of college students were responsible for potentially unconstitutional

infringements of free speech rights on many campuses.[28] The political uptake of campus misinformation in the fall of 2017 thus evolved quickly: from a federal education official endorsing disciplinary attitudes to campus speech (modeled on statements from University of Chicago administrators) to a powerful law enforcement official chillingly—and falsely—implying that many universities were infringing upon constitutional rights.

The foremost US law enforcement officials continued to help normalize the idea, from 2017 to 2019, that state investigation and regulation of college campuses might be warranted. In every case, federal officials' statements not only recycled tropes of campus misinformation; those statements also exhibited similarities with authoritarian rhetoric designed to undermine universities in other nations. Acting Attorney General Matthew Whitaker (who succeeded Sessions in office) testified before the US House of Representatives Oversight Committee on February 8, 2019. Early in his testimony, Whitaker cited the state of free speech on college campuses alongside border security and the opioid epidemic as urgent matters of federal law enforcement. Such federal involvement would, presumably, seek to find criminal wrongdoing by faculty, students, or administrators. Whitaker's proposal—criminalizing matters of free academic inquiry—was patently autocratic in spirit.

The next month, in March 2019, President Donald Trump issued an executive order that promised to withhold federal funding from universities unless they supported "free speech" according to an unnamed standard.[29] The language of campus misinformation was central to that order. "In particular," it read, "my Administration seeks to promote free and open debate on college and university campuses," which echoed the false premise of a free speech crisis in higher education. Trump's executive order also endorsed a basic premise of many arguments for viewpoint diversity: that institutions of higher education should "avoid creating environments that stifle competing perspectives, thereby potentially impeding beneficial research and undermining learning."[30] The central tropes of campus misinformation quoted in previous chapters and the content of this presidential order are essentially identical.[31]

US attorney general William Barr (who permanently replaced Whitaker in that office) also spoke ominously about alleged anticonservative speech in civil institutions—the third successive chief law enforcement officer in the nation to do so in a time of widespread campus misinformation. During an October 2019 address at the University of Notre Dame Law School, Barr alleged that "secularists and their allies have marshaled all the forces of mass communication, popular culture, the entertainment industry, and academia in an unremitting assault on religion and traditional values."[32] As in the case of Sessions's speech at Georgetown University, Barr made these claims about anticonservative biases in academia as a highly publicized invited speaker at a prestigious university. Barr's remarks, along with those of the other federal authorities cited in this chapter, suggest a selective and politically opportunistic approach to defending free speech. The federal government is empowered to intervene when one party infringes upon the First Amendment rights of another party—but not to ensure that members of the entertainment industries or academia demonstrate preferred levels of respect for religious beliefs and traditional values.

Note that Barr's language also echoed the 1971 Powell memorandum, which outlined an oft-imitated rationale for promoting conservative interests in key social institutions. Barr defined "academia" as Powell did: not as a mostly self-governing academic space, but as an important ideological front in a broader culture war among stereotypical partisan worldviews. Using government to tip the proverbial scales in favor of historically elite and hegemonic worldviews within that culture war is a very different thing from zealously defending the First Amendment rights of all students or faculty.

The words of these powerful federal officials and public figures suggest a collective commitment to First Amendment hardball, not to defending First Amendment freedoms in a genuinely egalitarian way. In hindsight, individual statements from powerful officials on the heels of largely manufactured controversies about higher education indicate a coordinated political campaign to steer public sentiment in favor of stronger federal regulation of university affairs. Growing populist support for leaders who claim to be concerned with free speech rights while advocating artificial litmus tests for university teaching and research—all to ostensibly protect traditional culture or heritage—is a common feature of rising authoritarianism. Leaders who use such tactics appropriate democratic terms and principles for antidemocratic ends: to exert power over independently functioning institutions.

The language of viewpoint diversity polemics, easily adopted as a hyperpartisan political tool, offers a potential rationale for placing unconstitutional preconditions on personal expression and academic freedom in higher education. Those unconstitutional preconditions include artificial and subjective standards of ideological balance or viewpoint parity, obeisance to traditional patriotism or religious values, and de facto classifications of specific campus protests and activism (counter-speech) as illegitimate or unlawful means of expression. Amplifications of campus misinformation by federal officials in this chapter should concern people from all sociopolitical orientations dedicated to comprehensive protections for First Amendment rights in higher education. The indispensable basis of comprehensive protections for First Amendment rights, whether in higher education or society at large, should be government noninterference to every extent possible. Efforts that heighten negative public opinion of higher education based on false claims about systemic corruption or states of emergency in universities are dangerous in a time of escalating authoritarian attacks on independent centers of learning.

A second wave of disturbing anti-education rhetoric modeled on campus misinformation, and equally consistent with rising authoritarianism, emerged during the 2020 presidential campaign. Manufactured grassroots outrage and falsehoods about critical race theory fueled escalating political attacks on diversity policies and multicultural content in educational systems—not only on college campuses but also, increasingly, in local school districts.[33] Those attacks emulated campus misinformation about leftist indoctrination in higher education. Increasingly popular polemics against campus culture in the mid-2010s, that is, provided templates for contrived controversies and rising anti-education sentiment in public school systems from 2020 forward.

A relatively small group of university scholars has contributed to critical race theory (CRT) in a relatively small number of universities since the late twentieth century (mostly, at first, in graduate-level teaching about legal or economic institutions and advanced scholarship on those same topics). The theory in question proposed that the most effective and empirically accurate way to study racism was not to ask whether individual people act in racist ways or believe themselves to be racist; teaching and research should examine, rather, how entire institutions function in systemically racist ways by denying access to all people of color as a basic function.

The academic subfield of critical race theory informed some interdisciplinary explorations of discrimination, inequality, and justice for decades, with little public notice until the late 2010s.[34] Indeed, critical race theory reflects a strong, uncontroversial consensus among professional historians and other scholars concerning the role of racism in the development of US civic institutions.[35] My remarks in previous chapters on massive resistance to desegregation in higher education provide an apt illustration of this voluminously documented historical reality. Until the late twentieth century, US institutions of higher education in general functioned by denying access to Black people—proudly so, in many cases, so that those institutions could promote themselves as academically exclusive and elite. Historic advances in civil rights and equality throughout US history did not occur in a vacuum; those advances were so improbable and revolutionary because reform movements consistently met fiercely entrenched resistance to affirming that all people are created equal. Simply put, critical race theory was seldom, if ever, discussed in political messaging prior to the late 2010s, and one of its basic principles reflects long-standing and academically uncontroversial historical consensus.[36] In an environment of widespread campus misinformation, however, the purposeful vilification of this hitherto obscure and empirically defensible theory became a primary organizing tool for Republican politicians during the 2020 presidential campaign.

I do not criticize manufactured outrage about critical race theory because Republican candidates for office foment it by promising to ban CRT from schools. I oppose such outrage because it promotes falsehoods about pro-diversity themes in higher education and, as such, resembles one-party attacks on educational institutions consistent with rising authoritarian sentiment. Claims that public schools now commonly teach critical race theory to politically indoctrinate children in extremist ideas, teaching them to "hate America," are false. Even if some schools *did* ask students to study ideas associated with critical race theory, however, they would have every right to do so in the most constructive academic spirit. Informing students that specific ideas exist and asking students to compare those ideas with others is both the essence of teaching and a constitutionally protected expression of academic freedom.

Allegations that schools now commonly teach critical race theory as a form of indoctrination rely on erroneous conflations of educational pro-diversity and anti-racist messages with critical race theory. Those conflations do not reveal an accurate understanding of critical race theory, but a twisted idea of it that portrays it as a radically anti-American ideology used to brainwash large parts of society. This conflation nevertheless popularized a politically reactionary shorthand based on falsehoods: the mere mention of critical race theory among conservative candidates in 2020 was designed to incite fear in suburban, predominantly white school districts over the idea that public schools had become threats to children and families. In this coded messaging, even school policies intended to help children understand the value of equality, diversity, and inclusion were divisive and unpatriotic.[37] Arguments about dangerous mob takeovers of college campuses thus supplied a potent template for reactionary politicians in 2020 who claimed that public schools had suddenly descended into a state of emergency based on a largely invented alternative reality of K–12 education. Such politicians increased grassroots support by pledging to ban pro-diversity or anti-racist content from schools in a manner consistent with recent authoritarian-friendly attacks on higher education in other nations.

Conservative leaders and Republican-controlled legislatures made good on those promises soon after the 2020 electoral cycle. Over the course of 2021, dozens of state governments in all parts of the United States introduced numerous bills intended to ban schools from teaching critical race theory. Those proposals served as pretext for further measures designed to restrict how teachers can discuss issues of racism, sexism, and inequality. Thirteen states in all parts of the nation successfully implemented those bans, whether through new legislation or other state administrative measures. Republican state lawmakers across the country continued to introduce more bills in the early 2020s that either banned critical race theory or regulated school discussions of racism, sexism, and other prejudices. Standing proposals and newly passed legislation of this kind demonstrated a coordinated national movement, not isolated incidents.[38]

Lawmakers frequently posed bans on critical race theory in schools alongside measures that promised to protect viewpoint diversity in state-funded education. Notable examples include the Florida viewpoint diversity measure that I noted in Chapter 1, which became state law alongside a ban on critical race theory, and measures in Texas and Arizona that require schools to teach "opposing" perspectives or "both sides" on topics like the Holocaust and slavery.[39] Upon being sworn in as Virginia governor on January 15, 2022, Glenn Youngkin issued an executive order that banned "inherently divisive concepts, like Critical Race Theory and its progeny," from Virginia public schools because those concepts suppress "diversity of ideas" in education.[40] Such twinned measures in state governments indicate the ultimately censorious nature of politically motivated arguments for viewpoint diversity examined throughout parts of this book. Those arguments imply, more accurately, an agenda for instituting obligatory viewpoint *parity* in education by using government to artificially elevate politically preferred perspectives while limiting or banning ideas and forms of speech that contradict them.

Parents and community members have every right to advocate for the quality and fairness of education in local school districts. Collaborative and constructive participation in school districts from parents and community members can positively enhance children's educational and social development, support school staff, and improve K–12 curricula. Scapegoating teachers and schools as sites of ideological indoctrination while banning parts of existing curricula based on blatant falsehoods does not promote those laudable goals. Such tactics are inconsistent with robust defenses of truly diverse academic viewpoints and open-minded, exploratory learning in educational settings. The adaptation of campus misinformation to misinformation about K–12 teaching created an anti–First Amendment "mania for book banning" in 2021—not a greater tolerance for ideological diversity and diverse free expression. Local grassroots organizers pressured libraires in schools and communities at this time to censor previously uncontroversial literary depictions of discrimination and multiculturalism, mostly by Black authors.[41]

Desegregation-era history teaches us, once again, that populist anger at local school boards for teaching unpatriotic or ideologically radical ideas implies a coordinated effort to limit the rights of many Americans. Pro-segregationist groups throughout the 1950s and 1960s repeatedly equated Black civil rights organizations like the NAACP with communism at a time of heightened paranoia over falsehoods about communist infiltrations of US institutions. Parents and community members in many predominantly white school districts devised an effective new tool of massive resistance to lawful desegregation by falsely claiming that dangerous ideas from radical Black organizations, or forms of ideological indoctrination, were flooding public schools. Such segregationist propaganda was designed to preserve systems of discrimination against Black students and families—an infringement of fundamental constitutional rights.[42]

Leaders of present-day parent and community groups dedicated to bans on critical race theory and regulation of pro-diversity messages in schools claim to be a new grassroots force in national politics.[43] Their erroneous arguments, scare tactics, and censorious goals, however, strikingly resemble pro-segregationist rhetoric about communism in school districts from the civil rights era. As in the 1950s and 1960s, reactionary outrage about discussions of race and racism in public schools reflect an invented conspiracy theory—a frightening but false narrative of shadowy campaigns to recruit children into ideological extremism and thereby erode traditional American culture.

The two contrived campaigns against education that I have described in this chapter—coordinated attacks on higher education and on local school boards—resemble documented phases of anti-education tactics in periods of rising authoritarian sentiment. Those tactics customarily center on campaigns to scapegoat parts of university curricula and school instruction for their alleged harms to society, which generate pretexts for initial forms of state regulation or censorship to "protect" the nation. Rising authoritarian populist movements in countries like Poland, Hungary, and Brazil have followed this pattern in their anti-education campaigns.[44] In 2018, the government of Poland banned any public acknowledgment of crimes that Poland committed during the Holocaust, including teaching about the historical fact of those crimes in schools.[45] In the same year, the Hungarian government removed gender studies from approved master's programs and forced Central European University, which was founded to promote liberal-democratic values in Central Europe, out of the country.[46] During his successful 2018 presidential election campaign in Brazil, moreover, Jair Bolsonaro promised "to combat the Marxist rubbish that has spread in educational institutions" as well as "gender ideology."[47] Leaders in these countries justified all such measures by claiming that international and decadent interests had turned the Polish, Hungarian, and Brazilian educational systems into spheres of dangerous leftist indoctrination.

Analogous versions of these pretenses now circulate in popular forms of campus misinformation. Such misinformation established a template for subsequent attacks on pro-diversity policies and classroom content in K–12 education, which resemble pro-segregationist attacks on public schools during the civil rights era. I noted in Chapter 5 that white supremacist propaganda flooded US college campuses during the 2017–2018 academic year—an important background fact in this context.[48] That propaganda scapegoated disciplines like gender studies and other fields that prioritize multiculturalism as sources of alleged national decline, much like recent anti-university movements abroad.[49] Indeed, the previously cited censorship or state regulation of universities in Poland, Hungary, and Brazil all satisfy white supremacist interests as an important element of pro-authoritarian populism. Banning historically accurate teaching about the Holocaust, curricula that question traditional masculine patriarchy, and so-called leftist economic and political theories are characteristic goals of white supremacist movements.

Some self-described US conservatives or libertarians now profess admiration for leaders like Hungarian president Viktor Orbán, who has not only exerted censorious control over universities but also sought to undermine free elections and freedom of the press in Hungary.[50] Connections among Republican politicians and European far-right Christian nationalists are currently evolving into an international political network devoted to defending the so-called defense of Western and Christian values. This international network opposes, in Orbán's words, "gender ideology and the LGBTQ lobby" as well as non-European migrants.[51] Former professor of psychology and bestselling author Jordan Peterson's unempirical diatribes about hostility to free speech in universities based on forms of teaching and research that examine sexual and gender inequality deserve mention in this context. His anti-university polemics became popular among US conservative groups in the late 2010s as Peterson also engaged in public displays of mutual admiration with Orbán, thus indicating a larger political and pseudo-intellectual pattern. All these figures express opposition to secular education as a prominent basis for their respective visions of *illiberal* democracy—a model of government that holds seemingly democratic elections but limits individual freedoms to maintain a traditionally Christian, patriarchal, and European (white) society.

Not all proposed uses of government power to ensure free speech and open debate on college campuses are the same. Using state power to decide which forms of university teaching and research demonstrate viewpoint diversity or ideological balance undermines First Amendment freedoms by interfering with people's ability to make judgments about the merits of academic content for themselves. Proposals to use federal offices to investigate whether forms of counter-speech on college campuses represent dangerous activities threaten First Amendment freedoms by potentially criminalizing some of those freedoms. The proper role of state or federal power with respect to free speech and academic freedom is (paraphrasing the First Amendment itself) to make *no* law at all, to introduce *no* artificial standards like viewpoint parity, civility, patriotism, or normative religious values whatsoever. Any state or federal measures should be used to ensure the *absence* of artificial standards in university speech and academic affairs. Falsehoods about speech crises in higher education or demands that schoolchildren should learn "both sides" in presentations of the Holocaust and slavery misinform the public about real threats to quality education, academic freedom, and the most democratic ways to protect them for everyone. There is a vast difference between state policies that ensure First Amendment freedoms for all and state policies that use First Amendment hardball to protect the speech of some groups over that of others.

Conclusion

The insights in this chapter about First Amendment hardball provide a hinge in the course of my overall argument. The words and standard argumentative turns that social groups adopt to describe various topics can have profound real-world consequences. Campus misinformation has popularized questionable interpretations of First Amendment freedoms that reactionary political actors adopted, in the early 2020s, to justify bans on academic content and state interference with educational institutions.

These disturbing and politically reactionary entailments of campus misinformation, which indicate democratic backsliding, prompt us to explore how the language of misinformation can undermine constructive democratic argument. Idioms of misinformation often draw us into wooly interpretations of fact or truth, pseudoscientific discourse about human behavior, and metadiscursive debates over semantics. Collaborative, flexible, and evidence-based argument designed to address critical problems can become difficult once communities get drawn into these linguistic culverts.

The next chapter examines arguably the master trope of campus misinformation: *orthodoxy*. That central figure of speech synthesizes the different
strains of discourse to establish a fashionable but ultimately obfuscating and
counterproductive way of talking about the state of higher education and its
role in democratic society. The present chapter has shown that adopting a
more constructive mode of democratic debate about higher education hinges
on understanding the difference between promoting First Amendment hardball and substantively defending First Amendment freedoms for everyone,
whether on college campuses or in society at large. Dispelling what I call the
myth of orthodoxy is a paramount final step toward that more constructive
mode of debate.

7
Orthodoxy

The misleading discourse about higher education that I have examined in this book ultimately redounds to a central term or concept: *orthodoxy*. Viewpoint diversity polemics consistently begin with and devolve upon the assertion that liberal, progressive, or secular orthodoxy—an ideological blind faith—dominates higher education today. That premise is not an original scholarly insight; it duplicates hyperpartisan hyperbole about "liberal orthodoxy" that appeared in publications like *National Review* beginning in the mid-1950s.[1] Cycles of campus misinformation that I detailed in previous chapters, which reactionary political figures have exploited to restrict First Amendment freedoms, all support a common strategic goal: to normalize manufactured warnings about the alleged extent of this orthodoxy in higher education and the dangers that it poses to free speech and open inquiry. Understanding how this interpretation of orthodoxy reshaped popular discourse about universities from the 2010s forward is a penultimate step toward adopting a more constructive framework of public debate over the state of higher education. In this chapter, I show how the omnipresent vocabulary of orthodoxy in campus misinformation has normalized restrictive, not expansive, ideals of personal expression and academic inquiry.

Orthodoxy is not an ordinary conversational term; it stands out in viewpoint diversity polemics as a consciously emphasized trope. The vocabulary of orthodoxy in campus misinformation illustrates, as such, a mode of strategic doublespeak. Accusations of stifling ideological orthodoxy in this context charge people who *oppose* traditionally hegemonic orthodoxies, rooted in Christian nationalism and male heteronormative authority, with espousing even more destructive orthodoxies themselves. Such strategic doublespeak sows confusion about what specific characteristics define genuinely discriminatory orthodoxies and how they function.

Throughout the early twenty-first century, self-described conservative Christian intellectuals alleged that US society has become too secular and too multicultural. Many of their arguments to this effect responded to the legalization of same-sex marriage and broader social acceptance of LGBTQ rights. Yale professor of jurisprudence Robert P. George, often described as "this country's most influential conservative thinker,"[2] pioneered the notion that secularism and multiculturalism constitute a nefarious orthodoxy that discriminates against conservative Christians. Commentary about the "secularist orthodoxy," the "new orthodoxy," or the "sexual liberationist orthodoxy" supplies a unifying thread across many of George's publications.[3] The various faces of this common orthodoxy, he claims, have operated "to crush those who dissented from" secular laws or popular opinion. I take no position on the merits of such claims unto themselves. I intend to highlight, rather, how exactingly networks of campus misinformation retrofitted the key terms and main logical turns of this conservative Christian discourse as an ostensible mode of commentary about higher education.

The conceit of a liberal orthodoxy in viewpoint diversity polemics did not emerge ex nihilo. The main tropes of campus misinformation imitate, almost wholesale, the language and logic of George's treatises and those of similar conservative Christian figures. Viewpoint diversity polemics revise the previously cited major premise about secular orthodoxy in civil institutions into a putative warning about the rise of a liberal or progressive orthodoxy "within scholarly culture."[4] George influentially advanced the premise that "anyone who dissents from the new orthodoxy must face antidiscrimination statues and ordinances and/or public shaming, ridiculing, and hounding."[5] Advocates for viewpoint diversity on college campuses contend that the liberal orthodoxy of higher education makes "people fear shame, ostracism, or any other form of social or professional retaliation for questioning or challenging a commonly held idea."[6] Such people, in viewpoint diversity discourse, fear unjust punishments for mere dissenting views as a result of campus diversity policies—just as George maintains that conservative Christians fear punishment, based on "antidiscrimination statues and ordinances," for their beliefs against same-sex marriage and recognition of LGBTQ rights.

Parallels between conservative Christian polemics about "secular orthodoxy" and viewpoint diversity polemics about "campus orthodoxy" run still deeper. Secular orthodoxy, according to George, punishes conservative Christians by denying natural law according to his definition of that concept: as a moral substrate, based on conservative religious beliefs, that should undergird civil laws. "Christians and other believers," George argues, "are right to defend their positions on key moral issues as *rationally* superior to the alternatives proposed by secular liberals."[7] Supporting the rights of LGBTQ people, women's reproductive rights, and nontraditional families might be popular; in George's terms, however, that democratic support simultaneously constitutes an attack on Christian values and freedom of conscience based on a rationally inferior worldview. Advocates of viewpoint diversity charge that the putative orthodoxy on college campuses punishes students and faculty who choose to believe in fundamental natural differences between certain kinds of human beings.[8] I noted in Chapter 1 that those beliefs in fundamental differences overwhelmingly concern unscientific ideas about genetic inequalities between white people and people of color or between men and women. Conservative Christian figures like George claim that the whims of secular opinion threaten to abolish "rationally superior" religious truths; viewpoint diversity polemics claim that the alleged abandonment of reason in favor of irrational opinions on college campuses inhibits the pursuit of elevated intellectual truth. George defines the perceived "clash of worldviews" that pits "morally conservative Jews, Christians, and other believers against secular liberals" as an epochal crisis of morality and culture.[9] Viewpoint diversity polemics posit that the rise of liberal orthodoxy on college campuses has created a historic crisis of free speech in the culture of higher education. It would be hard to imagine a more faithful approximation of George's argument about secular orthodoxy than viewpoint diversity polemics about campus orthodoxy.

Such arguments from self-described conservative Christian thinkers are a welcome sign of free religious expression. Those arguments warrant as much open-minded consideration as any other form of advocacy. George's claims nonetheless represent a narrow, not broadly representative, interpretation of both political conservatism and Christian theology. George himself admits as much by frequently distinguishing between conservative believers and religious denominations that espouse liberal values. Many religious communities, Christian or otherwise, recognize that secular government protects religious liberties by ensuring free religious practice in the private sphere without allowing any one religious orthodoxy to dominate the public sphere. We should encourage many principled contributions to debates over religious freedom and freedom of conscience in pluralistic society. My principal aim in this chapter is not to enter those debates per se, but to unify my analyses in prior chapters by demonstrating the profound doublespeak that agents of campus misinformation promote through the vocabulary of orthodoxy.

We can appreciate the main forms of such doublespeak by recognizing that viewpoint diversity polemics consist, to a large degree, of a borrowed partisan religious argument dressed in seemingly scientific verbiage. This fact explains why agents of campus misinformation, from apparently intellectual commentaries to hyperpartisan media, rely so deeply on tropes that evoke theological clashes and histories of religious persecution: *orthodoxy, heterodoxy, dogma, doctrine, heretics, blasphemy, tribunals, witch hunts, indoctrination, ostracism,* and many others. George's arguments about secular culture—the evident model of viewpoint diversity polemics—do not indict orthodoxy per se. He implies that disaster will ensue if conservative Christian orthodoxy can no longer vie for hegemony in civic institutions. This observation likely explains why viewpoint diversity polemics, for all their pretense of encouraging open debate and unfettered inquiry, incline toward a circumscribed definition of free speech based on the ideal of ideological "balance" or viewpoint parity among established partisan viewpoints.

The central trope of orthodoxy in campus misinformation thus sponsors two main forms of doublespeak in public discourse about higher education. First, advocates for viewpoint diversity on college campuses rely on a mélange of quasitheological concepts, pseudoscientific claims, and broad legalistic conceits. Careful and coherent arguments can effectively marry theological, scientific, and legal claims as part of a greater whole. I showed in previous chapters, however, that campus misinformation promotes rhetorically vivid but analytically wooly claims about tolerance, scientific evidence, and First Amendment freedoms. Second, viewpoint diversity polemics imply modified versions of conservative Christian arguments that characterize legal protections for LGBTQ rights (among other examples) as a symptom of profound crisis. The borrowed conceit of orthodoxy at the center of viewpoint diversity arguments originally justified secondary or limited rights for some human beings based on a narrow theological worldview. The vocabulary of orthodoxy in campus misinformation thus presents ever-shifting grounds of debate (quasi-theological, pseudoscientific, legalistic) in public discourse about higher learning. That vocabulary also paradoxically refashions a preexisting rationale for limiting the rights of specific historically disenfranchised groups into a defense of intellectual diversity and free speech for everyone.

I do not object to this kind of doublespeak on partisan grounds—liberal, conservative, or otherwise. I object to it because the highly contrived trope of orthodoxy promotes largely inaccurate ideas about university teaching and research. Those ideas provide pretexts, in turn, for additional state regulation and even censorship of free speech and academic freedom. The wave of proposed legislation in Republican-controlled state legislatures after the 2020 presidential election designed to censor academic content reveals the destructive influence of this doublespeak about orthodoxy. Numerous bills across dozens of state legislatures proposed to ban or punish "indoctrination," anti-American theories about "structural" or "systemic" discrimination, and "political, ideological or religious advocacy" in publicly funded education.[10] The shared language of these measures across so many states did not indicate evidence-based education policy but a coordinated effort to translate into law preexisting narratives about liberal orthodoxy in schools or universities. The commonest target of those bills—critical race theory—signifies an allegedly pernicious manifestation of campus orthodoxy in viewpoint diversity polemics. Such anti–First Amendment measures are one of the most significant indices of democratic backsliding in the current era. Those bills exemplify a one-party response to the false narrative that universities are flooding the rest of society with radical and unpatriotic orthodoxies.

We should have healthy debates about freedom of conscience, creeping conformism, and ideological rigidity in higher education as well as many other important institutions. Campus misinformation undermines the healthiest versions of those debates by popularizing a semantic muddle. That muddle redefines secularism—or *opposition* to rule based on religious orthodoxy—as rigid orthodoxy. The language of campus misinformation accordingly defines multicultural diversity as intellectually un-diverse and depicts the freely chosen policies of many dissimilar institutions as forcibly imposed dogma. Disentangling this muddle is a necessary prelude to identifying the basic principles of a more accurate and constructive framework of debate that better informs the public about the complexities of higher education.

The Conceit of Persecution

A basic narrative unites varieties of campus misinformation: radical orthodoxy has overtaken higher education—not only particular parts of some campuses, but the whole of most universities. Heterodox Academy influentially defines *the* problem in higher education as "the rise of orthodoxy within scholarly culture."[11] Jonathan Haidt helped to mainstream a redefinition of pro-diversity discourse on college campuses as "a new religion" in the pejorative sense of blind faith.[12] Similarly stated claims are routine among public figures allied with the viewpoint diversity movement. Princeton University professor of politics Keith Whittington laments students and faculty who prefer "dead dogma" to "living truth" that might challenge "the narrow confines of their preferred orthodoxy."[13] Powerful figures like former US attorney general William Barr and Florida senator Marco Rubio decry, respectively, "secular progressive orthodoxy" and the "new institutional orthodoxy" of critical race theory.[14] The University of Austin markets itself as a solution to this allegedly systemic blind faith by claiming to operate without "the illiberalism and censoriousness prevalent in America's most prestigious universities" and without political or religious affiliations (that is, without any orthodoxy).[15] Higher education, the story goes, is now a mode of thought control that persecutes heterodox thinkers, not an arena of academic freedom or open disagreement.

My understanding is that leaders of the viewpoint diversity movement make these assertions about enforced orthodoxy as mostly *literal* claims. Pundits and scholars who use these descriptions ritually compare the central orthodoxy in question, and the regimes of persecution that it allegedly fuels, to a cluster of historical analogies: religious wars in early modern Europe, the Spanish Inquisition, the Salem witch trials in colonial Massachusetts, the Red Scare or McCarthyism in the 1950s, and the Chinese Cultural Revolution of the 1960s and 1970s. Sociologist Christian Smith, for example, asks, "Whoever said inquisitions and witch hunts were things of the past?" "A big one is going on now," he contends, in the form of "progressive ortho-doxy" throughout academia.[16] Smith and Bari Weiss separately liken alleged "inquisitions and witch hunts" in universities to an "auto-da-fé," or a public ritual during the Spanish Inquisition in which heretics were burned alive.[17] Andrew Sullivan asserts that colleges now use "tribunals" to enforce the "or-thodoxy" of "Marxist" worldviews "hostile to the idea of a free society."[18] The ideological orthodoxy that allegedly dominates higher education today does not, according to this mode of discourse, metaphorically *resemble* horrific regimes of persecution. That so-called orthodoxy, advocates of viewpoint di-versity insist, *literally* manifests the same repressive human tendencies that fueled histories of extreme religious and political intolerance.

We have reached an important condensation point among the main nar-rative strains of campus misinformation. Agents of campus misinformation hold that a generation of coddled young people and coddling institutions have refashioned college campuses in the image of a psychologically irrational ideology. That ideology supposedly stems from obsessions with diversity and equality among coddled students and coddling professors. Such is the ortho-doxy of social justice that student and faculty groups reputedly impose on everyone else. Proponents of this narrative claim to demonstrate the roots of ideological zealotry in psychological analyses of student and faculty groups (based on the varieties of pseudoscience that I analyzed in Chapter 4). Those same proponents cite specious ideas about the First Amendment (which I examined in Chapter 6) to support their contention that such orthodoxy restricts liberties on college campuses just as horrific regimes of intolerance in modern history denied basic religious and political freedoms. Campus misin-formation thus consists, most comprehensively, in a vivid language designed to popularize a dystopian story about college campuses.

This ritually retold narrative among networks of campus misinforma-tion is thick with rhetorical twists and turns. The convoluted nature of that narrative implies a common melodramatic script more than sober and sub-stantive deliberations about distinct questions of academic freedom across many different institutions. This sort of reactionary metadiscourse, I noted in Chapter 3, typifies both ideological echo chambers and misinformation campaigns.

Melodramatic narratives or metadiscourses about campus orthodoxies in-deed restrict potential terms of debate to their most negative and extreme connotations. Linguist and bestselling author John McWhorter's criticism of contemporary anti-racism illustrates how viewpoint diversity discourse attempts to literalize the most radical definitions of orthodoxy. "I do not mean that these people's ideology is 'like' a religion," he unambiguously asserts. "I mean that it actually is a religion. An anthropologist would see no difference in type between Pentecostalism and this new form of anti-racism."[19] McWhorter insists that "we are witnessing the birth of a new reli-gion, just as Romans witnessed the birth of Christianity." He posits that "early Christians did not think of themselves as a 'religion,' either"; like contempo-rary anti-racist advocates, they also supposedly operated in blind faith by "not thinking for themselves." The evolution of pro-diversity arguments into anti-racist advocacy organizations, McWorther argues, is literally a new re-ligion in a specific sense: a blind faith that unthinking zealots seek to impose on other people.

A professional anthropologist *should* see vast differences between Pentecostalism and contemporary anti-racist organizations. If organized re-ligion refers to a group of freely assembled people who believe certain ideas and advocate for them vocally, then the implied definition of religion is so broad that it loses meaning as a coherent tool for understanding specific reli-gious communities. Cultural and historical analogies must demonstrate more tangible similarities than differences between two distinct circumstances if someone wants to assert that the analogy in question offers a persuasive perspective on reality. If someone claims that certain advocacy groups today are no different from early Christians in their adherence to a central dogma, moreover, then we will have to wait centuries for proof of that sweeping claim. Early Christians did not think of themselves as members of a single faith be-cause the Christian canon took centuries to form, across vast geographical expanses and myriad differences in scriptural interpretation.[20] Saying that intolerant anti-racist activists or other pro-diversity groups are literally the same as "early Christians" relies on reductive and acontextual doublespeak about both religion and social movements. That doublespeak takes us away from, rather than closer to, constructive dialogue about how such groups op-erate in real-world circumstances.

Other historical analogies designed to dramatize inquisitions and witch hunts on college campuses similarly draw us into a fog of frightening terminology and dark allusions rather than constructive deliberation about higher education. European wars of religion between Protestants and Catholics, which lasted from the sixteenth through the eighteenth centuries, frequently involved horrific levels of public torture and military destruction. The Salem witch trials occurred during a wave of hysteria about suspected supernatural forces throughout colonial Massachusetts in the 1690s. More than two hundred people were accused of being witches at this time; nineteen of them were executed by hanging. The Red Scare throughout the 1950s also reflected a wave of hysteria over mostly false allegations about communist infiltration of society; the event constituted one of the severest abuses of civil liberties in US history because state agencies targeted thousands of Americans as communist sympathizers often without evidence.

Assertions that equivalent regimes of intolerance and persecution are transpiring in hundreds, if not thousands, of universities are false on their face. Yet viewpoint diversity polemics commonly include unironic comparisons between the culture of those universities and the atrocities of the Chinese Cultural Revolution—a murderous sociopolitical movement that lasted for a decade. "The use of the Cultural Revolution to characterize the state of free speech on American campuses," according to Yangyang Cheng, a research scholar at Yale Law School, "reflects a fundamental misunderstanding of Chinese history and American society."[21] Productive debates in academia about potential forms of censorship, conformity, or hostility to new ideas are vital. The rhetoric of obfuscating cultural or historical analogy in campus misinformation undermines informed dialogue about what those institutional vices look like when they do arise and how best to address them from multiple constructive perspectives.

Uses of cultural and historical analogy can be constructive in public argument. Such analogies can help people to understand one circumstance in a new way as measured against a prior cultural or historical event—if telling similarities outweigh differences between them. Frequent analogies in viewpoint diversity polemics between college campuses and infamous histories of intolerance or persecution not only ignore profound differences among manifestly dissimilar circumstances. Those analogies also reinforce old patterns of sociopolitical invective based on familiar kinds of stereotypes.

Tropes of orthodoxy and heterodoxy that agents of campus misinformation use to characterize the state of higher education broadly imitate hyperpartisan political rhetoric. Liberal and conservative politicians both commonly use hyperpartisan labels to depict their opponents as ideological extremists in ways that recall past and present totalitarian movements. Sensationalized political journalism, I noted in Chapter 1, accommodates this rhetoric by featuring meta-debates about liberal and conservative ideologies, which fail to substantively inform the public about how politicians and political institutions operate. The result is seemingly entertaining and melodramatic political theatre based on abstract stereotypes rather than constructive deliberation in the public interest. The language and logic of viewpoint diversity reduces the state of higher education to academic equivalents of those partisan stereotypes: orthodox and heterodox rather than liberal and conservative. As in the case of sensationalized political journalism, this mode of discourse both narrows and cheapens public discourse about the realities of university teaching and research.

Yet this imitation of reductive political stereotypes in polemics about higher education illustrates only one part of the danger that sweeping narratives of orthodoxy on college campuses pose to principles of free speech and academic freedom. The image of unthinking ideological overseers that those narratives project is consistent with proto-authoritarian worldviews. Allegations about liberal orthodoxies on college campuses have created a pretext for attempted state censorship of First Amendment rights and academic freedom across the nation. We can better understand how this wildly hyperbolic rhetoric of orthodoxy, heterodoxy, and persecution provides that pretext by delineating its authoritarian-friendly entailments. I do so in the next section by explaining how that rhetoric characterizes democratic activities as threats to the allegedly proper order of things, views other people as representations of monolithic group identities or perpetual forces of conflict, and fetishizes violence. Demonstrating these proto-authoritarian entailments will cement the case for adopting a more intellectually insightful and democratically inclusive mode of public discourse about higher education.

The Language of Orthodoxy and Authoritarian Worldviews

Proto-authoritarian political arguments, I noted in Chapter 6, often distort the language of democratic ideals and social tolerance. Elite public figures who benefit from the status quo might characterize organized movements for structural change (that is, democratic threats to the undemocratic status quo) as radical and destructive forces. Arguing that people who promote liberal values are illiberal, that anti-fascist groups are fascist, that anti-racist organizations are racist, or that people who advocate social tolerance are intolerant is a rhetorical signature of creeping authoritarian sentiment. Jason Stanley coined the phrase "undermining propaganda" to explain how authoritarian groups undermine "a political ideal by using it to communicate a message that is inconsistent with it."[22] Dominating channels of public information with such obfuscating doublespeak can blunt the popular appeal of movements for democratic change by confusing the broader public about who stands for what while distracting from evidence of existing inequalities. This kind of rhetoric, I also noted in Chapter 6, is prevalent in spreading populist authoritarianism throughout Eastern Europe and Russia. Such proto-authoritarian rhetoric depicts university discussions of human diversity or multiculturalism as evidence of clandestine ideological agents seeking to impose their will on culture at large.

Polemics about liberal orthodoxy on US college campuses replicate strategically confusing depictions of advocates for democratic change as anti-democratic, or of programs designed to promote tolerance and diversity as intolerant and censorious. The doublespeak of phrases like "liberal orthodoxy" and "illiberal liberalism" suffuses present-day debates about higher education. Self-described Christian nationalists in Eastern Europe and Russia use phrases like "gender ideology," the "LGBTQ lobby," and "human rights fundamentalism" to falsely depict movements for greater democratic equality as parts of a single ideological conspiracy—or orthodoxy.[23] All such descriptions portray relatively powerless or historically disenfranchised groups as members of an increasingly powerful, if not all-powerful, syndicate.

Tales of rigidly enforced orthodoxy on college campuses accordingly depict democratic activities and freely chosen ideas as threats to social or political freedom. Consider Haidt's passive-voiced account of political activity in universities: "Everyone is pressured to take sides. Administrators are pressured to disinvite speakers. . . . Petitions are floated, and names of signers (and abstainers) are noted."[24] The activities that Haidt describes here, in language that invokes totalitarian circumstances, are patently democratic practices. University students and faculty from many different sociopolitical orientations are free to persuade other students and faculty to support specific proposals. They are free to organize petitions and monitor levels of support for their causes. Nonviolent social pressure is a nonpartisan resource of democratic advocacy. One of the cardinal values of higher education in a democratic society is that people not only earn academic degrees but can also acquire training in popular political participation. Students and faculty might acquire that training through trial and error; they might pursue it in naïve or unrealistic ways, support objectionable causes, and sometimes overstep the bounds of proper conduct. Every such hazard is an inherent feature of democratic participation in general, not ideologically intolerant campus environments. Depictions like the one quoted in this paragraph, which are common in viewpoint diversity polemics, falsely portray free on-campus political activities as elements of a covert plan to restrict other people's freedom.

Several other standard tropes in campus misinformation erroneously portray free political activities and freely chosen ideas as evidence of censorious ideological orthodoxy. The conceit of the "increasingly leftist professoriate" is a representative scare tactic.[25] Advocates of viewpoint diversity in higher education frequently cite surveys of faculty political opinions to support their claims about allegedly radical leftist conformity on college campuses.[26] Such alarmist claims, however, resemble common misuses of scientific evidence that I examined in Chapter 4. No centralized database of faculty political opinions in US higher education exists. The surveys in question are almost always voluntary, reflect dissimilar research methods, and record responses from only a fraction of faculty members across thousands of institutions. (This is admittedly a personal anecdote, but I have taught for over a quarter of a century at several different universities while holding memberships in several different scholarly societies and, thankfully, I have never encountered a survey of faculty political opinions.) Arguments that feign definitive knowledge of an "increasingly leftist professoriate" unscientifically equate a hypothetical statistical majority of faculty who hold stereotypically liberal views with a radical lockstep movement.

Suppose that we *could* definitively verify a majority-liberal university faculty (albeit based on political stereotypes). Even in that case, common premises in viewpoint diversity polemics still depict freely chosen political preferences among diverse individuals as automatic evidence of coordinated radicalism and intolerance. I do not object to the conceit of an increasingly leftist professoriate in defense of liberal ideas. I object to that conceit because it promotes specious assumptions about First Amendment freedoms and true diversity of opinion on college campuses.

Members of different organizations in a democratic society are free to choose their political affiliations. Presuming that a statistical majority of faculty members hold socially or politically liberal views and hypothesizing that university faculty in general constitute an increasingly radical leftist cabal are two very different things. Yet this kind of language symbolizes a core conceit of campus misinformation, which predominantly characterizes free political activity and freely chosen ideas as signs of centralized and repressive conspiracies.

Perceiving people with competing social or political ideas as representatives of a monolithic group or impersonal ideological force—as adherents to a lockstep orthodoxy—is also consistent with rising authoritarian discourse. Advocates of viewpoint diversity in higher education argue not only that a distinct ideological orthodoxy dominates college campuses; they further claim that this orthodoxy is a new religion, according to an extreme definition of religion as blind faith or brainwashed conformity. Members of this alleged new religion have supposedly lost the ability to think for themselves—hence the notions that college students are generationally irrational, easily triggered, and pathologically coddled or that university faculty have been indoctrinated into the language of diversity policies and seek to indoctrinate others in turn. Different members of university communities, in these descriptions, are not human agents with potentially valid ideas or experiences but interchangeable cogs in a conformist machinery—seemingly beyond persuasion or empathy. In Chapter 3, I showed that references to "mobs" or "mob justice" are prevalent in viewpoint diversity polemics. Such highly charged terms reduce the complexities of sundry political arguments and activities to the image of an inherently irrational and unintelligent mass.

McWhorter's treatise on contemporary anti-racist movements illustrates how such language classifies different people as mere expressions of monolithic group identity or impersonal ideological forces. Once again: anti-racism in such discourse comprises some of the allegedly worst evils that university discussions of diversity propagate in society at large. "We will need a crisper label for these problematic folk [anti-racist advocates]," McWhorter muses. He entertains monolithic labels like "social justice warriors," "the woke mob," and "Inquisitors" before ultimately deciding on a novel stereotype: "the Elect." McWhorter comprehensively frames his discussion of contemporary anti-racist discourse with a meditation on "what kind of people" the Elect are and how "these people" allegedly got that way. "Make no mistake," he warns readers: "these people are coming for your kids."[27] This terminology is antithetical to any pretense of intellectual openness and constructive disagreement.

Volumes of research in political rhetoric or argumentation theory conclude that appeals to an abstract and monolithic "them" versus "us" do not promote reciprocal and evidence-based dialogue about the pros and cons of different ideas or policies. Rather, according to professor of rhetoric and writing Patricia Roberts-Miller, such language "polarizes a complicated political situation" based on an insistence that "the world can be reduced to those who are with us and those who are against us."[28] The principal function of such appeals is to denigrate the motivations of opposing groups while burnishing the identity of one's own group—all of which undermines from the start opportunities for constructive, open-minded dialogue about differing interpretations of fact or policy.[29] Yet McWhorter's statements are only emphatic expressions of a general tendency in viewpoint diversity polemics to claim that many students and faculty across numerous college campuses are merely unthinking embodiments of a nefarious orthodoxy.

Members of historically disenfranchised communities and stereotypically progressive social groups undoubtedly reduce complex groups of people to derisive, monolithic labels as well. Some structurally disempowered groups do so because they lack many important resources and networks of influence aside from tactics of provocative or radical appeals. Meaningful intellectual leadership and commitment to difficult debates, however, require us to interrupt cycles of reductive stereotyping, not lean into them. Relatively privileged or elite public figures who participate in such stereotyping cannot credibly indict other groups for using equivalent tactics. This premise applies to educational and democratic exchanges alike. The truest tests of our commitments to intellectual openness and democratic deliberation do not arise when all parties to a conflict are reflexively civil or when consensus is easy. The most meaningful tests of those commitments arise, rather, when the temptation is greatest to view our opponents as mere stereotypes—as personifications of grand speculative theories about human behavior, unworthy of empathy or persuasion. Elevating and enriching public argument requires us to transcend the language of such reductive stereotypes or totalizing theories in search of a more flexible and inventive civic vernacular.

Orthodoxy, I have established, is not a neutral descriptor in campus misinformation. It connotes *repression* based on tales of an intolerant belief system. This observation explains the standard assortment of historical analogies that viewpoint diversity polemics cite to emphasize the severity of that perceived orthodoxy on college campuses. Advocates of viewpoint diversity maintain that student and faculty commitments to diversity in universities represent a new religious or political dogma. Such orthodoxy is allegedly akin to, say, religious persecution in early modern Europe, the Salem witch trials, McCarthyism, or the Chinese Cultural Revolution. Citing this litany of historical analogies makes little empirical sense as an attempt to demonstrate convincing parallels between past and present. Those analogies cohere, instead, around the false premise that commitments to diversity, equity, and social justice on college campuses naturally incline people toward violence.

Many signature elements of campus misinformation thus involve fetishistic descriptions of violence. Campus misinformation became popular during the late 2010s based, in large part, on repeatedly recycled anecdotes about disconnected incidents of violence on a small number of college campuses (predominantly encouraged or exploited by outside groups committed to fomenting conflict on those campuses). Such incidents were reprehensible. A constructive, evidence-based commitment to addressing violence in university systems, however, would avoid sensationalism and focus equally on the commonest patterns of violence in those systems—epidemic rates of sexual assault foremost among them.[30]

The plain subtext of columns about campus rage by op-ed writers like Sullivan and Weiss is that such evils pose violent threats to society at large.[31] Recall that comparisons of university culture to the gruesome spectacle of an auto-da-fé, or public burning of a heretic, appear in some viewpoint diversity polemics. I normally hesitate to cite tweets as evidence, but a telling announcement from the University of Austin deserves mention in this context. Weiss, as one of the leaders of the university, tweeted news of its founding faculty fellows in November 2021 by declaring that the university "will welcome witches who refuse to burn."[32] The symbolism of perpetual religious warfare is an inherently misguided lens through which to interpret the state of higher education in a democratic society. Reliance on that symbolism suggests a willingness to relinquish the project of open and collaborative inquiry among members of democratic society and claim the mantle of truth for factional purposes.

Such fetishistic discourse about violence in many forms of campus misinformation, which reinforces the basic premise of repressive ideological orthodoxy on college campuses, is also consistent with proto-authoritarian worldviews. Authoritarianism posits both history and politics as scenes of perpetual conflict among ideological, metaphysical, or even supernatural forces.[33] People and communities, in this worldview, are not self-determining agents who shape history, but characters destined to play out a transhistorical dramaturgy.[34] Depicting free political activity or freely chosen ideas as the mere zealotry of monolithic groups, of mobs operating in frenzied conformity, reflects motivations to perceive reality in that manner. Depicting overwhelmingly nonviolent educational settings and intellectual exchanges as contests among either literally warring or potentially warring factions similarly normalizes the idea of a raw and violent contest for power that requires the restoration of proper order.

Conclusion

This chapter has shown how viewpoint diversity polemics about higher education rely on confused and confusing redefinitions of language. Linguistically, this doctrine does not promote measured and evidence-based accounts of higher education. It functions principally to instill arguably positive phenomena in higher education with categorically negative meaning. Prominent examples in this chapter include characterizing pledges of equal access and opportunity for everyone as instruments of inequality and censorship or depicting the academic freedom to criticize leaders and institutions as signs of thoughtless orthodoxy.

Networks of campus misinformation have proven highly effective since the mid-2010s at normalizing claims about diversity policies and inclusion messages on college campuses that rest on such patterns of semantic shape-shifting. Doublespeak of this sort turns out to be an old partisan tactic of strategic obfuscation in new verbal clothing: people who advocate for human diversity actually oppose diversity, advocates for equality foment inequality, self-described liberals and progressives are illiberal and repressive, professed anti-fascists are the real fascists, and people who oppose racism and sexism are racist and sexist themselves. The omnipresent trope of orthodoxy in campus misinformation thus popularizes an inverted image of universities denuded of precise meaning and clear historical context.

Replacing this kind of solipsism with a more intellectually and democratically responsible mode of deliberation is critical. The doublespeak of campus misinformation has generated pretexts for political restrictions on academic freedoms, which continue to proliferate across the United States and abroad. Public tolerance for academic freedom is a hallmark of a healthy democracy; increasing political targeting of schools and universities is a hallmark of democratic backsliding or rising authoritarianism. We can and must do better than to allow cynical rhetorical quicksand of the sort examined in this chapter to further corrode public discourse about the essential goods *and* formidable challenges of higher education. My final chapter concludes this book by proposing a new—or at least a more ethically and empirically constructive—starting place for future deliberations about the state of college campuses as well as their role in democratic society.

8
Campus Information

Cynicism about higher education is not a form of expertise in higher education. Nostalgia for past eras of higher education—which featured less diverse
academic curricula and more elitist campus cultures—ill prepares us to address the rapidly changing state of college campuses and the many challenges
that they negotiate. There is nothing new in the sight of established pundits or
scholars dismissing the ideas of rising junior colleagues in order to burnish
their own intellectual authority. Novel insights, much less truth, seldom come
from that impulse.

Media personalities, op-ed writers, and academic figures hyperbolically claim that higher education is "broken" or "failing."[1] These sweeping
generalizations conjure, in hazy focus, some legitimate concerns about specific incidents or problems in parts of higher education. Ensuring that colleges
protect First Amendment rights, maintain positive learning environments,
and foster new forms of knowledge should be widely shared priorities. I readily
agree, moreover, that higher education *is* in trouble. Some of the forces that
most threaten it include political interference in education policy, unsustain-
able financial models, the widespread technological availability of knowledge,
and the fact that institutions created for privileged social classes are now being
asked to rapidly transform into multicultural centers of learning. However,
overreaching claims about coddled students or rigid ideological orthodoxies
among faculty cast an exceedingly wide and often misleading net. Those
claims de facto mischaracterize the conduct of myriad students and faculty
who manage the formidable challenges of higher learning in good faith. It is
therefore reasonable to question both the evidence and ethics of public figures, including some university scholars themselves, who present cynicism
about higher education or nostalgia for more elitist versions of it as a kind of
nonpartisan intellectual expertise.

Such questioning is vital work for members of democratic society in
general, not only for members of college campuses. In addition to the free
press, liberal arts colleges and research universities are some of society's
most important bulwarks against the dangers of misinformation. Popular
misinformation about universities undermines those bulwarks and often
represents an early-warning sign of rising authoritarian sentiment. Rampant

misinformation about political institutions, professional journalism, and scientific data has emerged in recent years as one of the leading threats to healthy democracy in the United States. Popular misinformation about one of our most important defenses against misinformation—colleges and universities—can only compound those threats.

This book has recommended tools for identifying and counteracting misinformation about higher education—and, by extension, numerous other social, political, or scientific topics. Those tools coalesce in a functional understanding of historical debates about institutional diversity, documented patterns in the genesis of misinformation, exploitations of anecdotal evidence, common misuses of scientific data, and quasi-authoritarian distortions of free-speech ideals. I have attempted to explain these tools in accessible and convenient form. Yet each one of them reflects academic literature that thousands of students and professors are probably studying as I type this sentence, in courses scattered across many different fields. Such tools of anti-misinformation can empower us to defend not only the mission of higher education, but also the quality of democratic information and decision-making writ large. The whole of this book demonstrates the need for that empowerment. This conclusion encourages readers to put it into practice by encouraging a better-informed and more constructive framework of debate about higher education in the current era.

One of the most common misapprehensions regarding academic argument or debate is that such exchanges consist primarily of airy speculation about esoteric topics or merely opinionated responses to academic content. Effective teaching and research exchanges should allow different people to offer competing interpretations of various topics or raise new ideas about them—but according to a structure of agreed-upon parameters. Those parameters should focus discussion around the most persuasive, evidence-based interpretations of academic topics.

I understand a *viewpoint* as a perspective that someone can hold even without clear evidence to support it or even if other people do not find that approach credible. The goal of academic discussion, I propose, is not to validate viewpoints at face value. *The goal of academic discussion is to help people turn viewpoints into arguments.* My understanding of an argument in this capacity assumes that it rests on credible evidence of some kind and that other people find it credible even if they draw competing conclusions from the evidence in question.

Why did the US Civil War start? Do countries with democratic governments go to war more often or less often than countries with non-democratic governments? Did the invention of modern mass media change human perceptions of time and space? How do scientists verify the safety and effectiveness of vaccines? The best way to develop a range of informed answers to these questions is to examine available evidence in dialogue with others according to reasonable principles of argument and interpretation. Shared principles of this kind should not predetermine interpretations of evidence; imagination and creativity are always important elements of that work. Yet shared principles of argument and interpretation *should* prevent someone from credibly asserting that Abraham Lincoln started a civil war by himself, that democracies are more warlike than autocracies, that modern mass media did not change human perceptions of time and space, or that scientists lack protocols for determining the safety of vaccines. People are free to adopt such claims as viewpoints, but those viewpoints will not withstand minimally informed debate as academic arguments.

A framework of discussion built on informed principles of interpretation encourages competing interpretations of evidence—but in ways that reinforce the impression of a relatively common empirical reality within which people with differing worldviews can coexist. A dynamic of this sort encourages freedom of thought and intellectual diversity while limiting opportunities for presenting misinformation as meritorious argument or engaging in caustic debate for its own sake. Academic dialogue so defined does not arbitrarily mandate *what* students and colleagues should either agree or disagree with; it advocates *how* students and colleagues can engage in the most constructive, evidence-based patterns of simultaneous agreement and disagreement. This is the spirit in which I offer the following principles of campus *information*.

Liberal arts education is an antidote to ideological indoctrination. No student is forced to attend a particular school, study a particular subject, or take a particular course. US higher education is built on *a choice-based structure* of application, enrollment, and attendance. University curricula in the liberal arts mold help students develop skills in academic self-advocacy in addition to instructing them in specific topics. Establishing a course of study that encourages students to freely choose their desired academic interests—across the natural sciences, social sciences, and humanities—is the defining premise of liberal arts education.

Yet students can also choose *not* to attend a liberal arts institution within the US higher education system. That system comprises thousands of different institutions, from community college networks and online degrees to professional or vocational schools. Journalist and bestselling author Jeffrey J. Selingo, an expert on trends in higher education, even speculates that US higher education has more individual institutions than necessary, meaning that the system might be *too* diverse and decentralized.[2] Higher education from the late twentieth century forward has become more attainable for people of color, women, international students, and people from structurally impoverished communities—or far less elitist in general. US higher education is built upon a structure of anti-indoctrination to the extent that it extends more choices of schools and programs of study to a wider variety of students than in any prior era.

Colleges do require students, faculty, and administrators to adhere to institutional codes of conduct and comply with campus policies pertaining to academic integrity, diversity and inclusion, or campus safety. Such requirements, however, are an important part of someone's *choice* to join a given educational community. Faith statements, which many private Christian universities require of all students and faculty, also illustrate common university policy obligations. Students and faculty from nonreligious backgrounds seek out such institutions and complete required faith statements or fulfill other faith-related obligations as a conscious choice in pursuit of education or employment. Being obliged to accept such conditions of entry, from required faith statements to diversity policies that apply to everyone, is not indoctrination.

Once enrolled in an academic major—as a choice among many options—students are also required to take certain classes. Those classes are required either as part of the student's chosen academic major or as general education credits prescribed by the college, school, or program to which the academic major belongs. In the case of major requirements, it would be odd for a student who holds strong social and political views to choose, among all available degree options, an academic major that challenges those views. A student in that circumstance would have chosen, among available educational options, to be in it—not forcibly indoctrinated.

In the case of general education requirements, most institutions based on the liberal arts model require students to take general education courses for a small number of skills-based courses. English composition and public speaking courses are typical examples. For most other general education requirements, however, students are required to choose from at least a few course options to fulfill a particular general education requirement (such as requirements for cultural experience or requirements for natural science, and so on, that each designate a cluster of approved courses from among several different departments). The trend of providing students with flexible options even for required general education courses further indicates how institutional diversity policies benefit all students. Such flexible options often recognize, for example, that basic writing and speaking courses should acknowledge cultural differences in styles of expression or that students with learning disabilities should not be forced to complete general education courses that effectively penalize them for those disabilities. The goal of such added flexibility is not to introduce more curricular choices simply for the sake of doing so, but to accentuate the overall quality of education for all types of students.

Institutions based on the liberal arts model do not force undergraduate students to signify agreement with specific belief systems, political views, or cultural norms. This premise constitutes one of the largest misnomers about courses in women's studies, gender studies, African American studies, philosophy, religion, and a wide variety of other courses centered on social, political, and cultural differences. Students admittedly *study* belief systems, political theories, or cultural norms with which they personally disagree in some courses—but they do so customarily to learn about the full scope of those subjects, whether in recently created interdisciplinary programs or in conventional areas of study. Being asked to consider or critically examine an unfamiliar belief, theory, or norm is an intrinsic part of education, not indoctrination.

In sum, attending a particular college or university, which offers a specific type of curriculum, is a choice. Once enrolled in a curriculum—by choice—most secular colleges and universities offer students a variety of ways to earn required types of credits, either in their academic major or as part of their general education. The case can be different at private religious schools, of course, which require theological instruction as part of general education or degree requirements—but, again, as a result of a student's choice to attend such an institution. These choice-based realities invalidate the fallacious premise that universities overwhelmingly pressure students and faculty to think and speak in uniform ways.

Institutional policies designed to promote diversity, equity, and inclusion on college campuses do not constitute an orthodoxy. If we define *orthodoxy* as a doctrine that institutions impose on people against their free will, then the term connotes two things at once: a common dogma *and* a centralized authority that imposes it. Myriad institutions of higher learning promote diversity policies in a *decentralized* manner: across public and private institutions, in secular as well as religious ones, throughout all parts of the nation. I try to avoid the language of political stereotypes. For the sake of argument, however, stereotypically liberal Ivy League colleges and Scripture-based Christian universities both promote diversity, equity, and inclusion messages. They do so to serve vastly different institutional goals, educational missions, and student communities. Common pro-diversity policies in higher education reflect decentralized and variably interpreted language choices, not the hierarchical imposition of a repressive orthodoxy.

The codified language of diversity at many dissimilar colleges and universities also manifests conscious efforts to *undo* ideological orthodoxies. The University of Mississippi, I previously noted, was the scene of prolonged mob violence intended to prevent lawful desegregation of publicly funded education in the 1960s. Massive resistance to desegregation concomitantly sought to enforce genuinely rigid ideological orthodoxies based on ideals of white, male, and heteronormative superiority. The University of Mississippi's diversity and community engagement standards express a commitment to undoing such rigid and historically recent orthodoxy by promoting "a self-transforming university" that "creates equitable opportunities for all," thus echoing the civil rights mantra of equal access to public institutions.[3] Many other southern institutions that resisted desegregation, from Vanderbilt University to the Virginia Military Institute (VMI), similarly promote commitments to undoing models of educational access based on discriminatory intellectual orthodoxies.[4] Vanderbilt University did not admit Black undergraduate students until the mid-1960s, and VMI continues to acknowledge unequal treatment of Black cadets (its honors system, for example, disproportionately expels them).[5] One of the reasons that stereotypically liberal Ivy League institutions publicize extensive diversity policies, moreover, is because elite northeastern institutions also discriminated against Black, Jewish, Asian American, and female applicants according to a variety of exclusionary devices, including quotas.[6] The language of such policies, across so many different institutions, has meaning principally as a de facto argument *against* historically narrow and sometimes violently enforced orthodoxies.

Universities that announce such commitments may or may not practice them in institutionally deep or consistent ways. Contemporary debates about the meaning of pro-diversity messages in higher education should acknowledge that frequently aspirational mission statements and policy language may constitute relatively meager instruments for achieving truly equal access to college campuses and equitable treatment within. Positive institutional talk does not necessarily translate into effective institutional practices. Some notably un-diverse corporations, for instance, coopt the language of institutional diversity and inclusion in their public relations strategies.[7]

Nonetheless, historically informed and empirically accurate discussions of diversity policies should begin by admitting that they exhibit *anti*-orthodox meaning and intent in universities. People can and should question on a case-by-case basis the effectiveness or wisdom of diversity language in higher education. Hyperbolically characterizing that language as evidence of forcibly imposed orthodoxy across diverse and decentralized institutions stifles evidence-based deliberation on the merits of pro-diversity messages from multiple constructive perspectives.

Institutional policies designed to promote diversity, equity, and inclusion on college campuses are not inherently liberal. Many different universities with stereotypically conservative missions in conservative regions of the United States have adopted those policies to promote individual rights, traditional social norms, and religious faith in higher learning. Notre Dame University, a private Catholic institution that requires all students to complete a course in theology, promotes "a spirit of inclusion" on its campus "for distinct reasons articulated in our Christian tradition." The university's inclusion policies "welcome all people, regardless of color, gender, religion, ethnicity, sexual orientation, social or economic class, and nationality" as well as "gay and lesbian members of this community." Notre Dame University defines this commitment to institutional diversity, equity, and inclusion as an expression of fidelity to both Catholic faith and social justice: "one of the essential tests of social justice within any Christian community is its abiding spirit of inclusion."[8] This distinguished private university promotes policy language that many partisan pundits and advocates of viewpoint diversity often malign as stereotypically liberal "virtue signaling" (or merely symbolic itemization of social identity categories) to uphold essential tenets of education aligned with Catholic beliefs.

Such stated commitments to diversity at Notre Dame University reflect broader trends among many private Christian institutions. The Council for Christian Colleges and Universities (CCCU) describes itself as a leading advocate of "Christ-centered higher education" across dozens of institutions dedicated to "faithfully relating scholarship and service to biblical truth."[9] CCCU institutions include Baylor University (Waco, Texas), Covenant College (Lookout Mountain, Georgia), Dallas Baptist University (Dallas, Texas), Kentucky Christian University (Grayson, Kentucky), Lipscomb University (Nashville, Tennessee), Messiah University (Mechanicsburg, Pennsylvania), Oral Roberts University (Tulsa, Oklahoma), and many others. The book *Diversity Matters: Race, Ethnicity, and the Future of Christian Higher Education* features contributions from administrators and faculty members across CCCU institutions that explain the importance of diversity, equity, and inclusion to Christian education.[10] Stated commitments to diversity from such institutions do not provide a complete portrait of all Christian universities. The fact that so many ostensibly conservative religious institutions embrace those principles, however, proves that diversity policies centered on categories like race, sex, and gender can support, if not *enhance*, both conservative and Christian values.

These observations lead to an even more comprehensive claim about the language of diversity policies. That language is neither liberal nor conservative. Pro-diversity messages represent pragmatic and adaptable idioms that dissimilar universities adopt for fittingly diverse reasons. As a primary framework of debate, the terminology of simple and monolithic political stereotypes promotes more obfuscation than clarity about which institutions freely adopt pro-diversity messages in higher education and why they choose to do so.

Some policy statements admittedly exceed the goal of promoting equitable and inclusive learning environments by proscribing preferred teaching or research practices in pursuit of that goal. John McWorther legitimately criticizes specific policy statements that overreach in this manner.[11] However, McWhorter's one-size-fits-all premise that such incidents of overreach evince a coordinated liberal orthodoxy creates unnecessary obstacles to understanding how those policies evolve and the most effective ways to correct them. His primary evidence of such a coordinated plot is a single job advertisement at San Diego State University—among thousands of annual job advertisements across thousands of institutions. The job advertisement sought candidates with experience in teaching, research, or mentoring involving underrepresented communities.[12] The unmysterious truth in this case is that academic programs employ many faculty in a variety of specialties; those programs are relatively free to seek applicants with desired kinds of experience in addition to many others. No candidate is forced to apply to the kind of position that McWhorter cites, and such a job advertisement applies to no university personnel outside of the program that issues it (usually with prior approval from multiple university offices). We can and should raise credible questions about potential misuses of diversity policies on a case-by-case basis. Falsely claiming that miscellaneous job advertisements or other collaboratively ratified policies reflect a pernicious liberal orthodoxy in higher education undermines constructive deliberation toward that end.

Many different institutions, including numerous stereotypically conservative colleges in stereotypically conservative communities, embrace diversity and inclusion policies to advance their chosen institutional missions on a decentralized basis. The critical issue of how to establish conditions of diversity and equal opportunity in relatively self-governing organizations without proscribing favored means to do so requires good-faith collaborative dialogue among all willing members of those organizations. For this reason, university diversity policies tend to exist in states of periodic review among campus constituencies, not as static legal codes. Promoting inaccurate narratives about coordinated liberal plots to explain abuses of diversity policies where they occur hinders informed deliberation about the best ways to prevent those abuses.

Institutional policies designed to promote diversity, equity, and inclusion on college campuses promote First Amendment ideals and academic freedom for all students and faculty. The premise that such policies create automatic infringements of free speech and inquiry is an illogical contrivance. The University of Oklahoma accurately describes this contrivance as a "false choice": "At OU, we will not accept the false choice of supporting either free expression or diversity. They are both essential. When we protect and strengthen one, we protect and strengthen the other."[13] Discrimination built into educational communities has historically operated in two primary ways: by systematically denying specific people equal access to those communities and by treating them unequally within. Recall the historic case of James Meredith, whom the University of Mississippi initially refused to enroll and then experienced persistent intimidation campaigns after he did so. College campuses that systematically exclude some qualified students or faculty fail to fully guarantee free speech and academic freedom for all students and faculty. Universities that tolerate hostility to the presence of *specific* students or faculty fail to fully guarantee those same liberties and freedoms for *all* students and faculty.

Pro-diversity messages in universities are, in this respect, pro–First Amendment and pro–academic freedom. Those messages reflect a straightforward argument: quality education requires institutions to ensure that a greater diversity of *all* students and faculty possess equal opportunities to exercise freedom of inquiry, speech, and conscience. The University of Oklahoma administration concisely summarizes this ideal harmony between free speech and institutional diversity: "Everyone has a voice, and each voice can and will be heard. In championing a broad notion of diversity, we protect a quintessentially American idea: that the doors of opportunity are open to all and everyone has something to contribute."[14] By contrast, institutions that admit only some students from certain kinds of backgrounds, narrowly define their academic curriculum to reflect status quo values, or limit discussions of curriculum according to artificial viewpoint parity potentially circumscribe First Amendment liberties and academic freedom.

The University of Oklahoma further attests that such potentially demarcated campus communities or academic curricula also present a circumscribed education in democracy. The idea that free speech and diversity harmonize, the administration states, "is at the very heart of our democracy, and great universities like OU nurture it by embracing diversity, equity, and inclusion on our campuses and instilling a culture of dignity and respect for all."[15] In the spring of 2022, a spate of faculty councils at publicly funded universities issued resolutions that similarly equate pro-diversity policies with First Amendment ideals and quality education. Faculty at institutions including Pennsylvania State University, the University of Texas at Austin, the University of Alabama, the University of Mississippi, and Ohio State University responded to rapidly increasing political interference with academic freedom. Their publicized resolutions overwhelmingly asserted that the ability of faculty to freely teach about racism, inequality, and all manner of political ideas while promoting diversity or multiculturalism is an essential to free speech and academic freedom in higher learning.[16] Faculty resolutions do not automatically set university policy, much less influence state law. Yet entire faculty senate bodies in expansive university systems openly debated and freely adopted such resolutions by large majority votes. This fact contradicts the notions that pro-diversity messages are inconsistent with academic freedom or democratic exchange and forcibly imposed by a small number of outspoken faculty.

Substantial systemic inequities in universities still exist. College administrations typically recognize that full diversity and inclusion are ideals against which to measure imperfect realities. Yet powerful figures throughout the nineteenth and twentieth centuries sought to preserve higher education as an elite and fundamentally unequal endeavor devoted to reproducing a narrowly defined intellectual community. The *comparatively* diverse and democratic state of many universities today manifests the very reality that those figures wanted to prohibit. By that measure, core premises of the viewpoint diversity doctrine—that present-day universities must choose between social justice and quality education—are both historically obtuse and empirically faulty. The fact that, on balance, higher education is far more academically diverse and functionally democratic than at any prior point in history invalidates the quintessential viewpoint diversity claim that ubiquitous pro-diversity messages on college campuses stifle free speech and academic freedom.

Public deliberations about the state of higher education should include multifaceted accounts of student bodies and the systemic hardships that many of them face. Students who constructively advocate for freely chosen political ideas in appropriate campus forums can acquire important educational experience in democratic participation as well as academic subjects. Teaching and research about political ideas or movements in universities is an integral part of myriad academic specialties. Relying on stereotypical categories of liberal and conservative identity to describe entire campus communities, however, implies a reductive and unimaginative approach to understanding the ideas, motivations, or behaviors of diverse academic populations. This concern is especially applicable to arguments that posit a deterministic understanding of stereotypical political identity. Such an understanding presupposes, in the context of higher education, that either liberal or conservative ideas determine the ideology that most college students hold or the psychology that most of them share as allegedly static human attributes. Higher education based on the liberal arts model offers an intrinsic opportunity to understand ourselves and other people without reliance on inherited stereotypes and without the impulse to scapegoat specific groups for shared problems.

Campus misinformation has helped to normalize reductive and deterministic discourse about college students based on political stereotypes. Such misinformation duplicates some of the most unfortunate aspects of sensationalist political journalism, predicated on ideals of artificial viewpoint parity or ideological balance, in debates about higher education. Sweeping generalizations about large student groups mislead the public about an important facet of all universities—the composition of undergraduate student communities—just as sensationalized political journalism presents a vastly simplified portrait of different political constituencies.

The fact that undergraduate student groups in an era of expanded access to higher learning are more diverse than ever, according to a greater variety of measurements, underscores the need for a multidimensional account of the people who comprise those groups. Some studies suggest that as many as 70 percent of college students attend school while working to pay for their education. A fraction of those students may work year-round, sometimes performing demanding labor in poor working conditions.[17] The normative image of college students as predominantly privileged people in their late teens or early twenties can be misleading: working adults constitute a significant part of the national undergraduate student population in an era of expanded educational opportunities. Appreciable numbers of university students suffer from combinations of economic insecurity, food insecurity, and homelessness.[18] Student debt from higher education loans, which college graduates often spend years paying off, may be a significant enough economic drag that it has become a national political issue.[19] Present-day undergraduate students have lived through two economic recessions (the Great Recession in the late 2000s and the 2020 recession) as well as a historic pandemic. Such systemic hardships disproportionately affect college students from historically disenfranchised communities. In sum, simply attending college now requires enormous commitment, labor, and self-advocacy for many students.

Broad generalizations about university student groups based on the language of inflexible political stereotypes misinform the public about the true social, political, and demographic diversity that those groups encompass.

Such generalizations distract from the numerous systemic challenges to accessible quality education that deserve greater attention in public discourse about college campuses. The health of important civic institutions hinges, to a large degree, on the success of students who struggle against formidable non-academic obstacles to simply earn their academic degrees. Elitist cynicism and heightened popular hostilities against colleges and universities only add to those burdens.

Teach to the topic—in the classroom and in public debates about higher education. Many university instructors share a shorthand for best practices in teaching. The concept of teaching to the topic, in my understanding, means encouraging students to make connections between classroom discussions and current affairs through the details of assigned course content. Teaching to the topic, in other words, helps students perceive real-world connections to academic study but avoids turning the classroom into a loosely structured forum for mere social, political, or moral opinions.

The temptation to make classroom discussion into that kind of forum can naturally arise in the wake of significant social or political events. Examples might include instructors' impulses to ask students about the latest political scandal in a course on political communication, disputes over the fate of Confederate monuments in a course on US history, or newly publicized findings about climate change in a course on earth science. Teaching to the topic means encouraging students to identify the most substantive versions of such connections by going deeper into the details of course content, not artificially forcing the latest public controversy into classroom discussion. In-depth study of core course topics, by this logic, simultaneously provides students with a new or different vantage on important facets of the wider world.

Public figures who allege that university instructors force atopical polemics about diversity and inequality into classroom discussions may not realize that many of those instructors are essentially teaching to the topic. Such allegations assume two common forms: pleas for a return to the so-called Western canon (or "great works") and proposals to abolish recently created academic disciplines that focus on race, sex, gender, and multiculturalism.

On the one hand, the notion that ideas about power, justice, or politics impede the discovery of truth through close study of the Western canon is anathema to many of the most representative works in that canon. Worldly debates over political authority, the arbitrariness of despotic power, differences between natural law and social convention, inequalities among social classes, masculine and feminine identity, and individual liberties suffuse vast portions of the Western canon. The premise holds true across the works of Aristotle, Cicero, Augustine, Shakespeare, Milton, Rousseau, and many others. Even Plato's discourses on heavenly truth or John Locke's forays into the depths of human consciousness were intended to inform the often crude and bloody field of real-world affairs. Decrying classroom discussions of oftentimes radical social and political theories by encouraging a return to the Western canon is oxymoronic. Using texts in that canon to refute existing authorities or hierarchies of knowledge, as many of their authors intended, is teaching to the topic.

On the other hand, disciplines that focus on racial and gender inequalities teach to the topic by exploring human realities that seldom appeared in prior eras of higher learning. Even traditional academic curricula that claimed to educate students in "universal" truths habitually omitted such realities of human existence. The accusation that newer disciplines offer merely esoteric or blithely ideological content suggests an intellectually parochial attitude toward university-level teaching and research. Thousands of students and faculty on college campuses recognize a fuller and more accurate portrait of the world in disciplines like African American studies, sex and gender studies, or Latinx studies. Teaching and research in those subject areas include contributions from a wide spectrum of scholars in the social sciences and humanities. Members of more long-standing academic disciplines, across the humanities and sciences, have freely adopted academic work on race, sex, gender, and multiculturalism to enrich their own teaching and research.

Dismissing entire academic programs that large numbers of students and faculty value does not exemplify a commitment to open-mindedness. Treating the varied ideas of scholars from multiple fields as a superficial exercise in groupthink does not indicate a commitment to intellectual diversity in pursuit of new ideas. Bemoaning an alleged lack of intellectual diversity on college campuses while reducing numerous academic explorations of human diversity to clumsy stereotypes is an internally contradictory position. Consulting newly created fields of study to enrich academic accounts of human diversity, however, and challenging academic traditions that claim authority over so-called truths about humanity *is* teaching to the topic.

Public figures in privileged positions have a responsibility to, in effect, teach to the topic in debates over the state of higher education. Even strident criticisms of university systems should reflect substantive homework about how various institutions of higher education function rather than the contrived metadiscourse of campus misinformation. That civic homework should include

- An understanding of the difference between campus misinformation and sound information about college or universities based on an array of relevant and reasonably accurate perspectives.
- A functional understanding of the history of US higher education, especially as it pertains to issues of academic freedom and diversity.
- Broad familiarity with the wealth of accessible information designed to assess learning environments and campus climates that universities routinely produce.
- A commitment to featuring diverse student, faculty, and administrator perspectives as an essential part of public debates about higher education.

I have shown throughout this book how campus misinformation imposes specious narratives about universities onto discussions of higher education rather than leaning into plentiful sources of information that contradict those narratives. Responsible discourse about higher education should teach to the topic by leaving the public better informed about the complex realities of university teaching, research, and administration—not more dedicated to cynical or nostalgic polemics that provide, at best, a highly selective understanding of those realities.

Members of the public also have the capacity to ensure that debates over the state of higher education teach to the topic. This capacity parallels the constructive role that college students can play in the classroom by ensuring that open academic discussion nonetheless works through course content rather than wandering above and beyond it. Citizens in general are potential collaborators in the production of knowledge about our most important institutions, just as students in classrooms are collaborators in the production of knowledge about academic subjects. Consumers of news and information have the capacity, if they choose to exercise it, to identify and counteract popular misinformation using the tools and techniques that I have recommended throughout this book. Asking that influential public figures with significant amounts of intellectual capital teach to the topic in debates about higher education is not simply an exercise in fact-checking or constructive argument. It is essential democratic work in era when misinformation about colleges and universities frequently presages antidemocratic restrictions on civil liberties.

Notes

Introduction

1. Andrew Atterbury and Juan Perez Jr., "Republicans Eye New Front in Education Wars: Making School Board Races Partisan," *Politico*, December 29, 2021, https://www.politico.com/news/2021/12/29/republicans-education-wars-school-board-races-526053; Olivia Beavers and Michael Stratford, "GOP Embraces Classroom Politics, Taking Cues from Youngkin," *Politico*, November 3, 2021, https://www.politico.com/news/2021/11/03/gop-classroom-politics-youngkin-519350; Stephanie Saul, "Energizing Conservative Voters, One School Board Election at a Time," *New York Times*, October 21, 2021, https://www.nytimes.com/2021/10/21/us/republicans-schools-critical-race-theory.html.
2. See W. Lance Bennett and Steven Livingston, eds., *The Disinformation Age: Politics, Technology, and Disruptive Communication in the United States* (New York: Cambridge University Press, 2020).
3. Brooks Jackson and Kathleen Hall Jamieson, *unSpun: Finding Facts in a World of Disinformation* (New York: Random House, 2007), viii.
4. See Ellie Bothwell, "Poland Trying to Destroy Universities' Independence, Warns Rector," *Times Higher Education*, November 23, 2020, https://www.timeshighered ucation.com/news/poland-trying-destroy-universities-independence-warns-rector; Dmitry Dubrovskiy, "Academic Rights in Russia and the Internationalization of Higher Education," *Academe* (American Association of University Professors), Fall 2019, https://www.aaup.org/article/academic-rights-russia-and-internationalization-higher-educat ion#.Ydh66FlOk2x; Diane Jeantet, "Brazil Education Overhaul Aims at Ousting 'Marxist Ideology,'" AP News, February 6, 2019, https://www.apnews.com/0fb07d84d14c4d948 f7028907c60f23f; Elizabeth Redden, "Hungary Officially Ends Gender Studies Programs," *Inside Higher Ed*, October 17, 2018, https://www.insidehighered.com/quicktakes/2018/10/17/hungary-officially-ends-gender-studies-programs; Marc Santora, "George Soros-Founded University Is Forced out of Hungary," *New York Times*, December 3, 2018, https://www.nytimes.com/2018/12/03/world/europe/soros-hungary-central-european-uni versity.html; Jason Stanley, "Fascism and the University," *Chronicle of Higher Education*, September 2, 2018, https://www-chronicle-com.ezaccess.libraries.psu.edu/article/Fas cismthe-University/244382; and Stanley, *How Fascism Works: The Politics of Us and Them* (New York: Random House, 2018), chapter 3.
5. Char Adams, Allan Smith, and Aadit Tambe, "Map: See Which States Have Passed Critical Race Theory Bills," NBC News, June 17, 2021, https://www.nbcnews.com/news/nbcblk/map-see-which-states-have-passed-critical-race-theory-bills-n1271215; Adrian Florido, "'We Can and Should Teach This History': New Bills Limit How Teachers Talk about Race," National Public Radio, May 25, 2021, https://www.npr.org/2021/05/25/1000273981/we-can-and-should-teach-this-history-new-bills-limit-how-teachers-talk-about-rac; Sarah Schwartz, "Map: Where Critical Race Theory Is under Attack," *Education Week*, June 11, 2021 (updated May 18, 2022), https://www.edweek.org/policy-politics/map-where-criti

cal-race-theory-is-under-attack/2021/06; Rashawn Ray and Alexandra Gibbons, "Why Are States Banning Critical Race Theory?," Brookings Institution, November 2021, https://www.brookings.edu/blog/fixgov/2021/07/02/why-are-states-banning-critical-race-theory/.

6. Gene Nichol, "Political Interference with Academic Freedom and Free Speech at Public Universities," *Academe* (American Association of University Professors), Fall 2019, https://www.aaup.org/article/political-interference-academic-freedom-and-free-speech-public-universities#.YhTsnJZOk2z.

7. "Anti-Palestinian Legislation," Palestine Legal, June 1, 2022, https://palestinelegal.org/rig httoboycott/.

8. "Restoring Free Speech on Campus," Goldwater Institute, January 30, 2017, https://goldwat erinstitute.org/campus-free-speech/.

9. Jeremy W. Peters, "In Name of Free Speech, States Crack Down on Campus Protests," *Washington Post*, June 14, 2018, https://www.nytimes.com/2018/06/14/us/politics/cam pus-speech-protests.html. See also Jennifer Tiedemann, "Nebraska Becomes Latest State to Consider Campus Free Speech Bill Based on Goldwater Institute Model," Goldwater Institute, January 5, 2018, https://goldwaterinstitute.org/article/nebraska-becomes-latest-state-to-consider-campus-free-speech-bill-based-on-goldwater-institute-model/.

10. "Free to Think 2021: Political Upheaval and Authoritarianism Threaten Academic Freedom and the Future of Higher Education," Scholars at Risk, December 9, 2021, https://www.scholarsatrisk.org/2021/12/free-to-think-2021-political-upheaval-and-authoritarianism-threaten-academic-freedom-and-the-future-of-higher-education/.

11. Greg Lukianoff and Jonathan Haidt, "The Coddling of the American Mind," *The Atlantic*, September 2015, https://www.theatlantic.com/magazine/archive/2015/09/the-coddling-of-the-american-mind/399356/.

12. Jannell Ross, "Obama Says Liberal College Students Should Not Be 'Coddled,'" *Washington Post*, September 15, 2015, https://www.washingtonpost.com/news/the-fix/wp/2015/09/15/obama-says-liberal-college-students-should-not-be-coddled-are-we-really-surprised/.

13. Alana Mastrangelo, "Review: Charlie Kirk's 'Campus Battlefield' Explains How to Fight the Death of Free Speech on Campus," Breitbart, November 23, 2018, https://www.breitb art.com/tech/2018/11/23/review-charlie-kirks-campus-battlefield-explains-how-to-fight-the-death-of-free-speech-on-campus/.

14. Sophie Tatum and Jordyn Phelps, "Trump Signs Executive Order Threatening Aid to Colleges If Speakers Silenced," ABC News, March 21, 2019, https://abcnews.go.com/Polit ics/trump-sign-executive-order-threatening-aid-colleges-speakers/story?id=61833503.

15. Áine Cain, "The Truth about Whether You Can Be Fired for Expressing Your Political Views at Work," *Business Insider*, January 20, 2017, http://www.businessinsider.com/you-can-be-fired-over-political-views-2017-1.

16. A host of commentaries support this conclusion. Political scientist Jeffrey Sachs explains that "the narrative" about college campuses that viewpoint diversity advocates promote is based on "myths." (Jeffrey Adam Sachs, "The 'Campus Free Speech Crisis' Is a Myth. Here Are the Facts," *Washington Post,* March 16, 2018, https://www.washingtonpost.com/news/monkey-cage/wp/2018/03/16/the-campus-free-speech-crisis-is-a-myth-here-are-the-facts/). The thesis that contemporary college students oppose free speech, English professor Aaron Hanlon explains, is simply "not true" (Aaron Hanlon, "Are Liberal College Students Creating a Free Speech Crisis? Not According to Data," NBC News, March 22, 2018, https://www.nbcnews.com/think/opinion/are-liberal-college-students-creating-free-speech-cri

sis-not-according-ncna858906). Both studies rely on thorough analyses of a range of available data. Adam Serwer writes that undue attention to issues of free speech on campuses has distracted from far more pressing state-based restrictions on First Amendment rights ("A Nation of Snowflakes," *The Atlantic*, September 26, 2017, https://www.theatlantic.com/politics/archive/2017/09/it-takes-a-nation-of-snowflakes/541050/).

17. Lee C. Bollinger, "Free Speech on Campus Is Doing Just Fine, Thank You," *The Atlantic*, June 12, 2019, https://www.theatlantic.com/ideas/archive/2019/06/free-speech-crisis-campus-isnt-real/591394/.

18. Sigal R. Ben-Porath, *Free Speech on Campus* (Philadelphia: University of Pennsylvania Press, 2017), 85.

19. Michael S. Roth, *Safe Enough Spaces: A Pragmatist's Guide to Inclusion, Free Speech, and Political Correctness on College Campuses* (New Haven: Yale University Press, 2019), 111.

20. "Fast Facts: Education Institutions," National Center for Educational Statistics, accessed February 5, 2022, https://nces.ed.gov/fastfacts/display.asp?id=84.

21. See Jerome Karabel, *The Chosen: The Hidden History of Admission and Exclusion at Harvard, Yale, and Princeton* (New York: Houghton Mifflin, 2005).

22. William G. Bowen and Derek Bok, *The Shape of the River: Long-Term Consequences of Considering Race in College and University Admissions* (Princeton, NJ: Princeton University Press, 1998), 293.

Chapter 1

1. See Yoel Inbar and Joris Lammers, "Political Diversity in Social and Personality Psychology," *Perspectives on Psychological Science* 7, no. 5 (2012): 496–503.

2. Caroline Anders, "In Push against 'Indoctrination,' DeSantis Mandates Surveys of Florida College Students' Beliefs," *Washington Post*, June 24, 2021, https://www.washingtonpost.com/education/2021/06/24/florida-intellectual-freedom-law-mandates-viewpoint-surveys/.

3. Michael S. Roth, *Safe Enough Spaces: A Pragmatist's Approach to Inclusion, Free Speech, and Political Correctness on College Campuses* (New Haven, CT: Yale University Press, 2019), ix.

4. For a helpful introduction to the scientific aspects of debates over affirmative action, see Kate Turetsky and Valerie Purdie-Vaughns, "What Science Has to Say about Affirmative Action," *Scientific American*, December 15, 2017, https://www.scientificamerican.com/article/what-science-has-to-say-about-affirmative-action/.

5. Lewis F. Powell Jr., "Attack on American Free Enterprise System," letter to US Chamber of Commerce, August 23, 1971, https://law2.wlu.edu/deptimages/Powell%20Archives/PowellMemorandumTypescript.pdf. All references to Powell in the paragraph are taken from this document.

6. Nicole Hemmer, "Eternally Frustrated by 'Liberal' Universities, Conservatives Now Want to Tear Them Down," *Vox*, March 8, 2017, https://www.vox.com/the-big-idea/2017/3/7/14841292/liberal-universities-conservative-faculty-sizzler-pc.

7. See "About Us," Foundation for Individual Rights in Education, accessed February 5, 2022, https://www.thefire.org/about-us/history/.

8. Alan Charles Kors and Harvey A. Silverglate, *The Shadow University: The Betrayal of Liberty on America's Campuses* (New York: Free Press, 1998), 174.

9. Hemmer, "Eternally Frustrated."

10. *Grutter v. Bollinger*, 539 U.S. 306, Justia, June 23, 2003, https://supreme.justia.com/cases/federal/us/539/306/.

11. "Students for Fair Admissions, Inc. v. President and Fellows of Harvard College (Harvard Corporation)," *Harvard Law Review*, May 10, 2021, https://harvardlawreview.org/2021/05/students-for-fair-admissions-inc-v-president-and-fellows-of-harvard-college/. In January 2022, the Supreme Court agreed to reexamine admissions policies at Harvard University and the University of North Carolina based on prior rulings. Both of those prior rulings upheld considerations for racial diversity in the admissions policies of each institution (Robert Barnes and Nick Anderson, "High Court to Revisit Stance on Affirmative Action," *Washington Post*, January 25, 2022).

12. See Thomas E. Wood and Malcolm J. Sherman, "Is Campus Racial Diversity Correlated with Educational Benefits?," *Academic Questions* 14 (2001): 72–88.

13. The publications of Yale professor of jurisprudence Robert P. George are essential sources of these tropes; see, for example, *The Clash of Orthodoxies: Law, Religion, and Morality in Crisis* (Wilmington, DE: ISI Books, 2001), and *Conscience and Its Enemies: Confronting the Dogmas of Liberal Secularism*, updated and expanded ed. (Wilmington, DE: ISI Books, 2016).

14. Examples of such research in multiple fields, which has accumulated for decades, include Devah Pager and Hana Shepherd, "The Sociology of Discrimination: Racial Discrimination in Employment, Housing, Credit, and Consumer Markets," *Annual Review of Sociology* 34 (2008): 181–209; Danyelle Solomon et al., "Systematic Inequality and Economic Opportunity," Center for American Progress, August 7, 2019, https://www.americanprogress.org/article/systematic-inequality-economic-opportunity/; "Structural Racism in America," Urban Institute, accessed February 5, 2022, https://www.urban.org/features/structural-racism-america; Ruqaiijah Yearby, "The Impact of Structural Racism in Employment and Wages on Minority Women's Health," *Human Rights Magazine* (American Bar Association), vol. 43, no. 3 (2018): https://www.americanbar.org/groups/crsj/publications/human_rights_magazine_home/the-state-of-healthcare-in-the-united-states/minority-womens-health/.

15. Ibram X. Kendi, *Stamped from the Beginning: The Definitive History of Racist Ideas in America* (New York: Nation Books, 2016), 311–312.

16. Kendi, *Stamped*, 426.

17. Kendi, 426.

18. "Apology to People of Color for APA's Role in Promoting, Perpetuating, and Failing to Challenge Racism, Racial Discrimination, and Human Hierarchy in U.S.," American Psychological Association Council of Representatives, October 29, 2021, https://www.apa.org/about/policy/racism-apology.

19. Ezekiel J. Dixon-Román, "Standardized Tests Like SAT and ACT Favor Students with Family Wealth," *Philadelphia Inquirer*, October 29, 2019, https://www.inquirer.com/opinion/commentary/sat-act-standardized-tests-equity-socioeconomic-status-wealth-20191029.html.

20. James Wellemeyer, "Wealthy Parents Spend up to $10,000 on SAT Prep for Their Kids," *MarketWatch*, July 7, 2019, https://www.marketwatch.com/story/some-wealthy-parents-are-dropping-up-to-10000-on-sat-test-prep-for-their-kids-2019-06-21.

21. Greg Lukianoff and Jonathan Haidt, *The Coddling of the American Mind: How Good Intentions and Bad Ideas Are Setting Up a Generation for Failure* (New York: Penguin, 2018), 258.

22. Lukianoff and Haidt, *Coddling*, 254. The authors' reasoning echoes Haidt's separate argument that truth and social justice conflict as campus missions. He reasons that commitments to "social justice" inhibit the pursuit of "truth" (based on viewpoint diversity); see "Why Universities Must Choose One Telos: Truth or Social Justice," Heterodox Academy, October 21, 2016, https://heterodoxacademy.org/blog/one-telos-truth-or-soc ial-justice-2/. In his own prior polemic (*Unlearning Liberty: Campus Censorship and the End of American Debate* [New York: Encounter, 2014], 32–33, 231–32), Lukianoff likens diversity policies to censorship.

23. For example, Lukianoff and Haidt, *Coddling*, 6–10, chapter 2.

24. See, for example, Mark Lilla, *The Shipwrecked Mind: On Political Reaction* (New York: New York Review of Books, 2016); Corey Robin, *The Reactionary Mind: Conservatism from Edmund Burke to Donald Trump*, 2nd ed. (New York: Oxford University Press, 2018).

25. *Regents of Univ. of California v. Bakke*, 438 U.S. 265 (1978), Justia, June 28, 1978, https://supreme.justia.com/cases/federal/us/438/265/.

26. Unfortunately, conservative figures have reverted to such rhetoric in recent election cycles insofar as defenses of European cultural heritage or warnings about the so-called loss of rights for white people have become politically advantageous again (Simon Clark, "How White Supremacy Returned to Mainstream Politics," Center for American Progress, July 1, 2020, https://www.americanprogress.org/article/white-supremacy-returned-mainstream-politics/).

27. Heather MacDonald, *The Diversity Delusion: How Race and Gender Pandering Corrupt the University and Undermine Our Culture* (New York: St. Martin's, 2018).

28. "The Benefits of Socioeconomically and Racially Integrated Schools and Classrooms," The Century Foundation, April 29, 2019, https://tcf.org/content/facts/the-benefits-of-socioe conomically-and-racially-integrated-schools-and-classrooms/#easy-footnote-bottom-1.

29. William G. Bowen and Derek Bok, *The Shape of the River: Long-Term Consequences of Considering Race in College and University Admissions* (Princeton, NJ: Princeton University Press, 1998), 267.

30. Leah Shafter, "The Case for Affirmative Action," Harvard Graduate School of Education, July 11, 2018, https://www.gse.harvard.edu/news/uk/18/07/case-affirmative-action.

31. Scott E. Page, *The Difference: How the Power of Diversity Creates Better Groups, Firms, Schools, and Societies* (Princeton, NJ: Princeton University Press, 2008).

32. Roth, *Safe Enough*, 17, 16.

33. See Nicole Hemmer, *Messengers of the Right: Conservative Media and the Transformation of American Politics* (Philadelphia: University of Pennsylvania Press, 2016), 85–87.

34. "A Case History of Ultra-Liberalism on the Campus," Manion Forum Broadcast #385, February 11, 1962. Hillsdale College is a much-admired institution in national conservative circles; Radio Free Hillsdale (WRFH 101.7), the campus radio station at Hillsdale College, archives some of Manion's broadcasts on its Soundcloud account: https://soundcloud.com/radiofreehillsdale/170104-125442-mz001.

35. William F. Buckley Jr., "Our Mission Statement," *National Review*, November 19, 1955, https://www.nationalreview.com/1955/11/our-mission-statement-william-f-buckley-jr/.

36. Eric Foner, *The Story of American Freedom* (New York: W. W. Norton, 1998), 122–123.

37. "Massive Resistance," Equal Justice Initiative, 2018, https://segregationinamerica.eji.org/report/massive-resistance.html.

38. "A History of Privilege in American Higher Education," Best Colleges, July 17, 2020, https://www.bestcolleges.com/blog/history-privilege-higher-education/.

39. Jonathan Hunt, "Communists and the Classroom: Radicals in U.S. Education, 1930–1960," *Composition Studies* 43, no. 2 (2015): 22–42. See also Erin Blakemore, "Did Communists Really Infiltrate American Schools?," *JSTOR Daily*, December 3, 2020, https://daily.jstor.org/did-communists-really-infiltrate-american-schools/.

40. Hunt, "Communists," 23.

41. "History," Best Colleges.

42. "Telecommunications Act of 1996," Federal Communications Commission, June 20, 2013, https://www.fcc.gov/general/telecommunications-act-1996.

43. For overviews of research on this issue, see Daniel E. Ho and Kevin M. Quinn, "Viewpoint Diversity and Media Consolidation: An Empirical Study," *Stanford Law Review* 61 (2009): 781–868; C. Edwin Baker, "Viewpoint Diversity and Media Ownership," *Federal Communications Law Journal* 61 (2009): 651–672; Gregory L. Rhode, *Minority Broadcast Ownership* (New York: Novinka, 2002).

44. Gadi Wolfsfeld, *Making Sense of Media and Politics: Five Principles in Political Communication* (New York: Routledge, 2011), 10.

45. Jonathan Mermin, "The Media's Independence Problem," *World Policy Journal* 21 (Fall 2004): 69.

46. See Thomas E. Patterson, *Informing the News: The Need for Knowledge-Based Journalism* (New York: Vintage, 2013).

47. W. Lance Bennett, *News: The Politics of Illusion,* 10th ed. (Chicago: University of Chicago Press, 2016), 15.

48. Bobby Allyn, "Facebook Keeps Data Secret, Letting Conservative Bias Claims Persist," National Public Radio, October 5, 2020, https://www.npr.org/2020/10/05/918520692/facebook-keeps-data-secret-letting-conservative-bias-claims-persist.

49. Sara Swann, "Despite Claims of Bias, Conservatives Thrive on Social Media, Study Shows," *Chicago Tribune*, February 1, 2021, https://www.chicagotribune.com/nation-world/ct-nw-conservatives-thrive-social-media-study-shows-20210201-zdscpcewyvha7n3wbt5q76c ywy-story.html.

50. Nancy K. Baym, "Social Media and the Struggle for Society," *Social Media + Society* (April–June 2015): 1–2; Amanda Lotz, "Profit, Not Free Speech, Governs Media Companies' Decisions on Controversy," The Conversation, August 10, 2018, https://theconversation.com/profit-not-free-speech-governs-media-companies-decisions-on-controversy-101292.

51. Shannon Bond, "Federal Trade Commission Refiles Suit Accusing Facebook of Illegal Monopoly," National Public Radio, August 19, 2021, https://www.npr.org/2021/08/19/102 9310979/federal-trade-commission-refiles-suit-accusing-facebook-of-illegal-monopoly.

52. Cristiano Lima, "A Whistleblower's Power: Four Key Takeaways from the Facebook Papers," *Washington Post*, October 26, 2021.

53. Some of Bret Stephens's opinions illustrate the resurgence of such erroneous ideas in academia and the media. He published an op-ed titled "The Secrets of Jewish Genius [Correction]" (*New York Times*, December 28, 2019). Stephens originally cited an anthropological paper to support his core premise about allegedly high levels of intelligence among Ashkenazi Jews relative to other ethnic groups. The subsequent republication of Stephens's column with a lengthy and elaborate editor's note conceded that at least one of the paper's authors was known to promote racist views in his work. The Southern Poverty

Law Center describes the author in question, former University of Utah anthropologist Henry Harpending, as a white nationalist whose work posits "the evolution" of "racial differences" as "the driving force behind all of modern history," and also as an advocate of eugenics ("Henry Harpending," Southern Poverty Law Center, accessed February 5, 2022, https://www.splcenter.org/fighting-hate/extremist-files/individual/henry-harpending). The editor's note attached to Stephens's column explained that the content of Harpending's and his coauthors' paper left "an impression with many readers that Mr. Stephens was arguing that Jews are genetically superior." The theory of Jewish genetic superiority is a common anti-Semitic trope; it appears in propaganda about alleged Jewish masterminds who secretly control financial institutions and the media. Hence the relevant intersection: many contemporary complaints about restrictions on free speech in academia concern scholars who attempt to promote scientifically false, often racist or anti-Semitic views as important new ideas; and figures in the media assist their cause by taking their so-called research or defenses of free speech at face value. For more, see Matthew Yglesias, "The Controversy over Bret Stephens's Jewish Genius Column, Explained," *Vox*, December 30, 2019, https://www.vox.com/policy-and-politics/2019/12/30/21042733/bret-stephens-jewish-iq-new-york-times.

54. Angela Saini, "Why Race Science Is on the Rise Again," *The Guardian*, May 18, 2019, https://www.theguardian.com/books/2019/may/18/race-science-on-the-rise-angela-saini;   see her *Superior: The Return of Race Science* (Boston: Beacon Press, 2019).

55. The much-publicized case of sociologist Noah Carl is a prime example. Cambridge University dismissed Carl in 2019 for promoting ideas about inherent racial differences as legitimate science. In some cases, those ideas overlapped with extremist propaganda. Noah protested his dismissal, and supporters defended him as an advocate of free speech (Sani, "Race Science"). Carl's case reflects a larger trend of university-affiliated scholars promoting erroneous arguments about the alleged meaning of racial differences as a defense of free speech. See, for example, Nathan Confas, "Research on Group Differences in Intelligence: A Defense of Free Inquiry," *Philosophical Psychology* 33 (2020): 125–147.

56. "About," *Quillette*, 2022, https://quillette.com/about/.

57. See Michael Biggs, "How Feminism Paved the Way for Transgenderism," *Quillette*, August 1, 2019, https://quillette.com/2019/08/01/how-feminism-paved-the-way-for-transgenderism/; Brian Boutwell and Kevin Beaver, "Criminology's Wonderland," *Quillette*, March 31, 2016, https://quillette.com/2016/03/31/criminologys-wonderland-why-almost-everything-you-know-about-crime-is-wrong/; Robert Plomin, "What Does Genetic Research Tell Us about Equal Opportunity and Meritocracy?," *Quillette*, October 15, 2018, https://quillette.com/2018/10/15/what-does-genetic-research-tell-us-about-equal-opportunity-and-meritocracy/; Bo Winegard and Ben Winegard, "A Tale of Two Bell Curves," *Quillette*, March 27, 2017, https://quillette.com/2017/03/27/a-tale-of-two-bell-curves/.

58. Donna Minkowitz, "Why Racists (and Liberals!) Keep Writing for *Quillette*," *The Nation*, December 5, 2019, https://www.thenation.com/article/archive/quillette-fascist-creep/.

59. National Human Genome Research Institute, Human Genome Project, December 22, 2020, https://www.genome.gov/human-genome-project.

60. See D. J. Witherspoon et al., "Genetic Similarities within and between Human Populations," *Genetics* 176 (May 2007): 351–359.

61. Witherspoon et al., "Genetic Similarities," explain a key sleight of hand on which race science relies. Minor genomic differences can be useful for classifying data according to specific populations, but those minor differences do not indicate superior or inferior genetics

between populations. Neither do such minor genomic differences contradict the fact that human genetic variations between populations is slight.

Chapter 2

1. Colleen Flaherty, "Trigger Unhappy," *Inside Higher Ed*, April 14, 2014, http://www.insideh ighered.com/news/2014/04/14/oberlin-backs-down-trigger-warnings-professors-who-teach-sensitive-material?utm_source=slate&utm_medium=referral&utm_term=part ner#sthash.7M9oFb0K.dpbs.

2. Editorial Board, "Warning: College Students, This Editorial May Upset You," *Los Angeles Times*, March 31, 2014, https://www.latimes.com/nation/la-ed-trigger-warnings-20140 331-story.html.

3. Judith Shulevitz, "In College and Hiding from Scary Ideas," *New York Times*, March 21, 2015, https://www.nytimes.com/2015/03/22/opinion/sunday/judith-shulevitz-hiding-from-scary-ideas.html.

4. A local newspaper chronicled events that led to the protests, the nature of student demands, and the historic consequences of student advocacy: Emma Vandelinder, "Racial Climate at MU: A Timeline of Incidents in Fall 2015," *Columbia Missourian*, November 6, 2015, https://www.columbiamissourian.com/news/higher_education/racial-climate-at-mu-a-timeline-of-incidents-in-fall-2015/article_0c96f986-84c6-11e5-a38f-2bd0aab0bf74.html.

5. Conor Friedersdorf, "Campus Activists Weaponize 'Safe Space,'" *The Atlantic*, November 10, 2015, https://www.theatlantic.com/politics/archive/2015/11/how-campus-activists-are-weaponizing-the-safe-space/415080/.

6. Jermaine Terrell Starr, "What the Press Didn't Get about Mizzou's Protests," *Washington Post*, December 15, 2015.

7. Nicole Hemmer, "Eternally Frustrated by 'Liberal' Universities, Conservatives Now Want to Tear Them Down," *Vox*, March 8, 2017, https://www.vox.com/the-big-idea/2017/3/7/ 14841292/liberal-universities-conservative-faculty-sizzler-pc.

8. William F. Buckley, *God and Man at Yale: The Superstitions of "Academic Freedom"* (Washington, DC: Regnery, 1951).

9. A keyword search for "viewpoint diversity" conducted on Nexis Uni, for example, from 2000 to 2019 shows the number of annual appearances of the phrase in both academic and popular periodicals averaged in the 30s and 40s from 2000 until 2015. But more than 100 results were returned for 2016, closely following the events at Oberlin College and the University of Missouri; 305 in 2017; and 253 in 2018.

10. "About," *Quillette*, 2022, https://quillette.com/about/.

11. "About Us," Heterodox Academy, 2022, https://heterodoxacademy.org/about-us/.

12. Hemmer, "Eternally Frustrated."

13. Jonathan Chait, "Not a Very P.C. Thing to Say: How the Language Police Are Perverting Liberalism," *New York*, January 27, 2015, http://nymag.com/intelligencer/2015/01/not-a-very-pc-thing-to-say.html?gtm=bottom&gtm=bottom. See also Jonathan Chait, "The 'Shut It Down!' Left and the War on the Liberal Mind, " *New York*, April 26, 2017, http:// nymag.com/daily/intelligencer/2017/04/the-shut-it-down-left-and-the-war-on-the-libe ral-mind.html.

14. Greg Lukianoff and Jonathan Haidt, "The Coddling of the American Mind," *The Atlantic*, September 2015, https://www.theatlantic.com/magazine/archive/2015/09/the-coddling-of-the-american-mind/399356/.

15. Carlo Davis, "Oberlin Amends Its Trigger-Warning Policy," *The New Republic*, April 9, 2014, https://newrepublic.com/article/117320/oberlin-amends-its-trigger-warning-policy.

16. Lindsay Holmes, "A Quick Lesson on What Trigger Warnings Actually Do," *Huffington Post*, February 6, 2017, https://www.huffpost.com/entry/university-of-chicago-trigger-warning_n_57bf16d9e4b085c1ff28176d; National Coalition Against Censorship, "What's All This about Trigger Warnings?," December 2015, https://ncac.org/wp-content/uploads/2015/11/NCAC-TriggerWarningReport.pdf.

17. Holmes, "Quick Lesson"; National Coalition Against Censorship, "Trigger Warnings?" Sloppy journalistic claims persistently make trigger warnings appear, quantitatively speaking, much more prevalent than they might be. One article reports, "About half U.S. professors use trigger warnings" (Olga Khazan, "The Real Problem with Trigger Warnings," *The Atlantic*, March 28, 2019, https://www.theatlantic.com/health/archive/2019/03/do-trigger-warnings-work/585871/). There is no way to know that information definitively (universities do not keep records on which professors use trigger warnings), and the source of that claim makes no such assertion. The original source is a single voluntary survey in 2016 sent to various institutions, which yielded approximately eight hundred responses (Anya Kamentz, "Half of Professors in NPR Ed Survey Have Used 'Trigger Warnings,'" National Public Radio, September 7, 2016, https://www.npr.org/sections/ed/2016/09/07/492979242/half-of-professors-in-npr-ed-survey-have-used-trigger-warnings). The results of that study do not support a general claim about how often all professors use trigger warnings or not.

18. Benjamin W. Bellet, Payton J. Jones, and Richard J. McNally, "Trigger Warning: Empirical Evidence Ahead," *Journal of Behavior Therapy and Experimental Psychology* 61 (2018): 134–141.

19. Pamela B. Paresky, "Harvard Study: Trigger Warnings Might Coddle the Mind," *Psychology Today*, August 3, 2018, https://www.psychologytoday.com/us/blog/happiness-and-the-pursuit-leadership/201808/harvard-study-trigger-warnings-might-coddle-the.

20. Wesley Lowery and Michael A. Fletcher, "'The Michael Brown Shooting Changed My Life,'" *Washington Post*, November 22, 2015, https://www.washingtonpost.com/business/economy/the-michael-brown-shooting-changed-my-life/2015/11/22/4ad12b94-8bac-11e5-acff-673ae92ddd2b_story.html?utm_term=.663564bfdbec; Arial Ruffin, "MU Community Creates Group Supporting Michael Brown," KOMU News, August 25, 2014, https://www.komu.com/news/mu-community-creates-group-supporting-michael-brown.

21. Michael Pearson, "A Timeline of the University of Missouri Protests," CNN, November 10, 2015, https://www.cnn.com/2015/11/09/us/missouri-protest-timeline/index.html.

22. Niraj Chokshi, "Militarized Police in Ferguson Unsettles Some; Pentagon Gives Cities Equipment," *Washington Post*, August 14, 2014, https://www.washingtonpost.com/politics/militarized-police-in-ferguson-unsettles-some-pentagon-gives-cities-equipment/2014/08/14/4651f670-2401-11e4-86ca-6f03cbd15c1a_story.html?utm_term=.f533148e9ef5.

23. Pearson, "Timeline"; Vandelinder, "Racial Climate"; Arial Ruffin, "MU Community Creates Group Supporting Michael Brown," KOMU News, August 25, 2014, https://www.komu.com/news/mu-community-creates-group-supporting-michael-brown.

24. Karen L. Cox, *No Common Ground: Confederate Monuments and the Ongoing Fight for Racial Justice* (Chapel Hill: University of North Carolina Press, 2021), 105.

25. See Adam H. Domby, *The False Cause: Fraud, Fabrication, and White Supremacy in Confederate Memory* (Charlottesville: University of Virginia Press, 2020); Stephen H. Monroe, *Heritage and Hate: Old South Rhetoric at Southern Universities* (Tuscaloosa: University of Alabama Press, 2021).

26. Hauser, Christine, "An Alabama Building Honors a Klan Leader," *New York Times*, February 8, 2022, https://www.nytimes.com/2022/02/08/us/alabama-kkk-autherine-lucy-foster.html.

27. Quoted in Domby, *False*, 19.

28. Domby, *False*, chapter 1.

29. See James W. Loewen and Edward H. Sebesta, eds., *The Confederate and Neo-Confederate Reader: The "Great Truth" about the "Lost Cause"* (Jackson: University of Mississippi Press, 2010).

30. Eric Foner, *The Story of American Freedom* (New York: W. W. Norton, 1998), 132.

31. Monroe, *Heritage*, 12.

32. "Massive Resistance," Equal Justice Initiative, 2018, https://segregationinamerica.eji.org/report/massive-resistance.html.

33. Monroe, *Heritage*, 12.

34. Joe Hernandez, "School Leaders Say HBCUs Are Undeterred after a Series of Bomb Threats," National Public Radio, February 8, 2022, https://www.npr.org/2022/02/08/1079294424/hbcu-bomb-threats-black-colleges.

35. Monroe, *Heritage*, 107–109.

36. Monroe, *Heritage*, 100.

37. Monroe, *Heritage*, 91.

38. Pearson, "Timeline"; Vandelinder, "Racial Climate."

39. See Monroe, *Heritage*, chapter 3.

40. Jason M. Vaughn, "Mizzou Protesters: Stay out of Our 'Safe Space' or We'll Call the Cops," *The Daily Beast*, November 9, 2015, https://www.thedailybeast.com/mizzou-protesters-stay-out-of-our-safe-space-or-well-call-the-cops.

41. Starr, "What the Press."

42. Ruth Marcus, "College Is Not for Coddling," *Washington Post*, November 10, 2015.

43. Kathleen Parker, "The 'Swaddled Generation,'" *Washington Post*, May 19, 2015. See also Catherine Rampell, "Wondering Whether Today's College Students Have Become Too Fragile?," *Washington Post*, May 13, 2016, https://www.washingtonpost.com/news/rampage/wp/2016/05/13/wondering-whether-todays-college-students-have-become-too-fragile-read-this-document/?utm_term=.1843bd1b88cc.

44. The colloquialism "safe space" is used in select contexts in higher education, but not in the manner that many media personalities claim. Faculty sometimes encourage students to share their views, regardless of social or political orientation, in the classroom to encourage openness for all perspectives. On-campus centers or offices that assist vulnerable student populations also use the colloquialism to assure students that they can seek assistance (for disability supports, to report an assault, or mental health issues, and so on) without fear of judgment or prejudice.

45. Office of the Dean of Students, University of Chicago, Welcome Letter to Class of 2020, August 2016, https://news.uchicago.edu/sites/default/files/attachments/Dear_Class_of_2020_Students.pdf.

46. Bret Stephens, "Our Best University President," *New York Times*, October 20, 2017.

47. Alex Morey, "University of Chicago's 'Academic Freedom' Letter a Win for Campus Speech," Foundation for Individual Rights in Education, August 25, 2016, https://www.thefire.org/u-chicagos-academic-freedom-letter-a-win-for-campus-speech/; Roger Pilon, "The University of Chicago Has No Room for Cyberbullies," *Cato Blog*, August 25, 2016, https://www.cato.org/blog/university-chicago-has-no-room-crybullies.

48. The contents of the letter reflected the work of a commission on campus speech and open intellectual inquiry that the university president convened in the months prior to August 2016. The purpose of the commission was to discuss university climate and policies amid growing national reports about campus activism.

49. Michael S. Roth, *Safe Enough Spaces: A Pragmatist's Guide to Inclusion, Free Speech, and Political Correctness on College Campuses* (New Haven, CT: Yale University Press, 2019), 25.

50. Report of the Committee on University Discipline for Disruptive Conduct, Provost, University of Chicago, June 2, 2017, https://provost.uchicago.edu/sites/default/files/DCCRevisedFinal%20%286-2-2017%29.pdf.

51. Sigal R. Ben-Porath, *Free Speech on Campus* (Philadelphia: University of Pennsylvania Press, 2017), 44.

52. "Adopting the Chicago Statement," Foundation for Individual Rights in Education, accessed February 5, 2022, https://www.thefire.org/get-involved/student-network/take-action/adopting-the-chicago-statement/.

53. See, for example, John Dewey, *Democracy and Education* (Mineola, NY: Dover Books, 2004).

Chapter 3

1. Frank D. LoMonte, "The Legislative Response to a Perceived 'Free Speech Crisis' on Campus," *Communications Lawyer* 34 (Winter 2019): 7–11.

2. Ben Mathis-Lilley, "Sweet Jesus, Will the NYT's Conservatives Ever Write about Anything but the 'Intolerant Left' Ever Again?," *Slate*, March 9, 2018, https://slate.com/news-and-politics/2018/03/david-brooks-times-conservatives.html.

3. See, for example, "Campus Speech," *The Federalist*, accessed February 9, 2022, http://thefederalist.com/tag/campus-speech/; Douglas Belkin, "Fear of Violent Protests Raises Cost of Free Speech on Campus," *Wall Street Journal*, October 22, 2017, https://www.wsj.com/articles/fear-of-violent-protests-raises-cost-of-free-speech-on-campus-1508670000; Jonathan Haidt and Greg Lukianoff, "Why It's a Bad Idea to Tell Students Words Are Violence," *The Atlantic*, July 18, 2017, https://www.theatlantic.com/education/archive/2017/07/why-its-a-bad-idea-to-tell-students-words-are-violence/533970/; Stanley Kurtz, "The Campus Free-Speech Crisis Deepens," *National Review*, September 27, 2017, https://www.nationalreview.com/corner/campus-free-speech-crisis-deepens/; Megan McArdle, "Campus Speech Is Threatened. but How Much?," *Washington Post*, April 13, 2018, https://www.washingtonpost.com/blogs/post-partisan/wp/2018/04/13/campus-free-speech-is-threatened-but-how-much/?utm_term=.248fbb950a76.

4. See Bradley Campbell and Jason Manning, *The Rise of Victimhood Culture: Microaggressions, Safe Spaces, and the New Culture Wars* (Cham, Switzerland: Palgrave Macmillan, 2018); Greg Lukianoff and Jonathan Haidt, *The Coddling of the American Mind: How Good Intentions and Bad Ideas Are Setting Up a Generation for Failure* (New York: Penguin,

2018); John Palfrey, *Safe Spaces, Brave Spaces: Diversity and Free Expression in Education* (Cambridge, MA: MIT Press, 2017).

Keith E. Whittington, *Speak Freely: Why Universities Must Defend Free Speech* (Princeton. NJ: Princeton University Press, 2018).

5. David Brooks, "Understanding Student Mobbists," *New York Times*, March 9, 2018.

6. David Brooks, "The Rise of the Amphibians," *New York Times*, February 16, 2018.

7. Bret Stephens, "The Dying Art of Disagreement," *New York Times*, September 24, 2017, https://www.nytimes.com/2017/09/24/opinion/dying-art-of-disagreement.html.

8. A variety of recent works from multiple academic fields illustrate such emphases on managing difficult conversations: Ulrich Baer, *What Snowflakes Get Right: Free Speech, Truth and Equality on Campus* (New York: Oxford University Press, 2019); Sigal R. Ben-Porath, *Free Speech on Campus* (Philadelphia: University of Pennsylvania Press, 2017); Erwin Chemerinsky and Howard Gillman, *Free Speech on Campus* (New Haven, CT: Yale University Press, 2017); Palfrey, *Safe Spaces, Brave Spaces*; Michael S. Roth, *Safe Enough Spaces: A Pragmatist's Approach to Inclusion, Free Speech, and Political Correctness on College Campuses* (New Haven, CT: Yale University Press, 2019). Other useful resources include special issues of academic journals devoted to these topics (see, for instance, Christina E. Wells, "The First Amendment, the University and Conflict: An Introduction to the Symposium," *Journal of Dispute Resolution 2* [2018]: 1–5) and the Pen America "Campus Free Speech Guide," accessed February 5, 2022, https://campusfreespeechguide.pen.org/.

9. For more information on this incident, see "Statement on the Christina Hoff Sommers Event at the Law School," *Lewis and Clark News*, March 9, 2018, https://www.lclark.edu/live/news/38367-statement-on-the-christina-hoff-sommers-event-at.

10. Bari Weiss, "We're All Fascists Now," *New York Times*, March 7, 2018, https://www.nytimes.com/2018/03/07/opinion/were-all-fascists-now.html.

11. Nicholas Kristoff, "Stop the Knee-Jerk Liberalism That Hurts Its Own Cause," *New York Times*, June 29, 2019, https://www.nytimes.com/2019/06/29/opinion/sunday/liberalism-united-states.html. In a 2016 column, Kristoff depicted events at Oberlin College as representative of universities in general (Nicholas Kristoff, "The Dangers of Echo Chambers on Campus," *New York Times*, December 10, 2016, https://www.nytimes.com/2016/12/10/opinion/sunday/the-dangers-of-echo-chambers-on-campus.html).

12. "*The Atlantic* Begins 'The Speech Wars' Reporting Project," *The Atlantic*, November 28, 2018, https://www.theatlantic.com/press-releases/archive/2018/11/the-atlantic-begins-the-speech-wars-reporting-project/576805/.

13. Andrew Sullivan, "We All Live on Campus Now," *New York Magazine*, February 9, 2018, https://nymag.com/intelligencer/2018/02/we-all-live-on-campus-now.html.

14. Anne Applebaum, "The New Puritans," *The Atlantic*, August 31, 2021, https://www.theatlantic.com/magazine/archive/2021/10/new-puritans-mob-justice-canceled/619818/.

15. Noah Rothman, *Unjust: Social Justice and the Unmaking of America* (Washington, DC: Gateway Editions, 2019), 3.

16. Robby Soave, *Panic Attack: Young Radicals in the Age of Trump* (New York: All Points, 2019), 71–73, 262.

17. Institute for Propaganda Analysis, "How to Detect Propaganda," in *Propaganda*, ed. Robert Jackall (New York: New York University Press, 1995), 219.

18. Out of the cited examples, Brooks was the rare columnist to directly quote a student.

19. In his February 2018 column ("Dying Art"), Stephens reproduced a student quotation from a school newspaper from several years prior.

20. Moira Weigel, "*The Coddling of the American Mind* Review—How Elite US Liberals Have Turned Rightwards," *The Guardian*, September 20, 2018, https://www.theguard ian.com/books/2018/sep/20/the-coddling-of-the-american-mind-review. Weigel deftly identified the reactionary, elitist, and self-consciously stylistic qualities of this discourse early on.

21. "Frequently Asked Questions," University of Austin, accessed February 5, 2022, https://www.uaustin.org/faq.

22. "News and Updates," University of Austin, accessed February 5, 2022, https://www.uaustin.org/news.

23. Heather Heying, "Can the University of Austin Spark a New Enlightenment?," *The Spectator*, November 18, 2021, https://spectatorworld.com/topic/university-austin-spark-new-enlightenment/; Ayaan Hirsi Ali, "American Education Needs a Revolution," UnHerd, November 11, 2021, https://unherd.com/2021/11/american-education-needs-a-revolut ion/; Joanna Williams, "The University of Austin Puts the Rest of Academia to Shame," *Spiked*, November 9, 2021, https://www.spiked-online.com/2021/11/09/the-university-of-austin-puts-the-rest-of-academia-to-shame/.

24. "Polish Ultra-conservatives Launch University to Mould New Elites," Reuters, May 28, 2021, https://www.reuters.com/world/polish-ultra-conservatives-launch-university-mould-new-elites-2021-05-28/.

25. "Who We Are," Ordo Iuris International Academy, accessed February 5, 2022, https://en.ordoiuris.pl/who-we-are.

26. "Polish," Reuters.

27. Elissa Nadworny, "As Elite Campuses Diversity, A 'Bias toward Privilege Exists," National Public Radio, March 5, 2019, https://www.npr.org/2019/03/05/699977122/as-elite-campu ses-diversify-a-bias-towards-privilege-persists.

Chapter 4

1. Robert P. Abelson, *Statistics as Principled Argument* (Hillsdale, NJ: Lawrence Erlbaum, 1995), 1.

2. Abelson, *Statistics*, xii.

3. See Abelson, chapter 1.

4. Erika Andersen, "True Fact: The Lack of Pirates Is Causing Global Warming," *Forbes*, March 23, 2012, https://www.forbes.com/sites/erikaandersen/2012/03/23/true-fact-the-lack-of-pirates-is-causing-global-warming/?fbclid=IwAR092jre-g0CMThJpzyNO2NQEpn3mXQd HLtqKlkhqGq8gSEeLogDjcbJdVg#b9a60423a679; Tyler Vigen, *Spurious Correlations* (New York: Hatchette, 2015).

5. See, for example, Tim Elmore, "What's Happening to College Students Today?," *Psychology Today*, November 30, 2015, https://www.psychologytoday.com/us/blog/artificial-matur ity/201511/what-s-happening-college-students-today.

6. Jean M. Twenge, *iGen: Why Today's Super-Connected Kids Are Growing Up Less Rebellious, More Tolerant, Less Happy—and Completely Unprepared for Adulthood—and What That Means for the Rest of Us*, reprint ed. (New York: Atria, 2017). See also Twenge's *Generation Me: Why Today's Young Americans Are More Confident, Assertive, Entitled—and More Miserable Than Ever*, rev. and updated ed. (New York: Atria, 2014).

7. Greg Lukianoff and Jonathan Haidt, *The Coddling of the American Mind: How Good Intentions and Bad Ideas Are Setting Up a Generation for Failure* (New York: Penguin, 2018), 24.

8. Lukianoff and Haidt, *Coddling*, 30.

9. See Lukianoff and Haidt, *Coddling*, chapter 7.

10. Nirmita Panchal et al., "The Implications of COVID-19 for Mental Health and Substance Use," Kaiser Family Foundation, February 10, 2021, https://www.kff.org/coronavi rus-covid-19/issue-brief/the-implications-of-covid-19-for-mental-health-and-substa nce-use/.

11. Amy Orben and Andrew K. Przybylski, "The Association between Adolescent Well-Being and Digital Technology Use," *Nature Human Behaviour* 3 (2019): 173–182.

12. Lydia Denworth, "The Kids (Who Use Tech) Seem to Be All Right," *Scientific American*, January 15, 2019, https://www.scientificamerican.com/article/the-kids-who-use-tech-seem-to-be-all-right/?redirect = 1.

13. Jacob Cohen, "The Earth Is Round (p < .05)," *American Psychologist* 49 (1994): 1001.

14. See also William H. O'Brien, Mary E. Kaplar, and Jennifer J. McGrath, "Broadly Based Causal Models of Behavior Disorders," in *Comprehensive Handbook of Psychological Assessment,* Volume 3: *Behavioral Assessment*, ed. Stephen N. Haynes and Elaine M. Heiby, 69–93 (Hoboken, NJ: Wiley, 2003).

15. Andrew Guess, Jonathan Nagler, and Joshua Tucker, "Less Than You Think: Prevalence and Predictors of Fake News Dissemination on Facebook," *Science Advances* 5 (2019), https://advances.sciencemag.org/content/5/1/eaau4586.

16. For helpful overviews of these trends in campus activism, see Chris Quintana, "Even in Fascism's Heyday, Anti-Fascists on Campus Were Controversial," *Chronicle of Higher Education*, April 12, 2017, https://www.chronicle.com/article/Even-in-Fascism-s-Heyday/239761; Angus Johnston, "Student Protests, Then and Now," *Chronicle of Higher Education*, December 11, 2015, https://www.chronicle.com/article/Student-Protests-ThenNow/234542.

17. Elspeth Reeve, "Every Every Every Generation Has Been the Me Me Me Generation," *The Atlantic*, May 9, 2013, https://www.theatlantic.com/national/archive/2013/05/me-generat ion-time/315151/.

18. Brent W. Roberts, Grant Edmonds, and Emily Grijalva, "It Is Developmental Me, Not Generation Me: Developmental Changes Are More Important Than Generational Changes in Narcissism," *Perspectives on Psychological Science* 5 (2010): 97.

19. Eunike Wetzel et al., "The Narcissism Epidemic Is Dead; Long Live the Narcissism Epidemic," *Psychological Science* 28 (2017): 1834.

20. Nick Roll, "The Kids Are Alright," *Inside Higher Ed*, October 13, 2017, https://www.ins idehighered.com/news/2017/10/13/research-says-college-students-no-more-narcissistic-previous-generations-age.

21. W. Lance Bennett, *News: The Politics of Illusion*, 10th ed. (Chicago: University of Chicago Press, 2016), 62–63.

22. Bennett, *News*, 62–63.

23. John Villasenor, "Views among College Students Regarding the First Amendment: Results from a New Survey," Brookings Institution, September 18, 2017, https://www.brookings. edu/blog/fixgov/2017/09/18/views-among-college-students-regarding-the-first-amendm ent-results-from-a-new-survey/.

24. Catherine Rampell, "A Chilling Study Shows How Hostile College Students Are toward Free Speech," *Washington Post*, September 18, 2017, https://www.washingtonpost.com/opini ons/a-chilling-study-shows-how-hostile-college-students-are-toward-free-speech/2017/ 09/18/cbb1a234-9ca8-11e7-9083-fbfddf6804c2_story.html?utm_term=.ae6f0aa167d8.

25. Terry Eastland, "Survey Confirms What Many Suspected: Free Speech Is in Trouble," *Weekly Standard*, September 20, 2017, https://www.weeklystandard.com/terry-eastland/ survey-confirms-what-many-suspected-free-speech-is-in-trouble.

26. Editorial Board, "James Madison Weeps," *Wall Street Journal*, September 19, 2017.

27. Lois Beckett, "'Junk Science': Experts Cast Doubt on Widely Cited College Free Speech Survey," *The Guardian*, September 22, 2017, https://www.theguardian.com/us-news/2017/ sep/22/college-free-speech-violence-survey-junk-science.

28. Villasenor said he planned "to publish a detailed analysis of the results in an academic paper," but "the timeliness of the topic" mandated immediate release of his findings (Villasenor, "Views").

29. Jeffrey Adam Sachs, "The 'Campus Free Speech Crisis' Is a Myth," *Washington Post*, March 16, 2018, https://www.washingtonpost.com/news/monkey-cage/wp/2018/03/16/the-cam pus-free-speech-crisis-is-a-myth-here-are-the-facts/?utm_term=.e4756b5b4588.

30. Abelson, *Statistics*, 155, 133.

31. Abelson, 132.

32. Benjamin W. Bellet et al., "Trigger Warning: Empirical Evidence Ahead," *Journal of Behavior Therapy and Experimental Psychology* 61 (2018): 134–141, https://www.sciencedir ect.com/science/article/pii/S0005791618301137?via%3Dihub.

33. Tom Ciccota, "Harvard Study: Trigger Warnings Increase Anxiety over 'Distressing' Content," *Breitbart*, July 30, 2018, https://www.breitbart.com/tech/2018/07/30/harv ard-study-trigger-warnings-increase-anxiety-over-distressing-content/; "Harvard Study: Trigger Warnings Actually Harmful to Students," *The College Fix*, July 29, 2018, https://www.thecollegefix.com/harvard-study-trigger-warnings-actually-harmful-to- students/; Ashe Schow, "STUDY: 'Trigger Warnings' Are Harmful to College Students," *The Daily Wire,* July 28, 2018, https://www.dailywire.com/news/33720/study-trigger-warni ngs-are-harmful-college-ashe-schow; Katherine Timpf, "Trigger Warnings Might Be Harmful, a Study Concludes," *National Review*, July 31, 2018, https://www.nationalreview. com/2018/07/study-says-trigger-warnings-might-harm-readers/.

34. Pamela B. Paresky, "Harvard Study: Trigger Warnings Might Coddle the Mind," *Psychology Today*, August 3, 2018, https://www.psychologytoday.com/us/blog/happiness-and-the- pursuit-leadership/201808/harvard-study-trigger-warnings-might-coddle-the.

35. Cynthia Meyersburg, "Harvard Study: Trigger Warnings May Impede Resilience," Foundation for Individual Rights in Education, August 1, 2018, https://www.thefire.org/ harvard-study-trigger-warnings-may-impede-resilience/.

36. Amazon Mechanical Turk, "Amazon Mechanical Turk," *Mturk*, accessed February 5, 2022, https://www.mturk.com/.

37. Lindsay Holmes, "A Quick Lesson on What Trigger Warnings Actually Do," *Huffington Post*, February 6, 2017, https://www.huffpost.com/entry/university-of-chicago-trigger- warning_n_57bf16d9e4b085c1ff28176d; "What's All This about Trigger Warnings?," National Coalition Against Censorship, December 2015, https://ncac.org/wp-content/ uploads/2015/11/NCAC-TriggerWarningReport.pdf.

38. Payton Jones, "Trigger Warning: Empirical Evidence Ahead," Heterodox Academy, September 12, 2018, https://heterodoxacademy.org/blog/trigger-warning-empirical-evidence-ahead/.

39. Abelson, *Statistics*, 10.

40. Mevagh Sanson, Deryn Strange, and Maryanne Gary, "Trigger Warnings Are Trivially Helpful at Reducing Negative Affect, Intrusive Thoughts, and Avoidance," *Clinical Psychological Science* (March 4, 2019): 778–793.

41. Sanson et al., "Trigger Warnings," 778.

42. Subsequent commentaries on trigger warnings continued to follow these patterns; see, for example, Olga Khazan, "The Real Problem with Trigger Warnings," *The Atlantic*, March 28, 2019, https://www.theatlantic.com/health/archive/2019/03/do-trigger-warnings-work/585871/; Shannon Palus, "The Latest Study on Trigger Warnings Finally Convinced Me They're Not Worth It," *Slate*, July 12, 2019, https://slate.com/technology/2019/07/trigger-warnings-research-shows-they-dont-work-might-hurt.html.

43. Sanson et al., "Trigger Warnings," 791.

44. Payton Jones, Benjamin Bellet, and Richard McNally, "Helping or Harming? The Effect of Trigger Warnings on Individuals with Trauma Histories," OSF Preprints, July 10, 2019, https://osf.io/axn6z/.

45. See Greg Lukianoff and Jonathan Haidt, "The Coddling of the American Mind," *The Atlantic*, September 2015, https://www.theatlantic.com/magazine/archive/2015/09/the-coddling-of-the-american-mind/399356/.

46. See, for example, classic works like William A. Belson, *The Design and Understanding of Survey Questions* (Aldershot, UK: Gower, 1981), and Seymour Sudman and Norman M. Bradburn, *Asking Questions: A Practical Guide to Questionnaire Design* (San Francisco: Jossey-Bass, 1982).

47. Fritz Strack and Norbert Schwarz, "Asking Questions: Measurement in the Social Sciences," in *Psychology's Territories: Historical and Contemporary Perspectives from Different Disciplines*, ed. Mitchell Ash and Thomas Sturm (Mahwah, NJ: Lawrence Erlbaum, 2007), 238.

48. "5 Common Survey Question Mistakes That'll Ruin Your Data," SurveyMonkey.com, accessed February 5, 2022, https://www.surveymonkey.com/mp/5-common-survey-mistakes-ruin-your-data/.

49. Knight Foundation 2017 College Student Survey, Knight Foundation (Washington, DC: Gallup, 2017), https://kf-site-production.s3.amazonaws.com/media_elements/files/000/000/147/original/Knight_Foundation_2017_Student_Survey_Questionnaire_1_.pdf.

50. Strack and Schwarz, "Asking," 229.

51. Phil Garland, "Question Order Matters," Survey Monkey, accessed February 5, 2022, https://www.surveymonkey.com/curiosity/question-order-matters/.

52. S. T. Stevens et al., "The Campus Expression Survey: A Heterodox Academy Project," 2017, https://2cnzc91figkyqqeq8390pgd1-wpengine.netdna-ssl.com/wp-content/uploads/2018/02/HxA-Campus-Expression-Survey-Guide.pdf.

53. Stevens et al., "Campus Expression."

54. Strack and Schwarz, "Asking," 229, 238. See also William A. Belson, *The Design and Understanding of Survey Questions* (Aldershot, UK: Gower, 1981); Stanley Le Baron Payne, *The Art of Asking Questions* (Princeton, NJ: Princeton University Press, 1951); Howard Schuman et al., "Context Effects on Survey Responses to Questions About Abortion," *Public Opinion Quarterly* vol. 45, no. 2 (Summer 1981): 216–223; Norbert Schwarz and Seymour

Sudman, eds., *Context Effects in Social and Psychological Research* (New York: Springer-Verlag, 1992).

55. Strack and Schwarz, "Asking," 232.
56. Strack and Schwarz, 230.
57. Stevens et al., "Campus Expression."
58. "Writing the Experimental Report: Methods, Results, and Discussion," Purdue Online Writing Lab, accessed February 5, 2022, https://owl.purdue.edu/owl/subject_specific_writ ing/writing_in_the_social_sciences/writing_in_psychology_experimental_report_writ ing/experimental_reports_2.html.
59. "User's Guide to FIRE's Disinvitation Database," Foundation for Individual Rights in Education, accessed February 5, 2022, https://www.thefire.org/research/disinvitation-database/users-guide-to-fires-campus-disinvitation-database/.
60. Brooks Jackson and Kathleen Hall Jamieson, *unSpun: Finding Facts in a World of Disinformation* (New York: Random House, 2007), 105.
61. Conor Friedersdorf, "The Glaring Evidence That Free Speech Is Threatened on Campus," *The Atlantic*, March 4, 2016, https://www.theatlantic.com/politics/archive/2016/03/the-glaring-evidence-that-free-speech-is-threatened-on-campus/471825/.
62. "Spotlight on Speech Codes 2017," Foundation for Individual Rights in Education, accessed February 5, 2022, https://www.thefire.org/spotlight/reports/spotlight-on-speech-codes-2017/.
63. Aaron R. Hanlon, "Why Colleges Have a Right to Reject Hateful Speakers Like Ann Coulter," *New Republic*, April 24, 2017, https://newrepublic.com/article/142218/colleges-right-reject-hateful-speakers-like-ann-coulter.
64. Erwin Chemerinsky and Howard Gillman, *Free Speech on Campus* (New Haven, CT: Yale University Press, 2017), 113.
65. Thomas Healy, "Who's Afraid of Free Speech?," *The Atlantic*, June 18, 2017, https://www.theatlantic.com/politics/archive/2017/06/whos-afraid-of-free-speech/530094/.

Chapter 5

1. Bill Maher, "Season 16, Episode 31," *Real Time with Bill Maher*, HBO, October 12, 2018, https://www.hbo.com/real-time-with-bill-maher/2018/31-episode-476.
2. Keith E. Whittington, *Speak Freely: Why Universities Must Defend Free Speech* (Princeton, NJ: Princeton University Press, 2018), 134.
3. Lee Jussim, "Stigmatizing Legitimate Dissent Threatens Freedom of Speech," Heterodox Academy, November 25, 2017, https://heterodoxacademy.org/blog/stigmatizing-legitim ate-dissent-threatens-freedom-of-speech/; Andrew Sullivan, "We All Live on Campus Now," *New York*, February 9, 2018, http://nymag.com/daily/intelligencer/2018/02/we-all-live-on-campus-now.html.
4. Peter W. Wood, "The Left Can't Stop Campus Riots Like Middlebury's Because Their Ideology Deserves Blame," *The Federalist*, March 14, 2017, http://thefederalist.com/2017/03/14/left-cant-stop-campus-riots-like-middleburys-ideology-deserves-blame/.
5. Jonathan Haidt, "Intimidation Is the New Normal on Campus," *Chronicle of Higher Education*, April 26, 2017, https://www.chronicle.com/article/intimidation-is-the-new-normal-on-campus/.

6. See Yangyang Cheng, "Cancel Culture Isn't the Real Threat to Academic Freedom," *The Atlantic*, November 23, 2021, https://www.theatlantic.com/international/archive/2021/11/china-academic-freedom-cultural-revolution-cancel-culture/620777/; Michael S. Roth, *Safe Enough Spaces: A Pragmatist's Approach to Inclusion, Free Speech, and Political Correctness on College Campuses* (New Haven, CT: Yale University Press, 2019), 78.

7. Jeffrey J. Selingo, "How Many Colleges and Universities Do We Really Need?," *Washington Post*, July 20, 2015, https://www.washingtonpost.com/news/grade-point/wp/2015/07/20/how-many-colleges-and-universities-do-we-really-need/?utm_term=.7c3083a954ee.

8. Carl Bialick, "The Latest Kentucky Riot Is Part of a Long, Destructive Sports Tradition," FiveThirtyEight, April 6, 2015, https://fivethirtyeight.com/features/the-latest-kentucky-riot-is-part-of-a-long-destructive-sports-tradition/.

9. "The Alt-Right on Campus: What Students Need to Know," Southern Poverty Law Center, August 10, 2017, https://www.splcenter.org/20170810/alt-right-campus-what-students-need-know.

10. Brooks Jackson and Kathleen Hall Jamieson, *unSpun: Finding Facts in a World of Disinformation* (New York: Random House, 2007), 105–106.

11. Sara Jaramillo, Zachary Horne, and Micah Goldwater, "The Impact of Anecdotal Information on Medical Decision-Making," OSF, May 15, 2019, https://osf.io/dkcwv/. See also Fernando Rodriguez, Rebecca Rhodes, Kevin Miller, and Priti Shah, "Examining the Influence of Anecdotal Stories and the Interplay of Individual Differences on Reasoning," *Thinking and Reasoning* 22 (2016): 274–296.

12. "Ex-Mizzou Professor Melissa Click, Fired over Protest Clash, Gets New Job," NBC News, September 4, 2016, https://www.nbcnews.com/news/us-news/ex-mizzou-professor-melissa-click-fired-over-protest-clash-gets-n642711.

13. The investigation later found that the student, Tim Thai, "was not a journalism student or working for a news outlet" at the time; Steve Kolowich, Brock Read, and Andy Thomason, "10 Revealing Details in the Melissa Click Investigation," *Chronicle of Higher Education*, February 26, 2016, https://www.chronicle.com/article/10-Revealing-Details-in-the/235502.

14. Katherine Timpf, "University Bans Snowball Fights and Water Guns," *National Review*, August 21, 2018, https://www.nationalreview.com/2018/08/university-bans-snowball-fights-and-water-guns/.

15. Scott Goss, "Delaware State University, Fox News, and the Snowball Story Heard 'round the World,'" Delaware Online, August 23, 2018, https://www.delawareonline.com/story/news/local/2018/08/23/dsu-fox-news-and-snowball-story-heard-round-world/1071412002/.

16. Madison Park and Kyung Lah, "Berkeley Protests of Yiannopoulos Caused $100,000 in Damage," CNN, February 2, 2017, https://www.cnn.com/2017/02/01/us/milo-yiannopoulos-berkeley/index.html.

17. Scott Jaschik, "Shouting Down a Lecture," *Inside Higher Ed*, March 3, 2017, https://www.insidehighered.com/news/2017/03/03/middlebury-students-shout-down-lecture-charles-murray; Allison Stanger, "Understanding the Angry Mob That Gave Me a Concussion," *New York Times*, March 13, 2017, https://www.nytimes.com/2017/03/13/opinion/understanding-the-angry-mob-that-gave-me-a-concussion.html.

18. For a timeline of key events, see Jasmine Kozak-Gilroy, "A Year of Events: A Timeline of Protests," *Cooper Point Journal*, May 31, 2017, http://www.cooperpointjournal.com/2017/05/31/a-year-of-events-a-time-line-of-protests/.

19. Research on organizational conflict is plentiful across multiple academic disciplines. Louis R. Pondy, "Organizational Conflict: Concepts and Models," *Administrative Science Quarterly* 12 (1967): 296–320, is a classic introductory study of organizational conflicts and contributing factors to them.

20. The Weinstein incident appeared to inflame long-simmering tensions over race, diversity, and inequality at the university. As in the case of student protests at the University of Missouri, national reports often omitted information about the full contributing factors and array of conflicts involved. See, for example, Georgie Hicks, "Students Questioned about Alleged Harassment: Allegations of Anti-Black Racism Ensue," *Cooper Point Journal*, May 24, 2017, http://www.cooperpointjournal.com/2017/05/24/students-questioned-about-alleged-harassment-allegations-of-anti-black-racism-ensue/.

21. "Fast Facts: College Crime," National Center for Education Statistics, 2018, https://nces.ed.gov/fastfacts/display.asp?id = 804.

22. See William Doyle, *An American Insurrection: James Meredith and the Battle of Oxford, Mississippi, 1962*, reprint ed. (New York: Anchor Books, 2003); James Meredith, *Three Years in Mississippi* (Oxford: University Press of Mississippi, 2019).

23. See "UM History of Integration," University of Mississippi, accessed February 5, 2022, https://50years.olemiss.edu/james-meredith/.

24. "Massive Resistance," Equal Justice Initiative, 2018, https://segregationinamerica.eji.org/report/massive-resistance.html.

25. "Massive Resistance," Equal Justice Initiative.

26. See "Massive Resistance," Virginia Museum of History and Culture, 2018, https://virginia history.org/learn/historical-book/chapter/massive-resistance.

27. "Massive Resistance," Equal Justice Initiative.

28. Nicole Hemmer, "A12," Past Punditry, August 6, 2018, http://www.pastpundit.com/a12.

29. P. Preston Reynolds, "UVA and the History of Race: Eugenics, the Racial Integrity Act, Health Disparities," *UVA Today*, January 9, 2020, https://news.virginia.edu/content/uva-and-history-race-eugenics-racial-integrity-act-health-disparities.

30. See Dmitry Dubrovskiy, "Academic Rights in Russia and the Internationalization of Higher Education," *Academe* (American Association of University Professors), Fall 2019, https://www.aaup.org/article/academic-rights-russia-and-internationalization-higher-education#.Ydh66FlOk2x; Jason Stanley, *How Fascism Works: The Politics of Us and Them* (New York: Random House, 2018), chapter 3.

31. "White Supremacist Propaganda Nearly Doubles on Campus in 2017–18 Academic Year," Anti-Defamation League, June 6, 2018, https://www.adl.org/resources/reports/white-supr emacist-propaganda-nearly-doubles-on-campus-in-2017-18-academic-year.

32. "Alt-Right," Southern Poverty Law Center.

33. Park and Lah, "Berkeley Protests."

34. Ray Villeda, "Conservative Speaker's Appearance Ignites Protests at NYU," NBC New York, February 2, 2017, https://www.nbcnewyork.com/news/local/NYU-Protests-Fights-Arre sts-Conservative-Speaker-Gavin-McInnes-412635693.html.

35. Max Blau, Sara Ganim and Chris Welch, "Richard Spencer's Appearance at Texas A&M Draws Protests," CNN, December 7, 2016, https://www.cnn.com/2016/12/06/politics/rich ard-spencer-texas-am/index.html; Joe Concha, "DePaul Cancels Conservative's Speech," *The Hill*, August 1, 2016, https://thehill.com/blogs/blog-briefing-room/news/289999-depaul-cancels-conservatives-speech; Scott Jaschik, "Speech, Interrupted," *Inside Higher Ed*, March 6, 2018, https://www.insidehighered.com/news/2018/03/06/students-interr

upt-several-portions-speech-christina-hoff-sommers; Dana Kampa, "Conservative Pundit Ben Shapiro Lectures to Turbulent Crowd on Safe Spaces, Freedom of Speech," *Badger Herald*, November 17, 2016, Madison, WI, https://badgerherald.com/news/2016/11/17/conservative-pundit-ben-shapiro-lectures-to-turbulent-crowd-on-safe-spaces-freedom-of-speech/; Madison Park, "Ben Shapiro Spoke at Berkeley as Protestors Gathered Outside," CNN, September 15, 2017, https://www.cnn.com/2017/09/14/us/berkeley-ben-shapiro-speech/index.html.

36. "Disinvitation Database," Foundation for Individual Rights in Education, accessed February 5, 2022, https://www.thefire.org/research/disinvitation-database/.

37. Milo Yiannopoulos, "How to Beat Me (Spoiler: You Won't)," *Breitbart*, March 21, 2016, https://www.breitbart.com/social-justice/2016/03/21/how-to-beat-me-spoiler-you-wont/.

38. Derek Robertson, "How 'Owning the Libs' Became the GOP's Chief Strategy," *Politico*, March 21, 2021, https://www.politico.com/news/magazine/2021/03/21/owning-the-libs-history-trump-politics-pop-culture-477203.

39. Camille Furst, "Colleges Targeted with Racist Zoom Bombings as White Supremacy Spikes," NBC Washington, April 15, 2021 https://www.nbcwashington.com/news/local/colleges-targeted-with-racist-zoom-bombings-as-white-supremacist-propaganda-spikes/2622296/; Elizabeth Redden, "'Zoombombing' Attacks Disrupt Classes," *Inside Higher Education*, March 26, 2020, https://www.insidehighered.com/news/2020/03/26/zoom-bombers-disrupt-online-classes-racist-pornographic-content.

40. "National Field Program," Turning Point USA, accessed February 5, 2022, https://www.tpusa.com/nfp.

41. "Events," Turning Point USA, accessed February 5, 2022, https://www.tpusa.com/events; Peter Stone, "Money and Misinformation: How Turning Point USA Became a Formidable Pro-Trump Force," *The Guardian*, October 23, 2021, https://www.theguardian.com/us-news/2021/oct/23/turning-point-rightwing-youth-group-critics-tactics.

42. Shapiro expresses Islamophobic, homophobic, and transphobic views, which overlap with white nationalist discourse ("Ben Shapiro," GLAAD, accessed February 5, 2022, https://www.glaad.org/gap/ben-shapiro; Jon Greenberg, "Ben Shaprio," PolitiFact, November 5, 2014, https://www.politifact.com/factchecks/2014/nov/05/ben-shapiro/shapiro-says-majority-muslims-are-radicals/). The Southern Poverty Law Center classifies Murray as an extremist whose views on race are based on spurious science with links to long-standing white supremacist groups ("Charles Murray," Southern Poverty Law Center, February 5, 2022, https://www.splcenter.org/fighting-hate/extremist-files/individual/charles-murray). Sommers's critiques of modern feminism, and her arguments that men are victims of diversity and inclusion programs, overlap with the priorities of men's rights activists who seek to normalize a doctrine of male supremacy ("Male Supremacy," Southern Poverty Law Center, February 5, 2022, https://www.splcenter.org/fighting-hate/extremist-files/ideology/male-supremacy). Yiannopoulos's public statements are replete with blatantly racist, anti-Semitic, and transphobic tropes ("Milo Yiannopoulos: Five Things to Know," Anti-Defamation League, February 5, 2022, https://www.adl.org/resources/backgrounders/milo-yiannopoulos-five-things-to-know). Spencer and McInnes proudly advocate bigoted and extremist ideas ("ADL Resource Identifies the Key Players of the Alt Right and Alt Lite," Anti-Defamation League, July 18, 2017, https://www.adl.org/news/press-releases/key-leaders-alt-right-vs-alt-lite).

43. See Emmanuel Chukwudi Eze, ed., *Race and the Enlightenment: A Reader* (Malden, MA: Blackwell, 1997).

44. See Peter Gay, *The Enlightenment: An Interpretation*, rev. ed. (New York: W. W. Norton, 1996), chapter 10.
45. Michalina Clifford-Vaughan, "Enlightenment and Education," *British Journal of Sociology* 14 (1963): 135.
46. Clifford-Vaughan, "Enlightenment," 135.
47. Ernst Cassirer, *The Philosophy of the Enlightenment*, updated ed., trans. Fritz C. A. Koelln and James P. Pettegrove (Princeton, NJ: Princeton University Press, 2009), 5–6.
48. Immanuel Kant, "What Is Enlightenment?, 1784," Internet History Sourcebooks Project, Fordham University, 1997, https://sourcebooks.fordham.edu/mod/kant-whatis.asp.

Chapter 6

1. Mark Tushnet, "Constitutional Hardball," *John Marshall Law Review* 37 (2004): 523.
2. Steven Levitsky and Daniel Ziblatt, *How Democracies Die* (New York: Crown, 2018), 109.
3. Lincoln Dahlberg, "Cyberlibertarianism," *Oxford Research Encyclopedia of Communication*, October 26, 2017, https://oxfordre.com/communication/view/10.1093/acrefore/978019 0228613.001.0001/acrefore-9780190228613-e-70.
4. Nicole Hemmer, "A12," Past Punditry, August 6, 2018, http://www.pastpundit.com/a12; Spencer Hawes and Sheryl Gay Stolberg, "White Nationalists March on University of Virginia," *New York Times*, August 12, 2017, https://www.nytimes.com/2017/08/11/us/white-nationalists-rally-charlottesville-virginia.html.
5. Erwin Chemerinsky and Howard Gillman, *Free Speech on Campus* (New Haven, CT: Yale University Press, 2017), 8.
6. S. G. Tallentyre (Evelyn Beatrice Hall), *The Friends of Voltaire* (New York: G. P. Putnam's Sons, 1907), 199.
7. Jason Stanley, *How Fascism Works* (New York: Random House, 2018), 42.
8. A strident argument in this vein: Robert C. Post, "There Is No 1st Amendment Right to Speak on a College Campus," *Vox*, December 31, 2017, https://www.vox.com/the-big-idea/2017/10/25/16526442/first-amendment-college-campuses-milo-spencer-protests.
9. Stanley Fish, "Free Speech Is Not an Academic Value," *Chronicle of Higher Education*, March 20, 2017, https://www.chronicle.com/article/Free-Speech-Is-Not-an-Academic/239536.
10. Michael S. Roth, *Safe Enough Spaces: A Pragmatist's Approach to Inclusion, Free Speech, and Political Correctness on College Campuses* (New Haven, CT: Yale University Press, 2019), 98. See also Ulrich Baer, *What Snowflakes Get Right: Free Speech and Truth on Campus* (New York: Oxford University Press, 2019), 11–12.
11. See Ryan Lizza, "Americans Tune In to 'Cancel Culture'—and Don't Like What They See," *Politico*, July 22, 2020, https://www.politico.com/news/2020/07/22/americans-cancel-culture-377412.
12. Perry Bacon Jr., "Why Attacking 'Cancel Culture' and 'Woke' People Is Becoming the GOP's New Political Strategy," *FiveThirtyEight*, March 17, 2021, https://fivethirtyeight.com/features/why-attacking-cancel-culture-and-woke-people-is-becoming-the-gops-new-political-strategy/; Danielle Kurtzleben, "When Republicans Attack 'Cancel Culture,' What Does It Mean?," National Public Radio, February 10, 2021, https://www.npr.org/2021/02/10/965815679/is-cancel-culture-the-future-of-the-gop.
13. "A Letter on Justice and Open Debate" (*Harper's*, July 7, 2020, https://harpers.org/a-letter-on-justice-and-open-debate/) is a paradigmatic example. The letter, signed by dozens of

artists, authors, and other notable public figures, expressed passive-voiced alarm about "institutional leaders" who, "in a spirit of panicked damage control, are delivering hasty and disproportionate punishments instead of considered reforms." The brief intellectual manifesto received substantial criticism for its vague and selective commitment to alleged injustices against people in predominantly elite or privileged positions; see Hannah Giorgis, "A Deeply Provincial View of Free Speech," *The Atlantic*, July 13, 2020, https://www.theatlantic.com/culture/archive/2020/07/harpers-letter-free-speech/614080/; Mary McNamara, "'Cancel Culture' Is Not the Problem. The Harper's Letter Is," *Los Angeles Times*, July 9, 2020, https://www.latimes.com/entertainment-arts/story/2020-07-09/cancel-culture-harpers-letter.

14. Thomas Healy, "Who's Afraid of Free Speech?," *The Atlantic*, June 18, 2017, https://www.theatlantic.com/politics/archive/2017/06/whos-afraid-of-free-speech/530094/.

15. Healy, "Who's Afraid?"

16. "Speech on Campus," American Civil Liberties Union, accessed February 5, 2022, https://www.aclu.org/other/speech-campus.

17. "Partnerships," Young America's Foundation, accessed February 5, 2022, https://www.yaf.org/partnerships/.

18. "Start a YAF Chapter," Young America's Foundation, February 5, 2022, https://students.yaf.org/young-americans-for-freedom/start-a-chapter/.

19. Eric Foner, *The Story of American Freedom* (New York: W. W. Norton, 1998), 312.

20. "National Field Program," Turning Point USA, accessed February 5, 2022, https://www.tpusa.com/nfp.

21. Amy Binder and Kate Wood, *Becoming Right: How Campuses Shape Young Conservatives* (Princeton, NJ: Princeton University Press, 2012), 76.

22. Binder and Wood, *Becoming*, 92.

23. For a full explication of this theory, see Karen Stenner, *The Authoritarian Dynamic* (New York: Cambridge University Press, 2005), chapter 2.

24. Elizabeth Redden, "Academic Freedom Front Lines," *Inside Higher Ed*, March 30, 2017, https://www.insidehighered.com/news/2017/03/30/hungary-and-russia-western-style-universities-are-under-threat.

25. Stanley, *How Fascism Works*, 50.

26. "Campus Free Speech," C-SPAN, October 26, 2017, https://www.c-span.org/video/?436331-1/hearing-focuses-college-campus-free-speech.

27. Betsy DeVos, "Remarks by Secretary DeVos to the National Constitution Center's Annual Constitution Day Celebration," US Department of Education, September 17, 2018, https://content.govdelivery.com/accounts/USED/bulletins/20dda95.

28. Lisa Marie Segarra, "Colleges Are an 'Echo Chamber of Political Correctness.' Read Jeff Sessions' Speech on Campus Free Speech," *Time*, September 26, 2017, http://time.com/4957604/jeff-sessions-georgetown-law-speech-transcript/.

29. "Executive Order: Improving Free Inquiry, Transparency, and Accountability at Colleges and Universities," American Presidency Project, March 21, 2019, https://www.presidency.ucsb.edu/documents/executive-order-13864-improving-free-inquiry-transparency-and-accountability-colleges-and. See also Maureen Groppe and Sean Rossman, "President Donald Trump, in CPAC Speech, Said He'll Sign 'Free Speech' Executive Order," *USA Today*, March 2, 2019, https://www.usatoday.com/story/news/politics/2019/03/02/donald-trump-cpac-president-speaks-following-cohen-hearing-korea/3039138002/; Andy Thomason, "Here's What Trump's Executive Order on Free Speech Says," *Chronicle of*

Higher Education, March 21, 2019, https://www.chronicle.com/article/Here-s-What-Trump-s/245943.

30. "Executive Order," American Presidency Project.

31. President Trump's subsequent "Executive Order on Combatting Anti-Semitism" is also relevant (Trump White House Archives, December 11, 2019, https://trumpwhitehouse.archi ves.gov/presidential-actions/executive-order-combating-anti-semitism/). The order effectively endorses taken-for-granted claims in conservative and right-wing media that college campuses harbor rising anti-Semitism. Such claims rely on a conflation of anti-Semitism with criticism against Israeli state policy: because some on-campus groups vocally criticize Israel, this logic falsely assumes, they must be anti-Semitic. Like the president's executive order on campus free speech, this order also arguably uses the pretext of combatting anti-Semitism as a device for regulating protected speech critical of Israeli policies or US policy toward Israel. Some self-described conservative and liberal commentators alike raised concerns about the order; see, for example, Manhattan Institute Fellow Heather MacDonald, "Trump's Executive Order on Anti-Semitism Might Be Well-Meaning, but It Could Limit Free Expression," Manhattan Institute, December 24, 2019, https://www. manhattan-institute.org/anti-semitism-executive-order-president-trump-campus-free-speech.

32. Jerry Lambe, "AG Barr: 'Secularists' and 'Pop Culture' Are Waging 'Unremitting Assault on Religion and Traditional Values,'" *Law and Crime*, October 12, 2019, https://lawandcr ime.com/high-profile/ag-barr-secularists-and-pop-culture-are-waging-unremitting-assa ult-on-religion-and-traditional-values/.

33. Andrew Atterbury and Juan Perez Jr., "Republicans Eye New Front in Education Wars: Making School Board Races Partisan," *Politico*, December 29, 2021, https://www. politico.com/news/2021/12/29/republicans-education-wars-school-board-races-526053; Olivia Beavers and Michael Stratford, "GOP Embraces Classroom Politics, Taking Cues from Youngkin," *Politico*, November 3, 2021, https://www.politico.com/news/2021/11/ 03/gop-classroom-politics-youngkin-519350; Stephanie Saul, "Energizing Conservative Voters, One School Board Election at a Time," *New York Times*, October 21, 2021, https:// www.nytimes.com/2021/10/21/us/republicans-schools-critical-race-theory.html.

34. Many publications explain critical race theory in detail for new readers. See Derek Bell, *Faces at the Bottom of the Well: The Permanence of Racism*, rev. ed. (New York: Basic Books, 2018); Kimberle Crenshaw, et al., eds., *Critical Race Theory: The Key Writings That Formed the Movement* (New York: New Press, 1996); Richard Delgado and Jean Stefancic, *Critical Race Theory: An Introduction*, 3rd ed. (New York: New York University Press, 2017).

35. Gary Peller, "I've Been a Critical Race Theorist for 30 Years," *Politico*, June 30, 2021, https:// www.politico.com/news/magazine/2021/06/30/critical-race-theory-lightning-rod-opinion-497046; Stephen Sawchuck, "What Is Critical Race Theory, and Why Is It under Attack?," *Education Week*, May 18, 2021, https://www.edweek.org/leadership/what-is-criti cal-race-theory-and-why-is-it-under-attack/2021/05.

36. See Peller, "Critical Race Theorist"; Sawchuck, "What Is."

37. Peter Greene, "Critical Race Theory Bans Are Expanding to Cover Broad Collection of Issues," *Forbes*, September 29, 2021, https://www.forbes.com/sites/petergreene/2021/ 09/29/critical-race-theory-bans-are-expanding-to-cover-broad-collection-of-issues/ ?sh=1381f56e5e5d.

38. Char Adams, Allan Smith and Aadit Tambe, "Map: See Which States Have Passed Critical Race Theory Bills," NBC News, June 17, 2021, https://www.nbcnews.com/news/nbcblk/

map-see-which-states-have-passed-critical-race-theory-bills-n1271215; Adrian Florido, "'We Can and Should Teach This History': New Bills Limit How Teachers Talk about Race," *National Public Radio*, May 25, 2021, https://www.npr.org/2021/05/25/1000273981/we-can-and-should-teach-this-history-new-bills-limit-how-teachers-talk-about-rac; Sarah Schwartz, "Map: Where Critical Race Theory Is under Attack," *Education Week*, June 11, 2021 (updated June 28, 2022), https://www.edweek.org/policy-politics/map-where-criti cal-race-theory-is-under-attack/2021/06; Rashawn Ray and Alexandra Gibbons, "Why Are States Banning Critical Race Theory?," Brookings Institution, November 2021, https://www.brookings.edu/blog/fixgov/2021/07/02/why-are-states-banning-critical-race-theory/.

39. Howard Fischer, "Arizona Bill Would Require Educators to Present Both Sides of 'Controversial Issues,'" KAWC, May 7, 2021, https://www.kawc.org/education/2021-05-07/arizona-bill-would-require-educators-to-present-both-sides-of-controversial-issues; Brian Lopez, "The Law That Prompted a School Administrator to Call for an 'Opposing' Perspective on the Holocaust Is Causing Confusion across Texas," *Texas Tribune*, October 15, 2021, https://www.texastribune.org/2021/10/15/Texas-critical-race-theory-law-confu ses-educators/.

40. Governor Glenn Youngkin, Executive Order Number One (2022): Ending the Use of Inherently Divisive Concepts, Including Critical Race Theory, and Restoring Excellence in K–12 Public Education in the Commonwealth, January 15, 2022, https://www.governor.virginia.gov/media/governorvirginiagov/governor-of-virginia/pdf/74---eo/74---eo/EO-1---ENDING-THE-USE-OF-INHERENTLY-DIVISIVE-CONCEPTS,-INCLUDING-CRITICAL-RACE-THEORY,-AND-RESTORING-EXCELLEN.pdf.

41. Michelle Goldberg, "A Frenzy of Book Banning," *Baltimore Sun*, December 7, 2021, https://www.baltimoresun.com/opinion/op-ed/bs-ed-op-1124-mgoldberg-book-banning-20211 207-xxwhd5mrrndudc65kpatftbhve-story.html.

42. Jeff Woods, *Black Struggle, Red Scare: Segregation and Anti-Communism in the South, 1948–1968* (Baton Rouge: Louisiana State University Press, 2004).

43. Tiffany Justice and Tina Descovich, "What 'School Board Moms' Really Want—And Why Candidates Ignore Us at Their Peril," *Washington Post*, November 8, 2021, https://www.was hingtonpost.com/opinions/2021/11/08/moms-for-liberty-education-elections/.

44. Jason Stanley, "Fascism and the University," *Chronicle of Higher Education*, September 2, 2018, https://www-chronicle-com.ezaccess.libraries.psu.edu/article/Fascismthe-Univers ity/244382.

45. Tara John, "Poland Just Passed a Holocaust Bill That Is Causing Outrage," *Time*, February 1, 2018, https://time.com/5128341/poland-holocaust-law/.

46. Elizabeth Redden, "Hungary Officially Ends Gender Studies Programs," *Inside Higher Ed*, October 17, 2018, https://www.insidehighered.com/quicktakes/2018/10/17/hungary-off icially-ends-gender-studies-programs; Marc Santora, "George Soros–Founded University Is Forced out of Hungary," *New York Times*, December 3, 2018, https://www.nytimes.com/2018/12/03/world/europe/soros-hungary-central-european-university.html.

47. Diane Jeantet, "Brazil Education Overhaul Aims at Ousting 'Marxist Ideology,'" AP News, February 6, 2019, https://www.apnews.com/0fb07d84d14c4d948f7028907c60f23f.

48. "White Supremacist Propaganda Nearly Doubles on Campus in 2017–18 Academic Year," Anti-Defamation League, June 6, 2018, https://www.adl.org/resources/reports/white-supr emacist-propaganda-nearly-doubles-on-campus-in-2017-18-academic-year.

49. Stanley, "Fascism."

50. Elisabeth Zerofsky, "How the American Right Fell in Love with Hungary," *New York Times*, October 19, 2021, https://www.nytimes.com/2021/10/19/magazine/viktor-Orbán-rod-dre her.html.
51. Ishaan Tharoor, "The GOP Alliance with Europe's Far-Right Deepens," *Washington Post*, October 12, 2021, https://www.washingtonpost.com/world/2021/10/12/republican-allia nce-europe-far-right/.

Chapter 7

1. William F. Buckley Jr., "Our Mission Statement," *National Review*, November 19, 1955, https://www.nationalreview.com/1955/11/our-mission-statement-william-f-buckley-jr/.
2. David D. Kirkpatrick, "The Right Hand of the Fathers," *New York Times Magazine*, December 20, 2009, 24–29.
3. Robert P. George, *The Clash of Orthodoxies: Law, Religion, and Morality in Crisis* (Wilmington, DE: ISI Books, 2001), chapter 1; *Conscience and Its Enemies: Confronting the Dogmas of Liberal Secularism*, updated and exp. ed. (Wilmington, DE: ISI Books, 2016), chapter 9, 29.
4. "The Problem," Heterodox Academy, accessed February 5, 2022, https://heterodoxacad emy.org/the-problem/.
5. George, *Conscience*, 107.
6. "Problem," Heterodox Academy.
7. George, *Clash*, 6. George also presents more concerted academic arguments about natural law theory in other writings, like *In Defense of Natural Law*, rev. ed. (New York: Oxford University Press, 2001).
8. Nathan Confas, "Research on Group Differences in Intelligence: A Defense of Free Inquiry," *Philosophical Psychology* 33 (2020): 125–147; Christian Smith, "An Academic Auto-da-Fé," *Chronicle of Higher Education*, July 23, 2012, https://www.chronicle.com/article/an-acade mic-auto-da-fe/; Bari Weiss, "Jonathan Haidt on the Cultural Roots of Campus Rage," *Wall Street Journal*, April 14, 2017, https://www.wsj.com/articles/jonathan-haidt-on-the-cultu ral-roots-of-campus-rage-1491000676; and Weiss, "We're All Fascists Now," *New York Times*, March 7, 2018, https://www.nytimes.com/2018/03/07/opinion/were-all-fascists-now.html.
9. George, *Clash*, 6.
10. Sarah Schwartz, "Map: Where Critical Race Theory Is under Attack," *Education Week*, June 11, 2021 (updated May 18, 2022), https://www.edweek.org/policy-politics/map-where-critical-race-theory-is-under-attack/2021/06.
11. "Problem," Heterodox Academy.
12. Weiss, "Campus Rage."
13. Keith E. Whittington, *Speak Freely: Why Universities Must Defend Free Speech* (Princeton, NJ: Princeton University Press), 130, 134.
14. Jeremy Beaman, "Barr Slams 'Secular Progressive Orthodoxy' in Schools," *Washington Examiner*, May 21, 2021, https://www.washingtonexaminer.com/news/william-barr-spe ech-slamming-progressive-orthodoxy; A. G. Gancarski, "Marco Rubio Attacks Critical Race Theory as 'New Institutional Orthodoxy,'" Florida Politics, June 16, 2021, https://flor idapolitics.com/archives/436121-crt-rubio/.

15. "Frequently Asked Questions," University of Austin, accessed February 5, 2022, https://www.uaustin.org/faq.

16. Smith, "Academic."

17. Weiss, "Campus Rage."

18. Andrew Sullivan, "We All Live on Campus Now," *New York*, February 9, 2018, https://nymag.com/intelligencer/2018/02/we-all-live-on-campus-now.html.

19. John McWhorter, *Woke Racism: How a New Religion Has Betrayed Black America* (New York: Penguin, 2021), 23.

20. A wealth of scholarship on this subject exists. Excellent and recently published introductory resources include Diarmaid MacCulloch, *Christianity: The First Three Thousand Years* (New York: Viking, 2010); Erin K. Vearncombe et al., *After Jesus before Christianity: A Historical Exploration of the First Two Centuries of Jesus Movements* (New York: Harper One, 2021).

21. Yangyang Cheng, "Cancel Culture Isn't the Real Threat to Academic Freedom," *The Atlantic*, November 23, 2021, https://www.theatlantic.com/international/archive/2021/11/china-academic-freedom-cultural-revolution-cancel-culture/620777/.

22. Jason Stanley, *How Propaganda Works* (Princeton, NJ: Princeton University Press, 2015), 57–68, 178.

23. Elissa Nadworny, "As Elite Campuses Diversify, a 'Bias toward Privilege Exists,'" National Public Radio, March 5, 2019, https://www.npr.org/2019/03/05/699977122/as-elite-campuses-diversify-a-bias-towards-privilege-persists; Ishaan Tharoor, "The GOP Alliance with Europe's Far-Right Deepens," *Washington Post*, October 12, 2021, https://www.washingtonpost.com/world/2021/10/12/republican-alliance-europe-far-right/.

24. Jonathan Haidt, "Intimidation Is the New Normal on Campus," *Chronicle of Higher Education*, April 26, 2017, https://www.chronicle.com/article/Intimidation-Is-the-New-Normal/239890.

25. Phillip W. Magness, "Tenured Radicals Are Real," *Chronicle of Higher Education*, September 24, 2020, https://www.chronicle.com/article/tenured-radicals-are-real.

26. See Sam Abrams, "Professors Moved Left since 1990s, Rest of Country Did Not," Heterodox Academy, January 9, 2016, https://heterodoxacademy.org/blog/professors-moved-left-but-country-did-not/; Samuel J. Abrams, "Why Colleges' Liberal Lean Is a Problem," *Chronicle of Higher Education*, March 5, 2017, https://www.chronicle.com/article/Why-Colleges-Liberal-Lean/239355; Jonathan Haidt and Lee Jussim, "Psychological Science and Viewpoint Diversity," Association for Psychological Science, January 29, 2016, https://www.psychologicalscience.org/observer/psychological-science-and-viewpoint-diversity; Magness, "Tenured"; Uwe Peters, Nathan Honeycutt, Andreas De Block, and Lee Jussim, "Ideological Diversity, Hostility, and Discrimination in Philosophy," *Philosophical Psychology* 33 (2020): 511–548.

27. McWhorter, *Woke*, 18–19, 3, 22.

28. Patricia Roberts-Miller, *Demagoguery and Democracy* (New York: The Experiment, 2017), 34. See also Roberts-Miller, *Rhetoric and Demagoguery* (Carbondale: Southern Illinois University Press, 2019).

29. Roberts-Miller, *Demagoguery*, 34–36.

30. "Campus Sexual Violence: Statistics," RAINN (Rape, Abuse, and Incest National Network), accessed February 5, 2022, https://www.rainn.org/statistics/campus-sexual-violence.

31. Weiss, "Fascists"; Sullivan, "We All."

32. Katherine Mangan, "A Planned University 'Dedicated to Truth' Will Welcome 'Witches Who Refuse to Burn,'" *Chronicle of Higher Education*, November 8, 2021, https://www. chronicle.com/article/a-planned-university-dedicated-to-truth-will-welcome-witches-who-refuse-to-burn.

33. Karen Stenner, *The Authoritarian Dynamic* (New York: Cambridge University Press, 2005), 267; see also Howard Gabennesch, "Authoritarianism as World View," *American Journal of Sociology* 77 (March 1972): 857–875.

34. Gabennesch, "Authoritarianism," 864; Stenner, *Authoritarian*, 267.

Chapter 8

1. See Joe Lonsdale, "America's Leadership Culture Is Rotten," *Washington Post*, November 22, 2021, https://www.washingtonpost.com/opinions/2021/11/22/joe-lonsdale-univers ity-of-austin/; Niall Ferguson, "I'm Helping to Start a New College Because Higher Ed Is Broken," *Bloomberg*, November 8, 2021, https://www.bloomberg.com/opinion/articles/ 2021-11-08/niall-ferguson-america-s-woke-universities-need-to-be-replaced.

2. Jeffrey J. Selingo, "How Many Colleges and Universities Do We Really Need?," *Washington Post*, July 20, 2015, https://www.washingtonpost.com/news/grade-point/wp/2015/07/20/ how-many-colleges-and-universities-do-we-really-need/?utm_term=.7c3083a954ee.

3. "Mission, Vision, and Values," University of Mississippi, accessed February 5, 2022, https:// dce.olemiss.edu/vision-mission-and-values/.

4. "Equity, Diversity, and Inclusion," Vanderbilt University, accessed February 5, 2022, https:// www.vanderbilt.edu/diversity/; "Statement on Diversity," Virginia Military Institute, accessed February 5, 2022, https://www.vmi.edu/about/governance/regulations-and-polic ies/statement-on-diversity/.

5. "A Look Back," Vanderbilt University, accessed February 5, 2022, https://www.vanderbilt. edu/celebratingblackhistory/look-back/; Ian Shapira, "VMI Will Change Honor System that Expels Black Cadets at Disproportionate Rates," *Washington Post*, February 5, 2022, https://www.washingtonpost.com/education/2022/02/05/vmi-honor-court-reforms/.

6. See Jerome Karabel, *The Chosen: The Hidden History of Admission and Exclusion at Harvard, Yale, and Princeton* (New York: Houghton Mifflin, 2005).

7. Kelly Dye and Golnaz Golnaraghi, "Organizational Benefits through Diversity Management: Theoretical Perspectives on the Business Case," in *The Oxford Handbook of Diversity in Organizations*, ed. Regine Bendl et al. (New York: Oxford University Press, 2015), 255–278.

8. "The Spirit of Inclusion at Notre Dame," Notre Dame University, accessed February 5, 2022, https://dulac.nd.edu/university-mission-and-vision/spirit-of-inclusion/.

9. "About," Council for Christian Colleges and Universities, accessed February 5, 2022, https://www.cccu.org/about/.

10. Karen A. Longman, ed., *Diversity Matters: Race, Ethnicity, and the Future of Christian Higher Education* (Abilene, TX: Abilene Christian University Press, 2017).

11. See John McWhorter, "Here's a Fact: We're Routinely Asked to Use Leftist Fictions," *New York Times*, November 22, 2021, https://www.nytimes.com/2021/11/19/opinion/ heres-a-fact-were-routinely-asked-to-use-leftist-fictions.html.

12. McWhorter, "Here's a Fact."

13. Joseph Harroz Jr., "Presidential Statement on the Intersection of First Amendment Freedoms and Diversity, Equity, and Inclusion at the University of Oklahoma," University of Oklahoma, accessed February 5, 2022, https://www.ou.edu/web/news_events/artic les/news_2021/presidential-statement-on-intersection-of-first-amendment-freed oms-and-dei-at-ou.
14. Harroz Jr., "Presidential Statement."
15. Harroz Jr.
16. Nick Anderson and Susan Svrluga, "College Faculty Are Fighting Back against State Bills on Critical Race Theory," *Washington Post*, February 19, 2022, https://www.washingtonp ost.com/education/2022/02/19/colleges-critical-race-theory-bills/; Megan Menchaca, "UT Faculty Council Passes Resolution Supporting Freedom to Teach Critical Race Theory," *Austin American-Statesman*, February 15, 2022, https://www.statesman.com/ story/news/2022/02/15/ut-faculty-council-passes-resolution-defending-teaching-criti cal-race-theory/6754421001/; Molly Minta, "UM Faculty Senate Latest to Oppose Anti-CRT Legislation," *Mississippi Today*, February 23, 2022, https://mississippitoday.org/2022/ 02/23/um-faculty-opposes-anti-critical-race-theory-legislation/; "Resolution in Support of Academic Freedom and Rejection of Attempts to Interfere with the Teaching of Racial and Social Justice," Senate Committees on Education Equity and Campus Environment; Faculty Affairs; Intra-University Relations, Pennsylvania State University, January 25, 2022, https://senate.psu.edu/files/2022/02/January-25-2022-Appendix-C-editorial-revisi ons.pdf.
17. Sara Goldrick-Rab, *Paying the Price: College Costs, Financial Aid, and the Betrayal of the American Dream* (Chicago: University of Chicago Press, 2016), 103, 107–108.
18. "Food Insecurity," Government Accountability Office, December 2018, https://www.gao. gov/assets/gao-19-95.pdf; Goldrick-Rab, *Paying*, chapter 5.
19. See Anshu Siripurapu and Mia Speier, "Is Rising Student Debt Harming the U.S. Economy?," Council on Foreign Relations, April 13, 2021, https://www.cfr.org/backgrounder/rising-student-debt-harming-us-economy.

Bibliography

Abelson, Robert P. *Statistics as Principled Argument*. Hillsdale, NJ: Lawrence Erlbaum, 1995.

"About." Council for Christian Colleges and Universities. Accessed February 5, 2022. https://www.cccu.org/about/.

"About." *Quillette*. Accessed February 5, 2022. https://quillette.com/about/.

"About Us." Foundation for Individual Rights in Education. Accessed February 5, 2022. https://www.thefire.org/about-us/history/.

"About Us." Heterodox Academy. Accessed February 5, 2022. https://heterodoxacademy.org/about-us/.

Abrams, Sam. "Professors Moved Left since 1990s, Rest of Country Did Not." Heterodox Academy, January 9, 2016. https://heterodoxacademy.org/blog/professors-moved-left-but-country-did-not/.

Abrams, Samuel J. "Why Colleges' Liberal Lean Is a Problem." *Chronicle of Higher Education*, March 5, 2017. https://www.chronicle.com/article/Why-Colleges-Liberal-Lean/239355.

Adams, Char, Allan Smith, and Aadit Tambe. "Map: See Which States Have Passed Critical Race Theory Bills." NBC News, June 17, 2021. https://www.nbcnews.com/news/nbcblk/map-see-which-states-have-passed-critical-race-theory-bills-n1271215.

"ADL Resource Identifies the Key Players of the Alt Right and Alt Lite." Anti-Defamation League, July 18, 2017. https://www.adl.org/news/press-releases/key-leaders-alt-right-vs-alt-lite.

"Adopting the Chicago Statement." Foundation for Individual Rights in Education. Accessed February 5, 2022. https://www.thefire.org/get-involved/student-network/take-action/adopting-the-chicago-statement/.

Ali, Ayaan Hirsi. "American Education Needs a Revolution." *UnHerd*, November 11, 2021. https://unherd.com/2021/11/american-education-needs-a-revolution/.

Allyn, Bobby. "Facebook Keeps Data Secret, Letting Conservative Bias Claims Persist." National Public Radio, October 5, 2020. https://www.npr.org/2020/10/05/918520692/facebook-keeps-data-secret-letting-conservative-bias-claims-persist.

"The Alt-Right on Campus: What Students Need to Know." Southern Poverty Law Center, August 10, 2017. https://www.splcenter.org/20170810/alt-right-campus-what-students-need-know.

Amazon Mechanical Turk. "Amazon Mechanical Turk." *Mturk*. Accessed February 5, 2022. https://www.mturk.com/.

Anders, Caroline. "In Push against 'Indoctrination,' DeSantis Mandates Surveys of Florida College Students' Beliefs." *Washington Post*, June 24, 2021. https://www.washingtonpost.com/education/2021/06/24/florida-intellectual-freedom-law-mandates-viewpoint-surveys/.

Andersen, Erika. "True Fact: The Lack of Pirates Is Causing Global Warming." *Forbes*, March 23, 2012. https://www.forbes.com/sites/erikaandersen/2012/03/23/true-fact-the-lack-of-pirates-is-causing-global-warming/?fbclid=IwAR092jre-g0CMThJpzyNO2NQEpn3mXQdHLtqKlkhqGq8gSEeLogDjcbJdVg#b9a60423a679.

Anderson, Nick, and Susan Svrluga. "College Faculty Are Fighting Back against State Bills on Critical Race Theory." *Washington Post*, February 19, 2022. https://www.washingtonpost.com/education/2022/02/19/colleges-critical-race-theory-bills/.

"Anti-Palestinian Legislation." Palestine Legal, June 1, 2022. https://palestinelegal.org/rightto boycott/.

"Apology to People of Color for APA's Role in Promoting, Perpetuating, and Failing to Challenge Racism, Racial Discrimination, and Human Hierarchy in U.S." American Psychological Association Council of Representatives, October 29, 2021. https://www.apa.org/about/pol icy/racism-apology.

Applebaum, Anne. "The New Puritans." The Atlantic, August 31, 2021. https://www.theatlantic. com/magazine/archive/2021/10/new-puritans-mob-justice-canceled/619818/.

"The Atlantic Begins 'The Speech Wars' Reporting Project." The Atlantic, November 28, 2018. https://www.theatlantic.com/press-releases/archive/2018/11/the-atlantic-begins-the-spe ech-wars-reporting-project/576805/.

Atterbury, Andrew, and Juan Perez Jr. "Republicans Eye New Front in Education Wars: Making School Board Races Partisan." Politico, December 29, 2021, https://www.politico.com/news/ 2021/12/29/republicans-education-wars-school-board-races-526053.

Bacon, Perry, Jr. "Why Attacking 'Cancel Culture' and 'Woke' People Is Becoming the GOP's New Political Strategy." FiveThirtyEight, March 17, 2021. https://fivethirtyeight.com/featu res/why-attacking-cancel-culture-and-woke-people-is-becoming-the-gops-new-political-strategy/.

Baer, Ulrich. What Snowflakes Get Right: Free Speech and Truth on Campus. New York: Oxford University Press, 2019.

Baker, C. Edwin. "Viewpoint Diversity and Media Ownership." Federal Communications Law Journal 61 (2009): 651–672.

Barnes, Robert, and Nick Anderson. "High Court to Revisit Stance on Affirmative Action." Washington Post, January 25, 2022.

Baym, Nancy K. "Social Media and the Struggle for Society." Social Media + Society (April–June 2015): 1–2.

Beaman, Jeremy. "Barr Slams 'Secular Progressive Orthodoxy' in Schools." Washington Examiner, May 21, 2021. https://www.washingtonexaminer.com/news/william-barr-spe ech-slamming-progressive-orthodoxy.

Beavers, Olivia, and Michael Stratford. "GOP Embraces Classroom Politics, Taking Cues from Youngkin." Politico, November 3, 2021. https://www.politico.com/news/2021/11/03/gop-classroom-politics-youngkin-519350.

Beckett, Lois. "'Junk Science': Experts Cast Doubt on Widely Cited College Free Speech Survey." The Guardian, September 22, 2017. https://www.theguardian.com/us-news/2017/sep/22/ college-free-speech-violence-survey-junk-science.

Belkin, Douglas. "Fear of Violent Protests Raises Cost of Free Speech on Campus." Wall Street Journal, October 22, 2017. https://www.wsj.com/articles/fear-of-violent-protests-raises-cost-of-free-speech-on-campus-1508670000.

Bell, Derek. Faces at the Bottom of the Well: The Permanence of Racism. Revised edition. New York: Basic Books, 2018.

Bellet, Benjamin W., Payton J. Jones, and Richard J. McNally. "Trigger Warning: Empirical Evidence Ahead." Journal of Behavior Therapy and Experimental Psychology 61 (2018): 134–141.

Belson, William A. The Design and Understanding of Survey Questions. Aldershot, UK: Gower, 1981.

"The Benefits of Socioeconomically and Racially Integrated Schools and Classrooms." The Century Foundation, April 29, 2019, https://tcf.org/content/facts/the-benefits-of-socioe conomically-and-racially-integrated-schools-and-classrooms/#easy-footnote-bottom-1.

"Ben Shapiro." GLAAD. Accessed February 5, 2022. https://www.glaad.org/gap/ben-shapiro.

Bennett, W. Lance. News: The Politics of Illusion, 10th ed. Chicago: University of Chicago Press, 2016.

Ben-Porath, Sigal R. *Free Speech on Campus*. Philadelphia: University of Pennsylvania Press, 2017.

Bennett, W. Lance, and Steven Livingston, eds. *The Disinformation Age: Politics, Technology, and Disruptive Communication in the United States*. New York: Cambridge University Press, 2020.

Bialick, Carl. "The Latest Kentucky Riot Is Part of a Long, Destructive Sports Tradition." FiveThirtyEight, April 6, 2015. https://fivethirtyeight.com/features/the-latest-kentucky-riot-is-part-of-a-long-destructive-sports-tradition/.

Biggs, Michael. "How Feminism Paved the Way for Transgenderism." *Quillette*, August 1, 2019. https://quillette.com/2019/08/01/how-feminism-paved-the-way-for-transgenderism/.

Binder, Amy, and Kate Wood. *Becoming Right: How Campuses Shape Young Conservatives*. Princeton, NJ: Princeton University Press, 2012.

Blakemore, Erin. "Did Communists Really Infiltrate American Schools?" *JSTOR Daily*, December 3, 2020. https://daily.jstor.org/did-communists-really-infiltrate-american-schools/.

Blau, Max, Sara Ganim, and Chris Welch. "Richard Spencer's Appearance at Texas A&M Draws Protests." CNN, December 7, 2016. https://www.cnn.com/2016/12/06/politics/richard-spencer-texas-am/index.html.

Bollinger, Lee C. "Free Speech on Campus Is Doing Just Fine, Thank You." *The Atlantic*, June 12, 2019. https://www.theatlantic.com/ideas/archive/2019/06/free-speech-crisis-campus-isnt-real/591394/.

Bond, Shannon. "Federal Trade Commission Refiles Suit Accusing Facebook of Illegal Monopoly." National Public Radio, August 19, 2021. https://www.npr.org/2021/08/19/1029310979/federal-trade-commission-refiles-suit-accusing-facebook-of-illegal-monopoly.

Bothwell, Ellie. "Poland Trying to Destroy Universities' Independence, Warns Rector." *Times Higher Education*, November 23, 2020. https://www.timeshighereducation.com/news/poland-trying-destroy-universities-independence-warns-rector.

Boutwell, Brian, and Kevin Beaver. "Criminology's Wonderland." *Quillette*, March 31, 2016. https://quillette.com/2016/03/31/criminologys-wonderland-why-almost-everything-you-know-about-crime-is-wrong/.

Bowen, William G., and Derek Bok. *The Shape of the River: Long-Term Consequences of Considering Race in College and University Admissions*. Princeton, NJ: Princeton University Press, 1998.

Brooks, David. "The Rise of the Amphibians." *New York Times*, February 16, 2018.

Brooks, David. "Understanding Student Mobbists." *New York Times*, March 8, 2018.

Buckley, William F. *God and Man at Yale: The Superstitions of "Academic Freedom."* Washington, DC: Regnery, 1951.

Buckley, William F. "Our Mission Statement." *National Review*, November 19, 1955. https://www.nationalreview.com/1955/11/our-mission-statement-william-f-buckley-jr/.

Cain, Áine. "The Truth about Whether You Can Be Fired for Expressing Your Political Views at Work." *Business Insider*, January 20, 2017. http://www.businessinsider.com/you-can-be-fired-over-political-views-2017-1.

Campbell, Bradley, and Jason Manning. *The Rise of Victimhood Culture: Microaggressions, Safe Spaces, and the New Culture Wars*. Cham, Switzerland: Palgrave Macmillan, 2018.

"Campus Free Speech." C-SPAN, October 26, 2017. https://www.c-span.org/video/?436331-1/hearing-focuses-college-campus-free-speech.

"Campus Free Speech Guide." PEN America. Accessed February 5, 2022. https://campusfreespeechguide.pen.org/.

"Campus Sexual Violence: Statistics." RAINN (Rape, Abuse, and Incest National Network). Accessed February 5, 2022. https://www.rainn.org/statistics/campus-sexual-violence.

"Campus Speech Archives." *The Federalist*. Accessed February 5, 2022. http://thefederalist. com/tag/campus-speech/.

"A Case History of Ultra-Liberalism on the Campus." Manion Forum Broadcast #385, February 11, 1962.

Cassirer, Ernst. *The Philosophy of the Enlightenment*. Updated edition. Translated by Fritz C. A. Koelln and James P. Pettegrove. Princeton, NJ: Princeton University Press, 2009.

Chait, Jonathan. "Not a Very P.C. Thing to Say: How the Language Police Are Perverting Liberalism." *New York*, January 27, 2015. http://nymag.com/intelligencer/2015/01/not-a-very-pc-thing-to-say.html?gtm=bottom&gtm=bottom.

Chait, Jonathan. "The 'Shut It Down!' Left and the War on the Liberal Mind." *New York*, April 26, 2017. http://nymag.com/daily/intelligencer/2017/04/the-shut-it-down-left-and-the-war-on-the-liberal-mind.html.

"Charles Murray." Southern Poverty Law Center. Accessed February 5, 2022. https://www. splcenter.org/fighting-hate/extremist-files/individual/charles-murray.

Chemerinsky, Erwin, and Howard Gillman. *Free Speech on Campus*. New Haven, CT: Yale University Press, 2017.

Cheng, Yangyang. "Cancel Culture Isn't the Real Threat to Academic Freedom." *The Atlantic*, November 23, 2021. https://www.theatlantic.com/international/archive/2021/11/china-academic-freedom-cultural-revolution-cancel-culture/620777/.

Chokshi, Niraj. "Militarized Police in Ferguson Unsettles Some; Pentagon Gives Cities Equipment." *Washington Post*, August 14, 2014. https://www.washingtonpost.com/politics/ militarized-police-in-ferguson-unsettles-some-pentagon-gives-cities-equipment/2014/08/ 14/4651f670-2401-11e4-86ca-6f03cbd15c1a_story.html?utm_term=.f533148e9ef5.

Chukwudi Eze, Emmanuel, ed. *Race and the Enlightenment: A Reader*. Malden, MA: Blackwell, 1997.

Ciccota, Tom. "Harvard Study: Trigger Warnings Increase Anxiety over 'Distressing' Content." *Breitbart*, July 30, 2018. https://www.breitbart.com/tech/2018/07/30/harvard-study-trigger-warnings-increase-anxiety-over-distressing-content/.

Clark, Simon. "How White Supremacy Returned to Mainstream Politics." Center for American Progress, July 1, 2020. https://www.americanprogress.org/article/white-supremacy-retur ned-mainstream-politics/.

Clifford-Vaughan, Michalina. "Enlightenment and Education." *British Journal of Sociology* 14 (1963): 135–143.

Cohen, Jacob. "The Earth Is Round (p < .05)." *American Psychologist* 49 (1994): 997–1003.

Concha, Joe. "DePaul Cancels Conservative's Speech." *The Hill*, August 1, 2016. https://thehill. com/blogs/blog-briefing-room/news/289999-depaul-cancels-conservatives-speech.

Confas, Nathan. "Research on Group Differences in Intelligence: A Defense of Free Inquiry." *Philosophical Psychology* 33 (2020): 125–147.

Crenshaw, Kimberle, et al., eds. *Critical Race Theory: The Key Writings That Formed the Movement*. New York: New Press, 1996.

Dahlberg, Lincoln. "Cyberlibertarianism." *Oxford Research Encyclopedia of Communication*, October 26, 2017. https://oxfordre.com/communication/view/10.1093/acrefore/978019 0228613.001.0001/acrefore-9780190228613-e-70.

Davis, Carlo. "Oberlin Amends Its Trigger-Warning Policy." *New Republic*, April 9, 2014. https://newrepublic.com/article/117320/oberlin-amends-its-trigger-warning-policy.

Delgado, Richard, and Jean Stefancic. *Critical Race Theory: An Introduction*. Third edition. New York: New York University Press, 2017.

Denworth, Lydia. "The Kids (Who Use Tech) Seem to Be All Right." *Scientific American*, January 15, 2019. https://www.scientificamerican.com/article/the-kids-who-use-tech-seem-to-be-all-right/?redirect=1.

DeVos, Betsy. "Remarks by Secretary DeVos to the National Constitution Center's Annual Constitution Day Celebration." U.S. Department of Education, September 17, 2018. https://www.ed.gov/news/speeches/remarks-secretary-devos-national-constitution-centers-ann ual-constitution-day-celebration.

Dewey, John. *Democracy and Education*. Mineola, NY: Dover Books, 2004.

"Disinvitation Database." Foundation for Individual Rights in Education. Accessed February 5, 2022. https://www.thefire.org/research/disinvitation-database/users-guide-to-fires-cam pus-disinvitation-database/.

Dixon-Román, Ezekiel J. "Standardized Tests Like SAT and ACT Favor Students with Family Wealth." *Philadelphia Inquirer*, October 29, 2019. https://www.inquirer.com/opinion/com mentary/sat-act-standardized-tests-equity-socioeconomic-status-wealth-20191029.html.

Domby, Adam H. *The False Cause: Fraud, Fabrication, and White Supremacy in Confederate Memory*. Charlottesville: University of Virginia, 2020.

Doyle, William. *An American Insurrection: James Meredith and the Battle of Oxford, Mississippi, 1962*. Reprint edition. New York: Anchor Books, 2003.

Dubrovskiy, Dmitry. "Academic Rights in Russia and the Internationalization of Higher Education." *Academe* (American Association of University Professors), Fall 2019. https://www.aaup.org/article/academic-rights-russia-and-internationalization-higher-education#. Ydh66FlOk2x.

Dye, Kelly, and Golnaz Golnaraghi. "Organizational Benefits through Diversity Management: Theoretical Perspectives on the Business Case." In *The Oxford Handbook of Diversity in Organizations*, edited by Regine Bendl et al., 255–278. New York: Oxford University Press, 2015.

Eastland, Terry. "Survey Confirms What Many Suspected: Free Speech Is in Trouble." *Weekly Standard*, September 20, 2017. https://www.weeklystandard.com/terry-eastland/survey-confirms-what-many-suspected-free-speech-is-in-trouble.

Editorial Board. "James Madison Weeps." *Wall Street Journal*, September 19, 2017.

Editorial Board. "Warning: College Students, This Editorial May Upset You." *Los Angeles Times*, March 31, 2014. https://www.latimes.com/nation/la-ed-trigger-warnings-20140331-story.html.

Elmore, Tim. "What's Happening to College Students Today?" *Psychology Today*, November 30, 2015. https://www.psychologytoday.com/us/blog/artificial-maturity/201511/what-s-happening-college-students-today.

"Equity, Diversity, and Inclusion." Vanderbilt University. Accessed February 5, 2022. https://www.vanderbilt.edu/diversity/.

"Events." Turning Point USA. Accessed February 5, 2022. https://www.tpusa.com/events.

"Executive Order: Improving Free Inquiry, Transparency, and Accountability at Colleges and Universities." American Presidency Project, March 21, 2019. https://www.presidency.ucsb. edu/documents/executive-order-13864-improving-free-inquiry-transparency-and-acc ountability-colleges-and.

"Executive Order on Combatting Anti-Semitism." Trump White House Archives, December 11, 2019. https://trumpwhitehouse.archives.gov/presidential-actions/executive-order-combating-anti-semitism/.

"Ex-Mizzou Professor Melissa Click, Fired over Protest Clash, Gets New Job." NBC News, September 4, 2016. https://www.nbcnews.com/news/us-news/ex-mizzou-professor-meli ssa-click-fired-over-protest-clash-gets-n642711.

"Fast Facts: College Crime." National Center for Education Statistics, 2018. https://nces.ed.gov/fastfacts/display.asp?id=804.

"Fast Facts: Education Institutions." National Center for Educational Statistics. Accessed February 5, 2022. https://nces.ed.gov/fastfacts/display.asp?id=84.

Ferguson, Niall. "I'm Helping to Start a New College Because Higher Ed Is Broken." *Bloomberg*, November 8, 2021. https://www.bloomberg.com/opinion/articles/2021-11-08/niall-fergu son-america-s-woke-universities-need-to-be-replaced.

Fischer, Howard. "Arizona Bill Would Require Educators to Present Both Sides of 'Controversial Issues.'" KAWC, May 7, 2021. https://www.kawc.org/education/2021-05-07/arizona-bill-would-require-educators-to-present-both-sides-of-controversial-issues.

Fish, Stanley. "Free Speech Is Not an Academic Value." *Chronicle of Higher Education*, March 20, 2017. https://www.chronicle.com/article/Free-Speech-Is-Not-an-Academic/239536.

"5 Common Survey Question Mistakes That'll Ruin Your Data." SurveyMonkey.com. Accessed February 5, 2022. https://www.surveymonkey.com/mp/5-common-survey-mistakes-ruin-your-data/.

Flaherty, Colleen. "Trigger Unhappy." *Inside Higher Ed*, April 14, 2014. http://www.insidehighe red.com/news/2014/04/14/oberlin-backs-down-trigger-warnings-professors-who-teach-sensitive-material?utm_source=slate&utm_medium=referral&utm_term=partner#sth ash.7M9oFb0K.dpbs.

Florido, Adrian. "'We Can and Should Teach This History': New Bills Limit How Teachers Talk about Race." National Public Radio, May 25, 2021. https://www.npr.org/2021/05/25/1000273 981/we-can-and-should-teach-this-history-new-bills-limit-how-teachers-talk-about-rac.

"Food Insecurity." Government Accountability Office, December 2018. https://www.gao.gov/assets/gao-19-95.pdf.

Foner, Eric. *The Story of American Freedom*. New York: W. W. Norton, 1998.

"Free to Think 2021: Report of the Scholars at Risk Academic Freedom Monitoring Project." Scholars at Risk. Accessed February 5, 2022. https://www.scholarsatrisk.org/wp-content/uploads/2021/12/Scholars-at-Risk-Free-to-Think-2021.pdf.

"Frequently Asked Questions." University of Austin. Accessed February 5, 2022. https://www.uaustin.org/faq.

Friedersdorf, Conor. "Campus Activists Weaponize 'Safe Space.'" *The Atlantic*, November 10, 2015. https://www.theatlantic.com/politics/archive/2015/11/how-campus-activists-are-weaponizing-the-safe-space/415080/.

Friedersdorf, Conor. "The Glaring Evidence That Free Speech Is Threatened on Campus." *The Atlantic*, March 4, 2016. https://www.theatlantic.com/politics/archive/2016/03/the-glaring-evidence-that-free-speech-is-threatened-on-campus/471825/.

Furst, Camille. "Colleges Targeted with Racist Zoom Bombings as White Supremacy Spikes." NBC Washington, April 15, 2021. https://www.nbcwashington.com/news/local/colleges-targeted-with-racist-zoom-bombings-as-white-supremacist-propaganda-spikes/2622296/.

Gabennesch, Howard. "Authoritarianism as World View." *American Journal of Sociology* 77 (March 1972): 857–875.

Gancarski, A. G. "Marco Rubio Attacks Critical Race Theory as 'New Institutional Orthodoxy.'" Florida Politics, June 16, 2021. https://floridapolitics.com/archives/436121-crt-rubio/.

Garland, Phil. "Question Order Matters." Survey Monkey. Accessed February 5, 2022. https://www.surveymonkey.com/curiosity/question-order-matters/.

Gay, Peter. *The Enlightenment: An Interpretation*. Revised edition. New York: W. W. Norton, 1996.

George, Robert P. *The Clash of Orthodoxies: Law, Religion, and Morality in Crisis*. Wilmington, DE: ISI Books, 2001.

George, Robert P. *Conscience and Its Enemies: Confronting the Dogmas of Liberal Secularism*. Updated and expanded edition. Wilmington, DE: ISI Books, 2016.

George, Robert P. *In Defense of Natural Law*. Revised edition. New York: Oxford University Press, 2001.

Giorgis, Hannah. "A Deeply Provincial View of Free Speech." *The Atlantic*, July 13, 2020. https://www.theatlantic.com/culture/archive/2020/07/harpers-letter-free-speech/614080/.

Goldberg, Michelle. "A Frenzy of Book Banning." *Baltimore Sun*, December 7, 2021. https://
www.baltimoresun.com/opinion/op-ed/bs-ed-op-1124-mgoldberg-book-banning-20211
207-xxwhd5mrrndudc65kpatftbhve-story.html.

Goldrick-Rab, Sara. *Paying the Price: College Costs, Financial Aid, and the Betrayal of the
American Dream*. Chicago: University of Chicago Press, 2016.

Goss, Scott. "Delaware State University, Fox News, and the Snowball Story Heard 'round the
World.'" Delaware Online, August 23, 2018. https://www.delawareonline.com/story/news/
local/2018/08/23/dsu-fox-news-and-snowball-story-heard-round-world/1071412002/.

Greenberg, Jon. "Ben Shapiro." PolitiFact, November 5, 2014. https://www.politifact.com/fac
tchecks/2014/nov/05/ben-shapiro/shapiro-says-majority-muslims-are-radicals/.

Greene, Peter. "Critical Race Theory Bans Are Expanding to Cover Broad Collection of Issues."
Forbes, September 29, 2021. https://www.forbes.com/sites/petergreene/2021/09/29/critical-
race-theory-bans-are-expanding-to-cover-broad-collection-of-issues/?sh=1381f56e5e5d.

Groppe, Maureen, and Sean Rossman. "President Donald Trump, in CPAC Speech, Said He'll
Sign 'Free Speech' Executive Order." *USA Today*, March 2, 2019. https://www.usatoday.com/
story/news/politics/2019/03/02/donald-trump-cpac-president-speaks-following-cohen-
hearing-korea/3039138002/.

Grutter v. Bollinger, 539 U.S. 306. Justia. Accessed February 5, 2022. https://supreme.justia.
com/cases/federal/us/539/306/.

Guess, Andrew, Jonathan Nagler, and Joshua Tucker. "Less Than You Think: Prevalence and
Predictors of Fake News Dissemination on Facebook." *Science Advances* 5 (2019). https://
advances.sciencemag.org/content/5/1/eaau4586.

Haidt, Jonathan. "Intimidation Is the New Normal on Campus." *Chronicle of Higher Education*,
April 26, 2017. https://www.chronicle.com/article/Intimidation-Is-the-New-Normal/
239890.

Haidt, Jonathan. "Why Universities Must Choose One Telos: Truth or Social Justice." Heterodox
Academy, October 21, 2016. https://heterodoxacademy.org/blog/one-telos-truth-or-social-
justice-2/.

Haidt, Jonathan, and Lee Jussim. "Psychological Science and Viewpoint Diversity." Association
for Psychological Science, January 29, 2016. https://www.psychologicalscience.org/obser
ver/psychological-science-and-viewpoint-diversity.

Haidt, Jonathan, and Greg Lukianoff. "Why It's a Bad Idea to Tell Students Words Are Violence."
The Atlantic, July 18, 2017. https://www.theatlantic.com/education/archive/2017/07/why-
its-a-bad-idea-to-tell-students-words-are-violence/533970/.

Hanlon, Aaron. "Are Liberal College Students Creating a Free Speech Crisis? Not According to
Data." NBC News, March 22, 2018. https://www.nbcnews.com/think/opinion/are-liberal-
college-students-creating-free-speech-crisis-not-according-ncna858906.

Hanlon, Aaron. "Why Colleges Have a Right to Reject Hateful Speakers Like Ann Coulter." *New
Republic*, April 24, 2017. https://newrepublic.com/article/142218/colleges-right-reject-hate
ful-speakers-like-ann-coulter.

Harroz, Joseph, Jr. "Presidential Statement on the Intersection of First Amendment Freedoms
and Diversity, Equity, and Inclusion at the University of Oklahoma." University of Oklahoma.
Accessed February 5, 2022. https://www.ou.edu/web/news_events/articles/news_2021/
presidential-statement-on-intersection-of-first-amendment-freedoms-and-dei-at-ou.

"Harvard Study: Trigger Warnings Actually Harmful to Students." *The College Fix*, July 29,
2018. https://www.thecollegefix.com/harvard-study-trigger-warnings-actually-harmful-to-
students/.

Hauser, Hauser. "An Alabama Building Honors a Klan Leader." *New York Times*, February 8,
2022. https://www.nytimes.com/2022/02/08/us/alabama-kkk-autherine-lucy-foster.html.

Healy, Thomas. "Who's Afraid of Free Speech?" *The Atlantic*, June 18, 2017. https://www.thea
tlantic.com/politics/archive/2017/06/whos-afraid-of-free-speech/530094/.

Hemmer, Nicole. "A12." Past Punditry, August 6, 2018. http://www.pastpundit.com/a12.

Hemmer, Nicole. "Eternally Frustrated by 'Liberal' Universities, Conservatives Now Want to Tear Them Down." *Vox*, March 8, 2017. https://www.vox.com/the-big-idea/2017/3/7/14841 292/liberal-universities-conservative-faculty-sizzler-pc.

Hemmer, Nicole. *Messengers of the Right: Conservative Media and the Transformation of American Politics*. Philadelphia: University of Pennsylvania Press, 2016.

"Henry Harpending." Southern Poverty Law Center. Accessed February 5, 2022. https://www.splcenter.org/fighting-hate/extremist-files/individual/henry-harpending.

Hernandez, Joe. "School Leaders Say HBCUs Are Undeterred after a Series of Bomb Threats." National Public Radio, February 8, 2022. https://www.npr.org/2022/02/08/1079294424/hbcu-bomb-threats-black-colleges.

Heying, Heather. "Can the University of Austin Spark a New Enlightenment?" *The Spectator*, November 18, 2021. https://spectatorworld.com/topic/university-austin-spark-new-enligh tenment/.

Hicks, Georgie. "Students Questioned about Alleged Harassment: Allegations of Anti-Black Racism Ensue." *Cooper Point Journal*, May 24, 2017. http://www.cooperpointjournal.com/2017/05/24/students-questioned-about-alleged-harassment-allegations-of-anti-black-rac ism-ensue/.

"A History of Privilege in American Higher Education." Best Colleges, July 17, 2020. https://www.bestcolleges.com/blog/history-privilege-higher-education/.

Ho, Daniel E., and Kevin M. Quinn. "Viewpoint Diversity and Media Consolidation: An Empirical Study." *Stanford Law Review* 61 (2009): 781–868.

Holmes, Lindsay. "A Quick Lesson on What Trigger Warnings Actually Do." *Huffington Post*, February 6, 2017. https://www.huffpost.com/entry/university-of-chicago-trigger-warning_n_57bf16d9e4b085c1ff28176d.

Hunt, Jonathan. "Communists and the Classroom: Radicals in U.S. Education, 1930–1960." *Composition Studies* 43, no. 2 (2015): 22–42.

Inbar, Yoel, and Joris Lammers. "Political Diversity in Social and Personality Psychology." *Perspectives on Psychological Science* 7, no. 5 (2012): 1–8.

Institute for Propaganda Analysis. "How to Detect Propaganda." In *Propaganda*, edited by Robert Jackall, 217–224. New York: New York University Press, 1995.

Jackson, Brooks, and Kathleen Hall Jamieson. *unSpun: Finding Facts in a World of Disinformation*. New York: Random House, 2007.

Jaramillo, Sara, Zachary Horne, and Micah Goldwater. "The Impact of Anecdotal Information on Medical Decision-Making." OSF, May 15, 2019. https://osf.io/dkcwv/.

Jaschik, Scott. "Shouting Down a Lecture." *Inside Higher Ed*, March 3, 2017. https://www.ins idehighered.com/news/2017/03/03/middlebury-students-shout-down-lecture-charles-murray.

Jaschik, Scott. "Speech, Interrupted." *Inside Higher Ed*, March 6, 2018. https://www.insideh ighered.com/news/2018/03/06/students-interrupt-several-portions-speech-christina-hoff-sommers.

Jeantet, Diane. "Brazil Education Overhaul Aims at Ousting 'Marxist Ideology.'" AP News, February 6, 2019. https://www.apnews.com/0fb07d84d14c4d948f7028907c60f23f.

John, Tara. "Poland Just Passed a Holocaust Bill That Is Causing Outrage." *Time*, February 1, 2018. https://time.com/5128341/poland-holocaust-law/.

Johnston, Angus. "Student Protests, Then and Now." *Chronicle of Higher Education*, December 11, 2015. https://www.chronicle.com/article/Student-Protests-ThenNow/234542.

Jones, Payton. "Trigger Warning: Empirical Evidence Ahead." Heterodox Academy, September 12, 2018. https://heterodoxacademy.org/blog/trigger-warning-empirical-evidence-ahead/.

Jones, Payton, Benjamin Bellet, and Richard McNally. "Helping or Harming? The Effect of Trigger Warnings on Individuals with Trauma Histories." OSF Preprints, July 10, 2019. https://osf.io/axn6z/.

Jussim, Lee. "Stigmatizing Legitimate Dissent Threatens Freedom of Speech." Heterodox Academy, November 25, 2017. https://heterodoxacademy.org/blog/stigmatizing-legitimate-dissent-threatens-freedom-of-speech/.

Justice, Tiffany, and Tina Descovich. "What 'School Board Moms' Really Want—And Why Candidates Ignore Us at Their Peril." *Washington Post*, November 8, 2021. https://www.washingtonpost.com/opinions/2021/11/08/moms-for-liberty-education-elections/.

Kamentz, Anya. "Half of Professors in NPR Ed Survey Have Used 'Trigger Warnings.'" National Public Radio, September 7, 2016. https://www.npr.org/sections/ed/2016/09/07/492979242/half-of-professors-in-npr-ed-survey-have-used-trigger-warnings.

Kampa, Dana. "Conservative Pundit Ben Shapiro Lectures to Turbulent Crowd on Safe Spaces, Freedom of Speech." *Badger Herald*, November 17, 2016. Madison, WI. https://badgerherald.com/news/2016/11/17/conservative-pundit-ben-shapiro-lectures-to-turbulent-crowd-on-safe-spaces-freedom-of-speech/.

Kant, Immanuel. "What Is Enlightenment?, 1784." Internet History Sourcebooks Project, Fordham University, 1997. https://sourcebooks.fordham.edu/mod/kant-whatis.asp.

Karabel, Jerome. *The Chosen: The Hidden History of Admission and Exclusion at Harvard, Yale, and Princeton*. New York: Houghton Mifflin, 2005.

Kendi, Ibram X. *Stamped from the Beginning: The Definitive History of Racist Ideas in America*. New York: Nation Books, 2016.

Khazan, Olga. "The Real Problem with Trigger Warnings." *The Atlantic*, March 28, 2019. https://www.theatlantic.com/health/archive/2019/03/do-trigger-warnings-work/585871/.

Kirkpatrick, David D. "The Right Hand of the Fathers." *New York Times Magazine*, December 20, 2009, 24–29.

Knight Foundation. 2017 College Student Survey. Washington, DC: Gallup. https://kf-site-production.s3.amazonaws.com/media_elements/files/000/000/147/original/Knight_Foundation_2017_Student_Survey_Questionnaire_1_.pdf.

Kolowich, Steve, Brock Read, and Andy Thomason. "10 Revealing Details in the Melissa Click Investigation." *Chronicle of Higher Education*, February 26, 2016. https://www.chronicle.com/article/10-Revealing-Details-in-the/235502.

Kors, Alan Charles, and Harvey A. Silverglate. *The Shadow University: The Betrayal of Liberty on America's Campuses*. New York: Free Press, 1998.

Kox, Karen L. *No Common Ground: Confederate Monuments and the Ongoing Fight for Racial Justice*. Chapel Hill: University of North Carolina Press, 2021.

Kozak-Gilroy, Jasmine. "A Year of Events: A Timeline of Protests." *Cooper Point Journal*, May 31, 2017. http://www.cooperpointjournal.com/2017/05/31/a-year-of-events-a-time-line-of-protests/.

Kristoff, Nicholas. "The Dangers of Echo Chambers on Campus." *New York Times*, December 10, 2016, https://www.nytimes.com/2016/12/10/opinion/sunday/the-dangers-of-echo-chambers-on-campus.html.

Kristoff, Nicholas. "Stop the Knee-Jerk Liberalism That Hurts Its Own Cause." *New York Times*, June 29, 2019. https://www.nytimes.com/2019/06/29/opinion/sunday/liberalism-united-states.html.

Kurtz, Stanley. "The Campus Free-Speech Crisis Deepens." *National Review*, September 27, 2017. https://www.nationalreview.com/corner/campus-free-speech-crisis-deepens/.

Kurtzleben, Danielle. "When Republicans Attack 'Cancel Culture,' What Does It Mean?" National Public Radio, February 10, 2021. https://www.npr.org/2021/02/10/965815679/is-cancel-culture-the-future-of-the-gop.

Lambe, Jerry. "AG Barr: 'Secularists' and 'Pop Culture' Are Waging 'Unremitting Assault on Religion and Traditional Values.'" *Law and Crime*, October 12, 2019. https://lawandcrime.com/high-profile/ag-barr-secularists-and-pop-culture-are-waging-unremitting-assault-on-religion-and-traditional-values/.

"A Letter on Justice and Open Debate." *Harper's*, July 7, 2020. https://harpers.org/a-letter-on-justice-and-open-debate/.

Levitsky, Steven, and Daniel Ziblatt. *How Democracies Die*. New York: Crown, 2018.

Lilla, Mark. *The Shipwrecked Mind: On Political Reaction*. New York: New York Review of Books, 2016.

Lima, Cristiano. "A Whistleblower's Power: Four Key Takeaways from the Facebook Papers." *Washington Post*, October 26, 2021.

Lizza, Ryan. "Americans Tune In to 'Cancel Culture'—and Don't Like What They See." *Politico*, July 22, 2020. https://www.politico.com/news/2020/07/22/americans-cancel-culture-377412.

Loewen, James W., and Edward H. Sebesta, eds. *The Confederate and Neo-Confederate Reader: The "Great Truth" about the "Lost Cause."* Jackson: University of Mississippi Press, 2010.

LoMonte, Frank D. "The Legislative Response to a Perceived 'Free Speech Crisis' on Campus." *Communications Lawyer* 34 (Winter 2019): 7–11. http://ezaccess.libraries.psu.edu/login?url=https://search-proquest-com.ezaccess.libraries.psu.edu/docview/2199858499?accountid=13158.

Longman, Karen A., ed. *Diversity Matters: Race, Ethnicity, and the Future of Christian Higher Education*. Abilene, TX: Abilene Christian University Press, 2017.

Lonsdale, Joe. "America's Leadership Culture Is Rotten." *Washington Post*, November 22, 2021. https://www.washingtonpost.com/opinions/2021/11/22/joe-lonsdale-university-of-austin/.

"A Look Back." Vanderbilt University. Accessed February 5, 2022. https://www.vanderbilt.edu/celebratingblackhistory/look-back/.

Lopez, Brian. "The Law That Prompted a School Administrator to Call for an 'Opposing' Perspective on the Holocaust Is Causing Confusion across Texas." *Texas Tribune*, October 15, 2021. https://www.texastribune.org/2021/10/15/Texas-critical-race-theory-law-confuses-educators/.

Lotz, Amanda. "Profit, Not Free Speech, Governs Media Companies' Decisions on Controversy." The Conversation, August 10, 2018. https://theconversation.com/profit-not-free-speech-governs-media-companies-decisions-on-controversy-101292.

Lowery, Wesley, and Michael A. Fletcher. "'The Michael Brown Shooting Changed My Life.'" *Washington Post*, November 22, 2015. https://www.washingtonpost.com/business/economy/the-michael-brown-shooting-changed-my-life/2015/11/22/4ad12b94-8bac-11e5-acff-673ae92ddd2b_story.html?utm_term=.663564bfdbec.

Lukianoff, Greg. *Unlearning Liberty: Campus Censorship and the End of American Debate*. New York: Encounter, 2014.

Lukianoff, Greg, and Jonathan Haidt. "The Coddling of the American Mind." *The Atlantic*, September 2015. https://www.theatlantic.com/magazine/archive/2015/09/the-coddling-of-the-american-mind/399356/.

Lukianoff, Greg, and Jonathan Haidt. *The Coddling of the American Mind: How Good Intentions and Bad Ideas Are Setting Up a Generation for Failure*. New York: Penguin, 2018.

MacCulloch, Diarmaid. *Christianity: The First Three Thousand Years*. New York: Viking, 2010.

MacDonald, Heather. *The Diversity Delusion: How Race and Gender Pandering Corrupt the University and Undermine Our Culture*. New York: St. Martin's, 2018.

MacDonald, Heather. "Trump's Executive Order on Anti-Semitism Might Be Well-Meaning, but It Could Limit Free Expression." Manhattan Institute, December 24, 2019. https://www.

manhattan-institute.org/anti-semitism-executive-order-president-trump-campus-free-speech.

Magness, Phillip W. "Tenured Radicals Are Real." *Chronicle of Higher Education*, September 24, 2020. https://www.chronicle.com/article/tenured-radicals-are-real.

Maher, Bill. "Season 16, Episode 31." *Real Time with Bill Maher.* HBO, October 12, 2018. https://www.hbo.com/real-time-with-bill-maher/2018/31-episode-476.

"Male Supremacy." Southern Poverty Law Center. Accessed February 5, 2022. https://www.splcenter.org/fighting-hate/extremist-files/ideology/male-supremacy.

Mangan, Katherine. "A Planned University 'Dedicated to Truth' Will Welcome 'Witches Who Refuse to Burn.'" *Chronicle of Higher Education*, November 8, 2021. https://www.chronicle.com/article/a-planned-university-dedicated-to-truth-will-welcome-witches-who-refuse-to-burn.

"Massive Resistance." Equal Justice Initiative. 2018. https://segregationinamerica.eji.org/report/massive-resistance.html.

"Massive Resistance." Virginia Museum of History and Culture. Accessed February 5, 2022, https://virginiahistory.org/learn/historical-book/chapter/massive-resistance.

Mastrangelo, Alana. "Review: Charlie Kirk's 'Campus Battlefield' Explains How to Fight the Death of Free Speech on Campus." *Breitbart*, November 23, 2018. https://www.breitbart.com/tech/2018/11/23/review-charlie-kirks-campus-battlefield-explains-how-to-fight-the-death-of-free-speech-on-campus/.

Mathis-Lilly, Ben. "Sweet Jesus, Will the NYT's Conservatives Ever Write about Anything but the 'Intolerant Left' Ever Again?" *Slate*, March 9, 2018. https://slate.com/news-and-politics/2018/03/david-brooks-times-conservatives.html.

McArdle, Megan. "Campus Free Speech Is Threatened. But How Much?" *Washington Post*, April 13, 2018. https://www.washingtonpost.com/blogs/post-partisan/wp/2018/04/13/campus-free-speech-is-threatened-but-how-much/?utm_term=.b4f6e6d1b057.

McNamara, Mary. "'Cancel Culture' Is Not the Problem. The Harper's Letter Is." *Los Angeles Times*, July 9, 2020. https://www.latimes.com/entertainment-arts/story/2020-07-09/cancel-culture-harpers-letter.

McWhorter, John. "Here's a Fact: We're Routinely Asked to Use Leftist Fictions." *New York Times*, November 22, 2021. https://www.nytimes.com/2021/11/19/opinion/heres-a-fact-were-routinely-asked-to-use-leftist-fictions.html.

McWhorter, John. *Woke Racism: How a New Religion Has Betrayed Black America.* New York: Penguin, 2021.

Menchaca, Megan. "UT Faculty Council Passes Resolution Supporting Freedom to Teach Critical Race Theory." *Austin American-Statesman*, February 15, 2022. https://www.statesman.com/story/news/2022/02/15/ut-faculty-council-passes-resolution-defending-teaching-critical-race-theory/6754421001/.

Meredith, James. *Three Years in Mississippi.* Oxford: University Press of Mississippi, 2019.

Mermin, Jonathan. "The Media's Independence Problem." *World Policy Journal* 21 (Fall 2004): 67–71.

Meyersburg, Cynthia. "Harvard Study: Trigger Warnings May Impede Resilience." Foundation for Individual Rights in Education. August 1, 2018. https://www.thefire.org/harvard-study-trigger-warnings-may-impede-resilience/.

"Milo Yiannopoulos: Five Things to Know." Anti-Defamation League. Accessed February 5, 2022. https://www.adl.org/resources/backgrounders/milo-yiannopoulos-five-things-to-know.

Minkowitz, Donna. "Why Racists (and Liberals!) Keep Writing for *Quillette*." *The Nation*, December 5, 2019. https://www.thenation.com/article/archive/quillette-fascist-creep/.

Minta, Molly. "UM Faculty Senate Latest to Oppose Anti-CRT Legislation." *Mississippi Today*, February 23, 2022. https://mississippitoday.org/2022/02/23/um-faculty-opposes-anti-critical-race-theory-legislation/.

"Mission, Vision, and Values." University of Mississippi. Accessed February 5, 2022. https://dce.olemiss.edu/vision-mission-and-values/.

Monroe, Stephen H. *Heritage and Hate: Old South Rhetoric at Southern Universities*. Tuscaloosa: University of Alabama Press, 2021.

Morey, Alex. "University of Chicago's 'Academic Freedom' Letter a Win for Campus Speech." Foundation for Individual Rights in Education, August 25, 2016. https://www.thefire.org/u-chicagos-academic-freedom-letter-a-win-for-campus-speech/.

Nadworny, Elissa. "As Elite Campuses Diversity, a 'Bias toward Privilege Exists." National Public Radio, March 5, 2019. https://www.npr.org/2019/03/05/699977122/as-elite-campuses-diversify-a-bias-towards-privilege-persists.

"National Field Program." Turning Point USA. Accessed February 5, 2022. https://www.tpusa.com/nfp.

National Human Genome Research Institute. Human Genome Project. Accessed February 5, 2022. https://www.genome.gov/human-genome-project.

"News and Updates." University of Austin. Accessed February 5, 2022. https://www.uaustin.org/news.

Nichol, Gene. "Political Interference with Academic Freedom and Free Speech at Public Universities." *Academe* (American Association of University Professors), Fall 2019. https://www.aaup.org/article/political-interference-academic-freedom-and-free-speech-public-universities#.YhTsnJZOk2z.

O'Brien, William H., Mary E. Kaplar, and Jennifer J. McGrath. "Broadly Based Causal Models of Behavior Disorders." In *Comprehensive Handbook of Psychological Assessment, Volume 3: Behavioral Assessment*, edited by Stephen N. Haynes and Elaine M. Heiby, 69–93. Hoboken, NJ: Wiley, 2003.

Office of the Dean of Students, University of Chicago. Welcome Letter to Class of 2020, August 2016. https://news.uchicago.edu/sites/default/files/attachments/Dear_Class_of_2020_Students.pdf.

Orben, Amy, and Andrew K. Przybylski. "The Association between Adolescent Well-Being and Digital Technology Use." *Nature Human Behaviour* 3 (2019): 173–182.

Page, Scott E. *The Difference: How the Power of Diversity Creates Better Groups, Firms, Schools, and Societies*. Princeton, NJ: Princeton University Press, 2008.

Pager, Devah, and Hana Shepherd. "The Sociology of Discrimination: Racial Discrimination in Employment, Housing, Credit, and Consumer Markets." *Annual Review of Sociology* 34 (2008): 181–209.

Palfrey, John. *Safe Spaces, Brave Spaces: Diversity and Free Expression in Education*. Cambridge, MA: MIT Press, 2017.

Palus, Shannon. "The Latest Study on Trigger Warnings Finally Convinced Me They're Not Worth It." *Slate*, July 12, 2019. https://slate.com/technology/2019/07/trigger-warnings-research-shows-they-dont-work-might-hurt.html.

Panchal, Nirmita, et al. "The Implications of COVID-19 for Mental Health and Substance Use." Kaiser Family Foundation, February 10, 2021. https://www.kff.org/coronavirus-covid-19/issue-brief/the-implications-of-covid-19-for-mental-health-and-substance-use/.

Paresky, Pamela B. "Harvard Study: Trigger Warnings Might Coddle the Mind." *Psychology Today*, August 3, 2018. https://www.psychologytoday.com/us/blog/happiness-and-the-pursuit-leadership/201808/harvard-study-trigger-warnings-might-coddle-the.

Park, Madison. "Ben Shapiro Spoke at Berkeley as Protestors Gathered Outside." CNN, September 15, 2017. https://www.cnn.com/2017/09/14/us/berkeley-ben-shapiro-speech/index.html.

Park, Madison, and Kyung Lah. "Berkeley Protests of Yiannopoulos Caused $100,000 In Damage." CNN, February 2, 2017. https://www.cnn.com/2017/02/01/us/milo-yiannopou los-berkeley/index.html.

Parker, Kathleen. "The 'Swaddled Generation.'" *Washington Post*, May 19, 2015.

"Partnerships." Young America's Foundation. Accessed February 5, 2022. https://www.yaf.org/partnerships/.

Patterson, Thomas E. *Informing the News: The Need for Knowledge-Based Journalism.* New York: Vintage, 2013.

Pearson, Michael. "A Timeline of the University of Missouri Protests." CNN, November 10, 2015. https://www.cnn.com/2015/11/09/us/missouri-protest-timeline/index.html.

Peller, Gary. "I've Been a Critical Race Theorist for 30 Years." *Politico*, June 30, 2021. https://www.politico.com/news/magazine/2021/06/30/critical-race-theory-lightning-rod-opin ion-497046.

Peters, Jeremy W. "In Name of Free Speech, States Crack Down on Campus Protests." *Washington Post*, June 14, 2018. https://www.nytimes.com/2018/06/14/us/politics/campus-speech-protests.html.

Peters, Uwe, Nathan Honeycutt, Andreas De Block, and Lee Jussim. "Ideological Diversity, Hostility, and Discrimination in Philosophy." *Philosophical Psychology* 33 (2020): 511–548.

Pilon, Roger. "The University of Chicago Has No Room for Cyberbullies." *Cato Blog*, August 25, 2016. https://www.cato.org/blog/university-chicago-has-no-room-crybullies.

Plomin, Robert. "What Does Genetic Research Tell Us about Equal Opportunity and Meritocracy?" *Quillette*, October 15, 2018. https://quillette.com/2018/10/15/what-does-genetic-research-tell-us-about-equal-opportunity-and-meritocracy/.

"Polish Ultra-conservatives Launch University to Mould New Elites." Reuters, May 28, 2021. https://www.reuters.com/world/polish-ultra-conservatives-launch-university-mould-new-elites-2021-05-28/.

Pondy, Louis R. "Organizational Conflict: Concepts and Models." *Administrative Science Quarterly* 12 (1967): 296–320.

Post, Robert C. "There Is No 1st Amendment Right to Speak on a College Campus." *Vox*, December 31, 2017. https://www.vox.com/the-big-idea/2017/10/25/16526442/first-amendment-college-campuses-milo-spencer-protests.

Powell, Lewis F., Jr. "Attack on American Free Enterprise System." Washington and Lee Law School, August 23, 1971. https://law2.wlu.edu/deptimages/Powell%20Archives/PowellM emorandumTypescript.pdf.

"The Problem." Heterodox Academy. Accessed February 5, 2022. https://heterodoxacademy. org/the-problem/.

Quintana, Chris. "Even in Fascism's Heyday, Anti-Fascists on Campus Were Controversial." *Chronicle of Higher Education*, April 12, 2017. https://www.chronicle.com/article/Even-in-Fascism-s-Heyday/239761.

Radio Free Hillsdale. WRFH 101.7. Accessed February 5, 2022. https://soundcloud.com/rad iofreehillsdale/170104-125442-mz001.

Rampell, Catherine. "A Chilling Study Shows How Hostile College Students Are toward Free Speech." *Washington Post*, September 18, 2017. https://www.washingtonpost.com/opinions/a-chilling-study-shows-how-hostile-college-students-are-toward-free-speech/2017/09/18/cbb1a234-9ca8-11e7-9083-fbfddf6804c2_story.html?utm_term=.ae6f0aa167d8.

Rampell, Catherine. "Wondering Whether Today's College Students Have Become Too Fragile?" *Washington Post*, May 13, 2016. https://www.washingtonpost.com/news/rampage/wp/2016/05/13/wondering-whether-todays-college-students-have-become-too-fragile-read-this-document/?utm_term=.1843bd1b88cc.

Ray, Rashawn, and Alexandra Gibbons. "Why Are States Banning Critical Race Theory?" Brookings Institution, November 2021. https://www.brookings.edu/blog/fixgov/2021/07/02/why-are-states-banning-critical-race-theory/.

Redden, Elizabeth. "Academic Freedom Front Lines." *Inside Higher Ed*, March 30, 2017. https://www.insidehighered.com/news/2017/03/30/hungary-and-russia-western-style-universities-are-under-threat.

Redden, Elizabeth. "Hungary Officially Ends Gender Studies Programs." *Inside Higher Ed*, October 17, 2018. https://www.insidehighered.com/quicktakes/2018/10/17/hungary-officially-ends-gender-studies-programs.

Redden, Elizabeth. "'Zoombombing' Attacks Disrupt Classes." *Inside Higher Education*, March 26, 2020. https://www.insidehighered.com/news/2020/03/26/zoombombers-disrupt-online-classes-racist-pornographic-content.

Reeve, Elspeth. "Every Every Every Generation Has Been the Me Me Me Generation." *The Atlantic*, May 9, 2013. https://www.theatlantic.com/national/archive/2013/05/me-generation-time/315151/.

Regents of Univ. of California v. Bakke, 438 U.S. 265 (1978). Justia, June 28, 1978. https://supreme.justia.com/cases/federal/us/438/265/.

Report of the Committee on University Discipline for Disruptive Conduct. Provost, University of Chicago, June 2, 2017. https://provost.uchicago.edu/sites/default/files/DCCRevisedFinal%20%286-2-2017%29.pdf.

"Resolution in Support of Academic Freedom and Rejection of Attempts to Interfere with the Teaching of Racial and Social Justice." Senate Committees on Education Equity and Campus Environment; Faculty Affairs; Intra-University Relations, Pennsylvania State University, January 25, 2022. https://senate.psu.edu/files/2022/02/January-25-2022-Appendix-C-editorial-revisions.pdf.

"Restoring Free Speech on Campus." Goldwater Institute, January 30, 2017. https://goldwaterinstitute.org/campus-free-speech/.

Reynolds, P. Preston. "UVA and the History of Race: Eugenics, the Racial Integrity Act, Health Disparities." *UVA Today*, January 9, 2020. https://news.virginia.edu/content/uva-and-history-race-eugenics-racial-integrity-act-health-disparities.

Rhode, Gregory L. *Minority Broadcast Ownership*. New York: Novinka, 2002.

Roberts, Brent W., Grant Edmonds, and Emily Grijalva. "It Is Developmental Me, Not Generation Me: Developmental Changes Are More Important Than Generational Changes in Narcissism." *Perspectives on Psychological Science* 5 (2010): 97–102.

Roberts-Miller, Patricia. *Demagoguery and Democracy*. New York: The Experiment, 2017.

Roberts-Miller, Patricia. *Rhetoric and Demagoguery*. Carbondale: Southern Illinois University Press, 2019.

Robertson, Derek. "How 'Owning the Libs' Became the GOP's Chief Strategy." *Politico*, March 21, 2021. https://www.politico.com/news/magazine/2021/03/21/owning-the-libs-history-trump-politics-pop-culture-477203.

Robin, Corey. *The Reactionary Mind: Conservatism from Edmund Burke to Donald Trump*. Second Edition. New York: Oxford University Press, 2018.

Rodriguez, Fernando, Rebecca Rhodes, Kevin Miller, and Priti Shah. "Examining the Influence of Anecdotal Stories and the Interplay of Individual Differences on Reasoning." *Thinking and Reasoning* 22 (2016): 274–296.

Roll, Nick. "The Kids Are Alright." *Inside Higher Ed*, October 13, 2017. https://www.insidehighered.com/news/2017/10/13/research-says-college-students-no-more-narcissistic-previous-generations-age.

Ross, Jannell. "Obama Says Liberal College Students Should Not Be 'Coddled.'" *Washington Post*, September 15, 2015. https://www.washingtonpost.com/news/the-fix/wp/2015/09/

15/obama-says-liberal-college-students-should-not-be-coddled-are-we-really-surprised/
?utm_term=.4982d3ff1779.

Roth, Michael S. *Safe Enough Spaces: A Pragmatist's Approach to Inclusion, Free Speech, and Political Correctness on College Campuses.* New Haven, CT: Yale University Press, 2019.

Rothman, Noah. *Unjust: Social Justice and the Unmaking of America.* Washington, DC: Gateway Editions, 2019.

Ruffin, Arial. "MU Community Creates Group Supporting Michael Brown." KOMU News, August 25, 2014. https://www.komu.com/news/mu-community-creates-group-supporting-michael-brown.

Sachs, Jeffrey Adam. "The 'Campus Free Speech Crisis' Is a Myth. Here Are the Facts." *Washington Post,* March 16, 2018. https://www.washingtonpost.com/news/monkey-cage/wp/2018/03/16/the-campus-free-speech-crisis-is-a-myth-here-are-the-facts/?utm_term=.33e1071e17d8.

Saini, Angela. "Why Race Science Is on the Rise Again." *The Guardian,* May 18, 2019. https://www.theguardian.com/books/2019/may/18/race-science-on-the-rise-angela-saini.

Saini, Angela. *Superior: The Return of Race Science.* Boston: Beacon Press, 2019.

Sanson, Mevagh, Deryn Strange, and Maryanne Gary. "Trigger Warnings Are Trivially Helpful at Reducing Negative Affect, Intrusive Thoughts, and Avoidance." *Clinical Psychological Science* (March 4, 2019): 778–793.

Santora, Marc. "George Soros–Founded University Is Forced out of Hungary." *New York Times,* December 3, 2018. https://www.nytimes.com/2018/12/03/world/europe/soros-hungary-central-european-university.html.

Saul, Stephanie. "Energizing Conservative Voters, One School Board Election at a Time." *New York Times,* October 21, 2021. https://www.nytimes.com/2021/10/21/us/republicans-schools-critical-race-theory.html.

Sawchuck, Stephen. "What Is Critical Race Theory, and Why Is It under Attack?" *Education Week,* May 18, 2021. https://www.edweek.org/leadership/what-is-critical-race-theory-and-why-is-it-under-attack/2021/05.

Schow, Ashe. "STUDY: 'Trigger Warnings' Are Harmful to College Students." *The Daily Wire,* July 28, 2018. https://www.dailywire.com/news/33720/study-trigger-warnings-are-harmful-college-ashe-schow.

Schwartz, Sarah. "Map: Where Critical Race Theory Is under Attack." *Education Week,* June 11, 2021 (updated May 18, 2022). https://www.edweek.org/policy-politics/map-where-critical-race-theory-is-under-attack/2021/06.

Segarra, Lisa Marie. "Colleges Are an 'Echo Chamber of Political Correctness.' Read Jeff Sessions' Speech on Campus Free Speech." *Time,* September 26, 2017. http://time.com/4957604/jeff-sessions-georgetown-law-speech-transcript/.

Selingo, Jeffrey J. "How Many Colleges and Universities Do We Really Need?" *Washington Post,* July 20, 2015. https://www.washingtonpost.com/news/grade-point/wp/2015/07/20/how-many-colleges-and-universities-do-we-really-need/?utm_term=.7c3083a954ee.

Serwer, Adam. "A Nation of Snowflakes." *The Atlantic,* September 26, 2017. https://www.theatlantic.com/politics/archive/2017/09/it-takes-a-nation-of-snowflakes/541050/.

Shafter, Leah. "The Case for Affirmative Action." Harvard Graduate School of Education, July 11, 2018. https://www.gse.harvard.edu/news/uk/18/07/case-affirmative-action.

Shapira, Ian. "VMI Will Change Honor System That Expels Black Cadets at Disproportionate Rates." *Washington Post,* February 5, 2022. https://www.washingtonpost.com/education/2022/02/05/vmi-honor-court-reforms/.

Shulevitz, Judith. "In College and Hiding from Scary Ideas." *New York Times,* March 21, 2015. https://www.nytimes.com/2015/03/22/opinion/sunday/judith-shulevitz-hiding-from-scary-ideas.html.

Siripurapu, Anshu, and Mia Speier. "Is Rising Student Debt Harming the U.S. Economy?" Council on Foreign Relations, April 13, 2021. https://www.cfr.org/backgrounder/rising-student-debt-harming-us-economy.

Smith, Christian. "An Academic Auto-da-Fé." *Chronicle of Higher Education*, July 23, 2012. https://www.chronicle.com/article/an-academic-auto-da-fe/.

Soave, Robby. *Panic Attack: Young Radicals in the Age of Trump*. New York: All Points, 2019.

Solomon, Danyelle, et al. "Structural Racism in America." Urban Institute. Accessed February 5, 2022. https://www.urban.org/features/structural-racism-america.

Solomon, Danyelle, et al. "Systematic Inequality and Economic Opportunity." Center for American Progress, August 7, 2019. https://www.americanprogress.org/article/systematic-inequality-economic-opportunity/.

"Speech on Campus." American Civil Liberties Union. Accessed February 5, 2022. https://www.aclu.org/other/speech-campus.

Spencer, Hawes, and Sheryl Gay Stolberg. "White Nationalists March on University of Virginia." *New York Times*, August 12, 2017. https://www.nytimes.com/2017/08/11/us/white-nationalists-rally-charlottesville-virginia.html.

"The Spirit of Inclusion at Notre Dame." Notre Dame University. Accessed February 5, 2022. https://dulac.nd.edu/university-mission-and-vision/spirit-of-inclusion/.

"Spotlight on Speech Codes 2017." Foundation for Individual Rights in Education. Accessed February 5, 2022. https://www.thefire.org/spotlight/reports/spotlight-on-speech-codes-2017/.

Stanger, Allison. "Understanding the Angry Mob That Gave Me a Concussion." *New York Times*, March 13, 2017. https://www.nytimes.com/2017/03/13/opinion/understanding-the-angry-mob-that-gave-me-a-concussion.html.

Stanley, Jason. "Fascism and the University." *Chronicle of Higher Education*, September 2, 2018. https://www-chronicle-com.ezaccess.libraries.psu.edu/article/Fascismthe-University/244382.

Stanley, Jason. *How Fascism Works*. New York: Random House, 2018.

Stanley, Jason. *How Propaganda Works*. Princeton, NJ: Princeton University Press, 2015.

"Start a YAF Chapter." Young America's Foundation, February 5, 2022. https://students.yaf.org/young-americans-for-freedom/start-a-chapter/.

"Statement on the Christina Hoff Sommers Event at the Law School." *Lewis and Clark News*, March 9, 2018. https://www.lclark.edu/live/news/38367-statement-on-the-christina-hoff-sommers-event-at.

"Statement on Diversity." Virginia Military Institute. Accessed February 5, 2022. https://www.vmi.edu/about/governance/regulations-and-policies/statement-on-diversity/.

Stenner, Karen. *The Authoritarian Dynamic*. New York: Cambridge University Press, 2005.

Stephens, Bret. "The Dying Art of Disagreement." *New York Times*, September 24, 2017. https://www.nytimes.com/2017/09/24/opinion/dying-art-of-disagreement.html.

Stephens, Bret. "Our Best University President." *New York Times*, October 20, 2017.

Stephens, Bret. "The Secrets of Jewish Genius [Correction]." *New York Times*, December 28, 2019.

Stevens, S. T., et al. "The Campus Expression Survey: A Heterodox Academy Project." 2017. https://2cnzc91figkyqqeq8390pgd1-wpengine.netdna-ssl.com/wp-content/uploads/2018/02/HxA-Campus-Expression-Survey-Guide.pdf.

Stone, Peter. "Money and Misinformation: How Turning Point USA Became a Formidable Pro-Trump Force." *The Guardian*, October 23, 2021. https://www.theguardian.com/us-news/2021/oct/23/turning-point-rightwing-youth-group-critics-tactics.

Strack, Fritz, and Norbert Schwarz. "Asking Questions: Measurement in the Social Sciences." In *Psychology's Territories: Historical and Contemporary Perspectives from Different Disciplines*, edited by Mitchell Ash and Thomas Sturm, 225–250. Mahwah, NJ: Lawrence Erlbaum, 2007.

"Students for Fair Admissions, Inc. v. President and Fellows of Harvard College (Harvard Corporation)." *Harvard Law Review*, May 10, 2021. https://harvardlawreview.org/2021/05/students-for-fair-admissions-inc-v-president-and-fellows-of-harvard-college/.

Sudman, Seymour, and Norman M. Bradburn. *Asking Questions: A Practical Guide to Questionnaire Design*. San Francisco: Jossey-Bass, 1982.

Sullivan, Andrew. "We All Live on Campus Now." *New York*, February 9, 2018. http://nymag.com/daily/intelligencer/2018/02/we-all-live-on-campus-now.html.

Swann, Sara. "Despite Claims of Bias, Conservatives Thrive on Social Media, Study Shows." *Chicago Tribune*, February 1, 2021. https://www.chicagotribune.com/nation-world/ct-nw-conservatives-thrive-social-media-study-shows-20210201-zdscpcewyvha7n3wbt5q76cywy-story.html.

Tallentyre, S. G. (Evelyn Beatrice Hall). *The Friends of Voltaire*. New York: G. P. Putnam's Sons, 1907.

"Telecommunications Act of 1996." Federal Communications Commission, June 20, 2013. https://www.fcc.gov/general/telecommunications-act-1996.

Tharoor, Ishaan. "The GOP Alliance with Europe's Far-Right Deepens." *Washington Post*, October 12, 2021. https://www.washingtonpost.com/world/2021/10/12/republican-alliance-europe-far-right/.

Thomason, Andy. "Here's What Trump's Executive Order on Free Speech Says." *Chronicle of Higher Education*, March 21, 2019. https://www.chronicle.com/article/Here-s-What-Trump-s/245943.

Tiedemann, Jennifer. "Nebraska Becomes Latest State to Consider Campus Free Speech Bill Based on Goldwater Institute Model." Goldwater Institute, January 5, 2018. https://goldwaterinstitute.org/article/nebraska-becomes-latest-state-to-consider-campus-free-speech-bill-based-on-goldwater-institute-model/.

Timpf, Katherine. "Trigger Warnings Might Be Harmful, a Study Concludes." *National Review*, July 31, 2018. https://www.nationalreview.com/2018/07/study-says-trigger-warnings-might-harm-readers/.

Timpf, Katherine. "University Bans Snowball Fights and Water Guns." *National Review*, August 21, 2018. https://www.nationalreview.com/2018/08/university-bans-snowball-fights-and-water-guns/.

Turetsky, Kate, and Valerie Purdie-Vaughns. "What Science Has to Say about Affirmative https://www.scientificamerican.com/article/what-science-has-to-say-about-affirmative-action/.

Tushnet, Mark. "Constitutional Hardball." *John Marshall Law Review* 37 (2004) 523–553.

Twenge, Jean M. *Generation Me: Why Today's Young Americans Are More Confident, Assertive, Entitled—and More Miserable Than Ever*. Revised and updated edition. New York: Atria, 2014.

Twenge, Jean M. *iGen: Why Today's Super-Connected Kids Are Growing Up Less Rebellious, More Tolerant, Less Happy—and Completely Unprepared for Adulthood—and What That Means for the Rest of Us*. Reprint edition. New York: Atria, 2017.

"UM History of Integration." University of Mississippi. Accessed February 5, 2022. https://50years.olemiss.edu/james-meredith/.

"User's Guide to FIRE's Disinvitation Database." Foundation for Individual Rights in Education. Accessed February 5, 2022. https://www.thefire.org/how-to-use-the-disinvitation-database/.

Vandelinder, Emma. "Racial Climate at MU: A Timeline of Incidents in Fall 2015." *Columbia Missourian*, November 6, 2015. https://www.columbiamissourian.com/news/higher_education/racial-climate-at-mu-a-timeline-of-incidents-in-fall-2015/article_0c96f986-84c6-11e5-a38f-2bd0aab0bf74.html.

Vaughn, Jason M. "Mizzou Protesters: Stay out of Our 'Safe Space' or We'll Call the Cops." *The Daily Beast*, November 9, 2015. https://www.thedailybeast.com/mizzou-protest ers-stay-out-of-our-safe-space-or-well-call-the-cops.

Vearncombe, Erin K., et al. *After Jesus before Christianity: A Historical Exploration of the First Two Centuries of Jesus Movements*. New York: Harper One, 2021.

Vigen, Tyler. *Spurious Correlations*. New York: Hatchette, 2015.

Villasenor, John. "Views among College Students Regarding the First Amendment: Results from a New Survey." Brookings Institution, September 18, 2017. https://www.brookings. edu/blog/fixgov/2017/09/18/views-among-college-students-regarding-the-first-amendm ent-results-from-a-new-survey/.

Villeda, Ray. "Conservative Speaker's Appearance Ignites Protests at NYU." NBC New York, February 2, 2017. https://www.nbcnewyork.com/news/local/NYU-Protests-Fights-Arrests-Conservative-Speaker-Gavin-McInnes-412635693.html.

Weigel, Moira. "*The Coddling of the American Mind* Review—How Elite US Liberals Have Turned Rightwards." *The Guardian*, September 20, 2018. https://www.theguardian.com/ books/2018/sep/20/the-coddling-of-the-american-mind-review.

Weiss, Bari. "Jonathan Haidt on the Cultural Roots of Campus Rage." *Wall Street Journal*, August 14, 2017. https://www.wsj.com/articles/jonathan-haidt-on-the-cultural-roots-of-campus-rage-1491000676.

Weiss, Bari. "We're All Fascists Now." *New York Times*, March 7, 2018. https://www.nytimes. com/2018/03/07/opinion/were-all-fascists-now.html.

Wellemeyer, James. "Wealthy Parents Spend up to $10,000 on SAT Prep for Their Kids." *MarketWatch*, July 7, 2019. https://www.marketwatch.com/story/some-wealthy-parents-are-dropping-up-to-10000-on-sat-test-prep-for-their-kids-2019-06-21.

Wells, Christina E. "The First Amendment, The University and Conflict: An Introduction to the Symposium." *Journal of Dispute Resolution 2* (2018): 1–5.

Wetzel, Eunike, et al. "The Narcissism Epidemic Is Dead; Long Live the Narcissism Epidemic." *Psychological Science* 28 (2017): 1833–1847.

"What's All This about Trigger Warnings?" National Coalition Against Censorship, December 2015. https://ncac.org/wp-content/uploads/2015/11/NCAC-TriggerWarningReport.pdf.

"White Supremacist Propaganda Nearly Doubles on Campus in 2017–18 Academic Year." Anti- Defamation League, June 6, 2018. https://www.adl.org/resources/reports/white-supr emacist-propaganda-nearly-doubles-on-campus-in-2017-18-academic-year.

Whittington, Keith E. *Speak Freely: Why Universities Must Defend Free Speech*. Princeton, NJ: Princeton University Press, 2018.

"Who We Are." Ordo Iuris International Academy. Accessed February 5, 2022. https:// en.ordoiuris.pl/who-we-are.

Williams, Joanna. "The University of Austin Puts the Rest of Academia to Shame." *Spiked*, November 9, 2021. https://www.spiked-online.com/2021/11/09/the-university-of-austin-puts-the-rest-of-academia-to-shame/.

Winegard, Bo, and Ben Winegard. "A Tale of Two Bell Curves." *Quillette*, March 27, 2017. https://quillette.com/2017/03/27/a-tale-of-two-bell-curves/.

Witherspoon, D. J., et al. "Genetic Similarities within and between Human Populations." *Genetics* 176 (May 2007): 351–359.

Wolfsfeld, Gadi. *Making Sense of Media and Politics: Five Principles in Political Communication*. New York: Routledge, 2011.

Wood, Peter W. "The Left Can't Stop Campus Riots Like Middlebury's Because Their Ideology Deserves Blame." *The Federalist*, March 14, 2017, http://thefederalist.com/2017/03/14/left-cant-stop-campus-riots-like-middleburys-ideology-deserves-blame/.

Wood, Thomas E., and Malcolm J. Sherman. "Is Campus Racial Diversity Correlated with Educational Benefits?" *Academic Questions* 14 (2001): 72–88.

Woods, Jeff. *Black Struggle, Red Scare: Segregation and Anti-Communism in the South, 1948–1968.* Baton Rouge: Louisiana State University Press, 2004.

"Writing the Experimental Report: Methods, Results, and Discussion." Purdue Online Writing Lab. Accessed February 5, 2022. https://owl.purdue.edu/owl/subject_specific_writing/writing_in_the_social_sciences/writing_in_psychology_experimental_report_writing/experimental_reports_2.html.

Yearby, Ruqaiijah. "The Impact of Structural Racism in Employment and Wages on Minority Women's Health." *Human Rights Magazine* (American Bar Association) 43, no. 3 (2018). https://www.americanbar.org/groups/crsj/publications/human_rights_magazine_home/the-state-of-healthcare-in-the-united-states/minority-womens-health/.

Yglesias, Matthew. "The Controversy over Bret Stephens's Jewish Genius Column, Explained." *Vox*, December 30, 2019. https://www.vox.com/policy-and-politics/2019/12/30/21042733/bret-stephens-jewish-iq-new-york-times.

Yiannopoulos, Milo. "How to Beat Me (Spoiler: You Won't)." *Breitbart*, March 21, 2016. https://www.breitbart.com/social-justice/2016/03/21/how-to-beat-me-spoiler-you-wont/.

Youngkin, Glenn. Executive Order Number One (2022): Ending the Use of Inherently Divisive Concepts, Including Critical Race Theory, and Restoring Excellence in K–12 Public Education in the Commonwealth, January 15, 2022. https://www.governor.virginia.gov/media/governorvirginiagov/governor-of-virginia/pdf/74---eo/74---eo/EO-1---ENDING-THE-USE-OF-INHERENTLY-DIVISIVE-CONCEPTS,-INCLUDING-CRITICAL-RACE-THEORY,-AND-RESTORING-EXCELLEN.pdf.

Zerofsky, Elisabeth. "How the American Right Fell in Love with Hungary." *New York Times*, October 19, 2021, https://www.nytimes.com/2021/10/19/magazine/viktor-Orbán-rod-dreher.html.

Index